Social Exclusion, Integration and Inclusive Policies

Social Exclusion, Integration and Inclusive Policies

Editors

V. Subramanyam
K. Sekhar

RAWAT PUBLICATIONS
Jaipur • New Delhi • Bangalore • Hyderabad • Guwahati

ISBN 81-316-0366-0

Published by
Prem Rawat for **Rawat Publications**
Satyam Apts, Sector 3, Jawahar Nagar, Jaipur 302 004 (India)
Phone: 0141 265 1748 / 7006 Fax: 0141 265 1748
E-mail: info@rawatbooks.com
Website: www.rawatbooks.com

New Delhi Office
4858/24, Ansari Road, Daryaganj, New Delhi 110 002
Phone: 011 2326 3290

Also at *Bangalore, Hyderabad* and *Guwahati*

Typeset by Rawat Computers, Jaipur
Printed at Chaman Enterprises, New Delhi

Contents

Foreword

Technology has changed fast but our minds have not changed at all. This sums up any treatise on inclusive policy. Throughout history, human beings have managed to treat their fellow beings not even as adjuncts by their 'reasoning' faculty. Marginalization has been the rule rather than the exception. Each age has seen a new form or variety of exclusion emerging thereby depriving the vast masses of their just entitlements.

Realizing the inherent dangers of these inequities, an attempt is being made in the contemporary times to provide access to everyone to what they need and deserve. If you seek peace, cultivate justice. As poverty anywhere is a threat to prosperity everywhere, injustice anywhere is a threat to justice everywhere. Understanding that human rights mean, right to be human and that human rights can never be realized if humans are treated in an inhuman or sub human manner, there has been a shift of focus on the subalterns.

For quite a long time it was mistakenly believed that growth will ensure justice- social, economic and political. But experience has proved that the trickle down does not take place and growth results in creation of islands of prosperity if safety nets are not provided. This has necessitated the just importance that is being accorded to inclusive policies. The systematized constraints can be appreciated only if the dimensions of social exclusion and integration are analysed in a holistic manner.

The book *Social Exclusion, Integration and Inclusive Policies* edited by Prof. V. Subramanyam and Dr K. Sekhar of the Centre for Study of Social Exclusion and Inclusive Policy, Andhra University is a compendium of papers presented at the national level workshop titled "Social Exclusion and Inclusive Policy with Special Reference to Weaker Sections of India" in March 2008. This book admirably serves the purpose of understanding the different nuances of inclusive policy. The centre is nascent but its contribution has been rich.

The book presents a mosaic of processes and levels of social exclusion. People who have a dominant share of values in the society are labeled as 'elite' and people who have a lesser share of values are labeled as weaker sections. Persons who have dominant share of social values may not necessarily have dominant share of political values. Any study on inclusive policy should not lose sight of this. Representative democracy will have any meaning only if there is participatory democracy in the real sense of the term. The participation will become meaningful only if emancipation precedes empowerment. In fact, emancipation is the heart and soul of inclusive policy and hence the ultimate of goal of inclusion should be effective participation. Therefore it is increasingly felt that growth and reducing poverty should be the major objectives of inclusive policy and economic development and social development need to go hand in hand. It is like walking on two legs. Ignoring any one of them will make the country limp along.

At a time when Martin Luther King's cherished wish expressed in a lucid statement – "I have a dream" – is coming true, I am sure this luminous book will provide the needed thrust to the theoretical discourse on inclusive policy.

31 May 2009

Prof. R. Venkata Rao
Vice-Chancellor
National Law School of India University
Bangalore

List of Contributors

Anita, G., Teacher Associate, Department of Journalism and Mass Communication, Andhra University, Visakhapatnam.

Arjun, P., Associate Professor, Department of Social Work, Andhra University, Visakhapatnam.

Babavali, N., Research Assistant, Centre for Study of Social Exclusion and Inclusive Policy, Andhra University, Visakhapatnam.

Behera, Deepak Kumar, Professor, Department of Anthropology, Sambalpur University, Jyothi Vihar, Sambalpur.

Chinna Rao, Y., Associate Professor, Programme for the Study of Discrimination and Exclusion, School of Social Sciences, Jawaharlal Nehru University, New Delhi.

Devarapalli, Jesurathnam, Lecturer, Department of Anthropology, Pondicherry University, Pondicherry.

Devi Prasad, B., Professor, Department of Social Work, Andhra University, Visakhapatnam.

Haranath, S., Teacher Associate, Department of Social Work, Andhra University, Visakhapatnam.

Indira Rani, N., Project Fellow Department of Social Work, Andhra University, Visakhapatnam.

Kishore Kumar, P., Programme Assistant, Gandhian Studies, Andhra University, Visakhapatnam.

Murthy, D.V.R., Associate Professor, Department of Journalism and Mass Communication, Andhra University, Visakhapatnam.

Nath, Nibedita, Research Scholar, Department of Anthropology, Sambalpur University, Jyothi Vihar, Sambalpur.

Pal, N.A.D, Teacher Associate, Department of Sociology, Andhra University, Visakhaptanam.

Patnaik, Rajesh, Social Anthropologist, Visakhapatnam.

Pradgna, C., Department of Basic and Humanities, GITAM University, Visakhapatnam.

Prakash, Jayasheela, Research Scholar, Department of Applied Economics, Andhra University, Visakhapatnam.

Pulla Rao, D., Department of Economics, Andhra University, Visakhapatnam.

Raja Kumar, D., Teacher Associate, Department of Sociology, Andhra University, Visakhaptanam.

Rama Mohan, K.R, Lecturer-cum-Assistant Director, Centre for Study of Social Exclusion and Inclusive Policy, Andhra University, Visakhapatnam.

Ramakrishna, R., Professor, Department of Applied Economics, Andhra University, Visakhapatnam.

Ramana, T.V., Teaching Associate, Department of Economics, Andhra University, Visakhapatnam.

Ranga Rao, A.B.S.V., Associate Professor, Department of Social Work, Programme Co-ordinator, Gandhian Studies Centre, Andhra University, Visakhapatnam.

Ratna Kumari, B., I/c Convenor, Dr Durgabai Deshmukh Centre for Women's Studies, Andhra University, Visakhapatnam.

Satya Pal, P.D., Department of Anthropology, Andhra University, Visakhapatnam.

Sekhar, K., Reader-cum-Deputy Director, Centre for Study of Social Exclusion and Inclusive Policy, Andhra University, Visakhapatnam.

Shakkeela, U.V., Post Doctoral Scholar, Kerala Council for Historical Research, Trivandrum, Kerala.

Sreemannarayana Murthy, V., Assistant Professor, Centre for SAARC Studies, Andhra University, Visakhapatnam.

Srivirajarani, J., Research Assistant, Centre for Study of Social Exclusion and Inclusive Policy, Andhra University, Visakhapatnam.

Subba Rao, P., Reader-cum-Deputy Director, Centre for Study of Social Exclusion and Inclusive Policy, Andhra University, Visakhapatnam.

Subramanyam, V., Director, Centre for Study of Social Exclusion and Inclusive Policy, Andhra University, Visakhapatnam.

Tata Rao, D., Research Scholar, Department of Sociology, Andhra University, Visakhapatnam.

Introduction

V. Subramanyam and K. Sekhar

Social exclusion is a process by which individuals or households experience deprivation either of resources or of social links to the wider community or society. Since the seminal work of Rene Lenoir (1974) of France on social exclusion, it became the central theme of social policy in many European countries. The French establishment defined social exclusion as a rupture of social bonds. A broader framework of the understanding of social exclusion suggests that it is the process that excludes individuals, groups and aggregates from full participation in the society in which they live. According to Silver (1995), exclusion must include the following: a livelihood; secure, permanent employment; earnings; property, credit, or land; minimal or prevailing consumption levels; education, skills, and cultural capital; the welfare state; citizenship and legal equality; democratic participation; public goods; the nation or the dominant race; family and sociability; humanity, respect, fulfilment and understanding.

Sen (2000) holds that exclusion from social relations can lead to other deprivations that further limit our living opportunities. It can thus be constitutively a part of capability deprivation as well as instrumentally a cause of diverse capability failures. In the Indian context, exclusion revolves around institutions that discriminate, isolate, shame and deprive subordinate groups on the basis of identities like caste, religion and gender (Thorat and Newman, 2007). Succinctly put, in India, exclusion is based on caste and patriarchal systems. The rigid barriers of caste not only practise the most pungent form of exclusion but also regulate economic life. Inequality is the organizing principle of the caste-based hierarchy, which spews discrimination and has kept numerous groups outside the gamut of Hindu social life. The end product of this kind of exclusion for thousands of years has resulted in disempowerment of a vast multitude of population. In India, the most rigorous form of exclusion is practised by the institution of caste, followed by income, ethnicity, gender, religion and territory. The contours of the exclusion perpetuated by these variables constantly change with the context and actors. So is the intensity of the discrimination.

Throughout recorded history we find numerous movements that aimed at ending caste-based discrimination and integrating the vulnerable sections into the mainstream. The heterodox sects that fought against the entrenched priestly class and its tenets fashioned by rules of purity and pollution, the lower-castes-led Bhakti movement which called for equality through spiritual awakening, the reform movements during the colonial era and finally the nationalist movement that encompassed freedom struggle as well as reform sought to end the exclusionary dispensation of the social order. Their egalitarian philosophy and democratically constructed agenda accorded great importance to social justice and empowerment of the weak. The Constitution of India is the best document that upholds and effectively articulates the ideology of inclusion and seeks to uplift the marginalized through a range of programmes.

Since the dawn of independence the Government of India as well as the state governments introduced a number of policies and programmes for the empowerment of the Dalits, backward classes, tribes, religious minorities and women. In spite of consistent and gigantic efforts by the government as well as by civil society these marginalized groups have not progressed on the expected lines. They continue to experience exclusion at various levels and in different contexts and it is not uncommon to see the Scheduled Castes (SCs) being treated as untouchables in majority of the villages in India. Not only upper castes but also dominant backward classes commit atrocities on them. The reservation policies have undoubtedly effected a considerable change in the lives of the oppressed sections, but the majority is still found to be outside the realm of the progress and economic empowerment.

The discourse on social policy has undergone a sea change in the wake of globalization, which has a profound impact on the dynamics of the labour market and has brought the issue of caste-based economic discrimination to the fore. Hence, the need to re-examine the concept of exclusion and reframe the policy appears conspicuous. Keeping this in view, the University Grants Commission (UGC) had established Centres for Study of Social Exclusion and Inclusive Policy in 35 universities under the Tenth and Eleventh Plan periods. Since the universities are primary spaces where exclusion can be studied, understood and transcended, they were sanctioned these centres. The centres have to offer new insights into the problem of exclusion and conceptualize discrimination exclusion and inclusion based on caste/ethnicity and religion. It should be the endeavour of the centres to develop an understanding of discrimination at an empirical level and formulate policies for protecting the rights of these groups and eradicating the problem of exclusion and discrimination.

The Centre for Study of Social Exclusion and Inclusive Policy, Andhra University, is one of the thirty-five centres. In line with the stated objectives of the centres it organized a national level workshop titled "Social Exclusion and Inclusive Policy with Special Reference to Weaker Sections of India" in March 2008. The basic aims of the workshop were to understand the processes and levels of social exclusion to which the marginalized communities are subject and identify new areas of intervention. The workshop also discussed and deliberated on the existing policies, ideologies and initiatives meant for the empowerment of the underprivileged. In accordance with the guidelines given, the UGC had tried to develop an analytical framework to critically examine the concepts of exclusion and disparity and evolve inclusive strategies for enabling the marginalized groups to participate fully in the economic, educational and social institutions that define social membership.

The papers presented at the workshop are divided into the following four sections:

(i) Concept and Theory of Social Exclusion and Inclusive Policy
(ii) Excluded Groups
(iii) Gender Issues
(iv) Thinkers, Inclusion and Integration

Concept and Theory of Social Exclusion and Inclusive Policy

In a detailed overview of the concept of social exclusion and inclusive policy, V. Subramanyam delineated the extent and forms of exclusion. He offered a comprehensive picture of the process of exclusion and argued that social exclusion and poverty are deeply interconnected. He argued that the link between poverty and gender inequality which restricts opportunity is a natural corollary of patriarchy. Restricted opportunity leads to capability deprivation which obviously results in poverty. The author listed out several forms of exclusion. They are: (i) geographic isolation, (ii) barriers to entry, (iii) corruption, (iv) intimidation and (v) physical violence. The excluded groups according to the author are (i) the poor, (ii) women, (iii) the elderly, (iv) ethnic groups, (v) the disabled, (vi) HIV/AIDS-infected and (vii) widows. He concluded that due to the growing corruption in the state apparatus it is difficult for people to seek redress against exclusion and escape poverty. The strengthening of social safety networks and the inclusive measures will certainly help the excluded groups fight discrimination effectively.

V. Subramanyam in his paper "Contextual Social Exclusion and Inclusion of Weaker Sections in a Multi-Caste Village of Andhra Pradesh" provides empirical evidence of social discrimination and inequality in a multi-caste village 'Mandur' in Guntur district. The population of the village comprises five important categories of population such as forward castes, other backward castes (OBCs), Scheduled Castes (SCs), Scheduled Tribes (STs) and religious minorities. The paper argues that the discrimination against lower castes is based on land distribution pattern, while political discrimination is associated with wealth and power of different castes. The paper also records contextual exclusion which depends on the economic functions and social and religious ceremonies. It highlights the Jajmani system and the ensuing relations between the Dalits and the touchable castes. The traditional leaders of the village are from the dominant castes and hence their unilateral decisions reflect their hegemonic attitude. The author found the Dalits and other lower castes to be very poor and hence their negotiating abilities were also low.

In a paper titled "Social Exclusion and the Dalits in India" Y. Chinna Rao attempted to give a comprehensive definition of the term exclusion. Quoting Rene Lenoir and Sen, Rao states that in India exclusion is embedded in societal interrelations and institutions that exclude, discriminate, isolate and deprive some groups on the basis of the groups' identities such as caste and ethnicity. He argues that the caste and untouchability-based exclusion and discrimination can be categorized in the economic, civil, cultural and political spheres, as the exclusion and denial of equal opportunity in economic spheres would necessarily operate through markets and non-market transactions and exchange. The paper is about social exclusion in the field of higher education, particularly the universities. It reveals that most of the central universities have not filled most of the posts falling in reservation categories. The situation is too alarming to ignore. The author laments that if institutions of higher learning ignore social justice, what could be the situation in other spaces.

The paper by Rajesh Patnaik titled "Socio-cultural Anthropology and Social Exclusion: From Simple Description to Complex Process" throws light on some of the customs and traditions of Kolam of Satmala Plateau. The author narrates the practice of some villages preventing the Kolams from using their traditional route to carry their clan symbol 'Ayak' to the banks of River Godavari. He argues that it is an instance of excluding the Kolams from their own ancestral socio-cultural spatial zone and focuses on environmental exclusion with ramifications of socio-cultural and religious nature. His paper was essentially of ethnographic nature, which according to Geertz (1973) is 'thick description'. The term is in contrast with overt observable behaviour, observation and superficial description that are said to be 'thin'.

One can move from this thin description to a thick description which as Geertz states is the main objective of ethnography. Presenting an absorbing ethnographic account of the beliefs, customs and traditions of the Kolam tribe the author mentions about their strong belief that the Ayak if displeased would cause destruction. The fact that the castes out of fear for the powers of the Ayak objected to it being taken through their villages indicates the growing index of sanskritization. The paper concludes that the politicization of the villages had resulted in declining respect for traditional reciprocal statuses and obligations and while the analysis of social exclusion is adequate to formulate a policy to direct the village Panchayats to permit the procession of the Ayak, the thick description is useful for a much deeper understanding of the issues and socio-psychological understanding of the illegal ban.

The role played by Phule and Ambedkar in the emancipation of the depressed classes was exemplary. Their formulation that only adequate representations can establish an equitable social order has been the ideological basis for almost all the political formations. P.D. Satya Pal, in his paper titled "From Culture of Reservations to Culture of Representations: Phule–Ambedkarite Agenda for Social Inclusion in India" holds that the interface between ideology and social order which caused social, economic and political exclusion of the Bahujans in India was comprehensively exposed by Jotirao Phule and Ambedkar. But for their exhumation of the structural exclusion the dubious role of religion as an engine of oppression would not have come to light. The paper examines the incompatibility of the ideology of exclusion with that of inclusion in Indian republic, which is yet to become a total social democracy.

The paper is critical of Brahmanical ideology around which the caste system revolves and the elements of Brahmanical cosmology that proclaim inequalities to be built into the very nature of the categories of people, natural objects, food, occupation and even gods themselves. The Brahmanical metaphysics and ethics rationalize inequality as natural and legitimize the social order. Dwelling on the arduous struggle launched by personalities like Sahu Maharaj, Phule, Ambedkar, Narayana Guru and Periyar against the structural exclusion of the Brahmanical system the author finds their insights very crucial to the understanding of the societal process in terms of exclusion and inclusion. Drawing on the Phule–Ambedkar exposition of exclusion perpetuated by the caste system the author highlights the less noticed fact that the Brahmanical system thrusts strange and undesirable identities and nomenclatures like Anarya, Pisacha, Atishudra, etc., on the Bahujans.

The paper lists the levels of exclusion and calls the Brahmanical system to represent group-based exclusion, as it is the social group that bears the brunt of exclusion, not the individual. Individuals and the family have no relevance in the Hindu scheme of things as it is only caste which matters and confers membership on individuals. One of the first instances of demanding for representations was the one by Phule who in 1882 asked the Hunter Commission to facilitate the representations to all communities based on their proportion of population in the fields of education, employment, agriculture, industry and bureaucracy of the country. The paper urges the civil society to develop and inculcate social and moral conscience in order to build a cohesive, inclusive and vibrant society.

Deepak Kumar Behera and Nibedita Nath in their paper titled "The So-Called Development and Dispossession: An Analysis of Land and Forest Rights of the Socially Excluded Project Affected Tribal People" bring forth the trying conditions of the displaced people due to the construction of the Upper Indravati Hydro-electric project in Orissa. The authors reveal that there were 5,988 families, out of which 43.31 per cent belonged to Scheduled Tribes (STs) and 40.19 per cent belonged to Scheduled Castes (SCs). The data explain that the oft-repeated phrase "some should sacrifice for the common benefits of all or in national interests" came true in their case. The Project Affected Persons (PAPs) as ever are underprivileged and impoverished and continue to suffer from impoverishment and disempowerment. The claims of the government that the displaced have been rehabilitated are false.

Excluded Groups

The Scheduled Tribes (STs) in India are the most exploited and displaced lot. Since ages they are denied their entitlements and are robbed of their livelihoods. Ignorance of rights and lack of organization had contributed to their marginalization. V. Subramanyam, J. Srivirajarani and N. Babavali in their paper titled "Scheduled Tribes and Rights Discourse" discuss the plight of the Adivasis in the context of development initiatives. They also give an exhaustive list of the constitutional provisions devised to safeguard the interests of the Adivasis.

Planned development undoubtedly has ushered in significant changes in the lives of the people. But, the tribes owing to several reasons have not enjoyed the fruits of development. Land alienation is one of those reasons. The non-tribals for the past few centuries have been encroaching upon the tribal lands which ultimately led to the worst kind of alienation. The paper provides, details about the methods of land grabbing by the outsiders and the attendant unrest among the tribes and informs that lack of proper health and educational facilities had added to the woes of the indigenous people. The paper suggests for advocacy by activist groups and objective research by academic establishments in regard to tribal problems.

In their paper titled "Tribal Population and Development Policies: A Critical Analysis", J. Srivirajarani and V. Subramanyam highlight the increasing growth rate of tribal population in the country. The paper provides exhaustive information about the tribal demographics of India. It also presents a detailed list of development programmes designed for the welfare of the indigenous groups. The authors drive home the point that despite the increasing number of schemes and programmes the quantum of development had not commensurated them. They also suggest that the Census has to include caste-wise and tribe-wise population and meticulous care needs to be taken during enumeration.

Suggesting an interactive model for inclusive education for the tribes, K.R. Rama Mohan delineated the National Educational Policies

(1986 and 1992) and programmes that aim to raise the literacy levels of the tribal groups. He raised a very pertinent question with regard to inclusion in education that how far is it justifiable to educate the tribal students in exclusive residential schools by segregating them from the rest? He felt that this kind of segregation would rob the tribal children of the opportunity of interaction with their peers in mainstream schools and such isolation contradicts the fact that skills and knowledge are acquired only through interaction with peer groups and intercultural dialogue. The author's model calls for exchange programmes that enable both the tribal and non-tribal students to learn about each other's culture and lifestyles. He suggested that the teachers need to be well trained to impart education to students from diverse backgrounds and for that they got to know about 'culture therapy' propounded by Spindler (1963).

R. Ramakrishna, Jayasheela Prakash and D. Tata Rao, in their paper titled "Role of SHGs in the Empowerment of Weaker Sections: Strategies for the Upliftment through Inclusive Policies", emphasize the proposition that in contemporary development economics people's participation is the central theme for poverty reduction initiatives. In line with the proposition, the Self-Help Group (SHG) method is found to be very effective in realizing the goal of empowerment of low-income households. The paper is based on a study of 300 SHG households in Sabbavaram mandal of Visakhapatnam district. Multi-stage sampling technique was used in the selection of units in the study area. The study has clearly established that the SHG experiment has reduced the intensity of poverty among the sample households and the non-SHG households were lagging behind the SHG households as far as socio-economic and nutritional development were concerned.

N. Indira Rani, S. Haranath and B. Devi Prasad, in their paper titled "Are the Current Educational Policies Inclusive of Tribals?", present an analysis of the educational deprivation of tribals and its relation to their exclusion. The authors discuss the reasons for the backwardness of the tribes in regard to education and other development indicators under three broad categories. The first category implies the problems and difficulties at the level of the conception of educational policy with reference to tribal communities and its implementation. The second category includes internal constraints related to problems associated with the school system in tribal areas, the curriculum content, medium of instruction, pedagogy, academic supervision, monitoring and teacher-related problems. The third category refers to problems related to social, economic and cultural background of tribals and psychological problems of first-generation leaders. The paper concludes that factors like inadequate facilities, pattern of curriculum, poverty, etc., exclude tribal children from the educational endeavour.

V. Sreemannarayana Murthy brought to the fore the dichotomous relationship between the Dalits and the intermediary castes, especially the backward classes. The crux of the arguments presented in the paper titled "Assertion of Rights and Ensuing Reprisals: Atrocities on Dalits in Andhra Pradesh" is that the Shudras have turned out to be the worst oppressors of the Dalits in several parts of the country. Though the backward classes also make use of the affirmative action policies, most of them, in fact, never constitute an excluded group. The author analyses the problem from the functionalist perspective and holds the process of sanskritization responsible for the casteist and reactionary tendencies among the intermediary castes of whom the backward classes constitute the majority. He argues that the intermediary caste groups are a part and parcel of the *jajmani* system and hence constitute an important segment of the Hindu social organization, while the Dalits have always remained outside the pale of the Hindu social structure and ordained by the religious texts to be excluded from participation in the social institutions. The quantum of humiliation and disempowerment experienced by the backward classes as they claim is negligible compared to the crudest form of untouchability and systemic exclusion thrust on the Scheduled Castes (SCs). Hence, the author denounces the demands of the intermediary castes for reservations at par with the Dalits.

Citing numerous instances of atrocities against the Dalits by the intermediary/backward classes in Andhra Pradesh, the author refutes the imaginary and politically manufactured slogan of Dalit-OBC unity. In 1983 the Kamma gentry killed four Dalits at Padiorikuppam, Chittor district. In 1985 Kamma landlords affiliated to the Telugu Desam party killed seven Dalits in Karamchedu village of Prakasam district. In 1987 the same group killed one Dalit in Neerukonda village, Krishna district. In 1986 landlords belonging to the Koppula Velama caste, a dominant backward class, killed one Dalit at Gudiada, Vizianagaram district, and in 2005 people belonging to the Gandla caste, a backward class and by no means dominant, killed five Dalits at Vempeta, Kurnool district. Similarly in 1977 at Belchi, Bihar, the

Kurmi (intermediary backward class) landlords killed eleven Dalits. The paper expresses concern over the continuing discrimination against dalits and their lack of knowledge about the constitutional provisions meant to protect their rights. It recommends for a monitoring mechanism to provide immediate relief for the victims of caste oppression.

P. Subba Rao and T.V. Ramana, in their paper titled "A Study of Child Labour in the Hotel Industry in Kakinada", found that most of the children working in hotels belonged to the downtrodden sections. Child labour is a ubiquitous problem which closely intertwined with poverty throws a challenge to the public policy. Increasing urbanization and the consequent migration from villages, rising poverty levels and expanding informal sector have contributed to the increasing number of child labourers. Andhra Pradesh accounts for 14.5 per cent of the total number of child labourers in the country.

The paper is based on a study of child labour in the hotel industry at Kakinada city, East Godavari district. The authors interviewed seventy children and collected the secondary information from government departments, NGOs, newspaper reports and Census reports. In Kakinada, children below 6 years of age constitute 11 per cent of the population. The authors discovered a link between caste status and child labour. Some caste groups, especially the upper castes, consider it demeaning to send their children to work despite gnawing poverty, while the lower castes with reasonable incomes may prefer to send their children to work. Hence the problem of child labour to some extent is associated with caste practices. The study found that the habit of consuming liquor by the head of the family often landed the family in financial crisis, resulting in the discontinuation of the studies of children and subsequently their employment in the informal sector. Gender discrimination is another reason for the large presence of girl child labourers. It was found that most of the respondents did not get adequate food and medical care. The study called for strict implementation of birth control measures. A massive campaign involving the NGOs and peer groups should be launched against child labour.

The Chenchu are one of the few living examples of foraging people of India displaying the cultural features of the Paleolithic period. They inhabit the Nallamalai Hills, the southernmost part of the Eastern Ghats. The dense Nallamalai forests are abode to the Chenchu who over the centuries have developed distinct cultural patterns and lifestyles. Jesurathnam Devarapalli, in a paper titled "The Concomitant Effects of Geographical and Cultural Isolation on Chenchu Leading to Social Exclusion" documents the socio-cultural traits of the Chenchu and provides the readers with first-hand information about the incursions of the outsiders and the consequent developments. The paper reveals that the ethnocentric attitude of the Chenchu resists developmental initiatives, and the intrusion of outsiders into their habitat had led to the degradation of the environment as a result of which the sources of sustenance got shrunk. The 'middlemen' as elsewhere have been playing a dubious role in the affairs of the Chenchu. Their insulation over the centuries has resulted in their alienation.

The literacy rates among the Scheduled Tribes (STs) are very low. Despite the efforts of the government and the civil society the enrolment at the upper primary stage is very discouraging. It is found that the dropout rate of ST girls is the highest in Andhra Pradesh. D. Pulla Rao, in his paper titled "Population, Literacy and Educational Status of Scheduled Tribes in India", recommends for providing greater incentives to the girl children of ST communities to ensure their attendance at schools. He suggests for enlisting the services of the voluntary agencies in this regard and establishing more schools in the vicinity of tribal areas. The author also calls for starting mobile schools, mosque schools, non-graded schools, learning post-schools, etc., and involvement of parents of the tribal children in the educational process of the children. The author delineates the constitutional provisions dealing with the tribals and gives the statistical profile of the primary and upper primary schools and the net enrolment rates in several states in India.

N.A.D. Pal and D. Raja Kumar, in their paper titled "Exclusion of Dalits in India: A Violation of Human Rights", elucidate the concept of Dalits and their position. Tracing the origin of the word, the authors explain its etymological meaning and the context in which it was used. The caste system based on iniquitous social hierarchy has always operated on the principles of segregation and discrimination. Exclusion has been the most important indicator for the preservation of the system. Legislative action in the form of constitutional safeguards and based on the philosophy of inclusion has ushered in significant changes in the power relations and resulted in the empowerment of Dalits.

Disability creates and increases poverty by increasing isolation and economic strain not just for the disabled person but also for the entire family. The disabled therefore are found to be the poorest of the poor in developing countries. S. Haranath, N. Indira Rani and P. Arjun, in their paper titled "Social Exclusion and the Disabled", discussed the issues of the persons with disabilities who constitute an excluded group. According to conservative estimates, the number of disabled people across the world is around 600 million. Among them 335 million live below the poverty line. The paper classifies groups with different kinds of disabilities, viz., disabled women, people with severe and or multiple disabilities, people with mental illness, disabled people in disaster situations and disabled people in institutions. The authors also suggest several methods to be adopted while working with persons with disabilities. Social model is the most important of all the models. The authors make the following recommendations:

(i) Strengthen leadership of people with disabilities with special emphasis on disabled women. Facilitate the participation of women with disability in other women's movements.
(ii) Facilitate critical analysis of the structural causes of disability.
(iii) Campaign for the formulation of new laws.
(iv) Identify and address specific rehabilitation needs of PWD in extreme circumstances.
(v) Create state and national level networks.

Gender Issues

C. Pradgna in her paper titled "Hindu Code Bill: A *Coup De Grace* to Systemic Gender Exclusion in India" underscores the historical fact that the sexist ideology reinforced by religion relegated women to subhuman existence through structural exclusion from economic, social, political and religious roles in the country. The author argues that the highly restricted female role confines women to 'inside' activities and thrusts natural inferiority complex on women. The author describes the Hindu Code Bill as the perfect socio-legal instrument for gender inclusion towards a humane society and highlights the debate over the recent Women Reservation Bill which is viewed as a powerful tool for the inclusion of women in the political arena. The Hindu Code Bill lays down the following prescriptions:

- The abolition of castes as a necessary requirement for a valid marriage
- The prescription of monogamy
- Right to divorce
- Right to property to women

The author argues that by pitching the conscience against the orthodoxy, Ambedkar shook the very structure and foundations of the caste society. In doing so he continued the legacy of Phule and Buddha. The author explicitly makes it clear that the Brahmanical forces including upper caste women time and again proved that they were against any concessions to the underprivileged and hence they were also against 33 per cent reservation for women. Since the Indian society consists of multiple patriarchies and layers of gender that are integral to the Brahmanical order, these Brahmanical hierarchies prompt different experiences, perceptions and behaviours of women belonging to different castes and classes towards their common oppressions. Finally, the author calls upon the civil society and the educated sections to create a moral consciousness and build a humane society.

B. Ratna Kumari in her paper titled "Ambedkar and Women's Rights" presents a comprehensive account of Ambedkar's gigantic efforts to ameliorate the conditions of women. The author highlights Ambedkar's pro-woman stand and consistent opposition to the dominant Brahmanical ideology which was anti-women and discusses his contribution to the legislation facilitating empowerment of women. The author also delineates Ambedkar's engagement with the twin causes of Dalit emancipation as well as women empowerment and documents the events that led to his resignation from the central cabinet.

D.V.R. Murthy and G. Anita probed into the caste composition of women journalists working in media organizations. In their paper titled "Women Employment in Media: A Case Study of Andhra Pradesh" the authors made an attempt to ascertain the caste composition of women in media. They used survey methods while adopting purposive sampling methods to collect data pertaining to the study. The study interpreted the large presence of respondents from forward castes in the media to the increase in the number of jobs in the private sector. The authors argue that since most of the media organizations are owned by forward castes the recruitment is likely to be influenced by their caste bias. The authors attribute the underrepresentation of Dalit issues in the media to the large presence of upper castes.

U.V. Shakkeela dealt at length with reform movement during the colonial era. She unfolded several interesting details regarding the vacillating attitude of some of the reformers in course of their struggle against social evils. Her paper titled "Social Exclusion of Women in

India Under Colonialism" informs that Rammohan Roy was always ambiguous when it came to taking a firm stand on enacting law against *sati*. Debendranath Tagore and Eshwar Chandra Vidyasagar were not as progressive as their public image. Same was the case with Ranade, who gave in to the pressure of his family members and married an 11-year-old girl after the death of his wife. The author concludes that despite such shortcomings the reform movement during the colonial era inspired the later-day legislation which to a great extent ameliorated the conditions of women.

Thinkers, Inclusion and Integration

K. Sekhar and N. Babavali in their paper titled "Rammanohar Lohia's Social Philosophy and Inclusive Politics: An Assessment" analyse the politics and ideology of Rammanohar Lohia, the Socialist leader. The authors critically examine the stand taken by Lohia on a range of issues concerning the state as well as society. The credit of forcing the institution of caste to subdue its vigour and punctiliousness in the twentieth century largely goes to the triumvirate of Periyar, Ambedkar and Lohia. Among the three, Lohia was the youngest and deeply involved in parliamentary politics. The authors point out that Lohia was the first Socialist leader who could comprehend the importance of caste and its divisive character and wished caste to be grounded in the ideology of the Socialists. The throws light on Lohia's fight against caste inequalities, specifically the Dvija dominance. A man of sharp intellect and unwavering commitment to the cause of social justice, Lohia formulated several strategies to cut the dominance of Dvijas to size, the most important of them was to increase the representation of the Shudras, Harijans, Adivasis, minorities and women in the state and central legislatures.

Lohia, due to some inconsistencies, was criticized by several quarters. His uncharitable remarks against Nehru were never accepted by even enemies of the latter. His farfetched conclusions regarding linguistic issues and probity in public life or moral stand in politics were too idealistic to be followed or emulated. The paper concludes that the sterling contribution of Lohia to the discourse on caste and empowerment of the depressed classes overshadow his inconsistencies.

P. Kishore Kumar and A.B.S.V. Ranga Rao discussed Gandhi's vision of inclusiveness in relation to the removal of untouchability. Their paper titled "Removal of Untouchability: Gandhi's Vision of Inclusiveness" examines the Gandhian method of fighting the derogatory and inhuman practice. Gandhi attempted to fight out social justice on four fronts – social, moral, political and educational. He prevailed on the people to treat the religious sanctions that support untouchability as symbols of social stigma. He perceived it as an essentially moral problem and felt that it could be eradicated by a change in the hearts of caste Hindus. Gandhi combined the struggle for freedom with the reform, as the latter, for him, had a transcendental value far surpassing Swaraj. The paper seeks to highlight the persistent efforts of Gandhi to eradicate untouchability.

The above papers provide an exhaustive material an social exclusion. In addition to covering a range of areas and raise several questions pertaining to exclusion and policy framework. The contributors had critically examined the phenomenon of exclusion in the light of social movements, legislation, globalization, changing nature of labour market and ideology. The papers while analysing and critiquing issues, that include caste discrimination, gender discrimination, child labour, problems of tribes, advocacy for representations and problems of the displaced and disabled offer vital insights about the concept and contexts of exclusion and develop new perspectives concerning integration and policy formulation.

References

Geertz, Clifford. 1973. *The Interpretation of Cultures: Selected Essays,* Basic Books, New York.

Lenoir, Rene. 1914. *Les Exclus: Un Francais Sur Dix.* Editions du Seuil, Paris.

Sen, Amartya. 2000. *Development as Freedom,* Anchor Books, Random House, New York.

Silver, H. 1995. "Reconceptualising Social Disadvantage: Three Paradigms of Social Exclusion" in G. Rodgers, C. Gore and J. Figueireds (eds) *Social Exclusion: Phetoric, Reality and Responses,* Geneva, International Institute of Labour Studies.

Spindler, George. 1963. "The Transmission of American Culture" in G. Spindler (ed) *Education and Culture,* New York, Halt, Rinehart and Winsten.

Thorat Sukhdeo and S. Katherine Newman, 2007 "Caste and Discrimination: Causes, Consequences and Remedies" in Sukhdeo Thorat, Prasant Negi, Samir Kumar Mohapatra and Narendra Kumar (eds), *Labour Market Discrimination and Urban Sector,* Research Series, Social Exclusion 1.1, New Delhi, Indian Institute of Dalit Studies.

1

Contextual Social Exclusion and Inclusion of Weaker Sections in a Multi-Caste Village of Andhra Pradesh

V. Subramanyam

Caste-based hierarchy reflects iniquitous social order and social ordering of different communities in India. Such social arrangement has kept the majority of the communities socially excluded. According to the People of India (PoP) project (2002), there are 4,694 different castes in India. All these caste groups are classified into different categories according to their levels of development and discrimination to which they were subject. They are classified as forward castes, backward classes, Scheduled Castes (SCs), Scheduled Tribes (STs) and religious minorities. To balance the inequalities existing in different forms, the Government of India has provided certain privileges for the 3,654 (77.84%) deprived communities in the areas of education and employment.

The state of Andhra Pradesh has 389 castes – the highest among all the states. From among them there are 59 Scheduled Castes, 33 Scheduled Tribes, 103 Other Backward Classes (OBCs) and the rest (194) include the forward castes and linguistic and religious minorities. The proportion of SCs, STs and OBCs when compared to the forward castes is very high both at the national and state levels. However, the percentage of reservation extended to these communities by the constitution is not in proportion to their population.

Social Discrimination, Inequality and Equality

Inequality is a ubiquitous phenomenon. Though it is apparent everywhere, the forms and magnitude are different across societies. The traditional social system in rural India is mainly centred on the caste structure, its organization and caste identities. The caste system is the basis for examining the social discrimination, inequality and the levels of equality between the members belonging to different endogamous groups. The ramifications of caste system are widely seen in villages, when compared to that of urban areas.

In rural India, the division of labour is determined on the lines of gender, caste and age set. In a multi-caste village, the caste hierarchy clearly envisages the existing social discrimination and inequality between different castes. Inter- and intra-caste relations in different spheres of rural life have to be taken into consideration to identify the social discrimination, inequality and equality among different endogamous groups. Gender issues are also important as they serve to examine the existing discrimination and inequality.

Sociological studies have mainly dwelt on three aspects or forms about the rural society such as the structure of caste, the system of classes and finally the distribution of power. Social inequality is a perennial problem as it creates high and low positions and the principles on the basis of which it exists determine the distribution of social resources among individuals, families and groups (Sharma, 1997). The traditional Indian society was based on the premise of inequality and hierarchical values that permeated every sphere of collective life. The stress on hierarchy was particularly conspicuous in the legal order of Hindu society.

The principle of equality of opportunity has an important place in the transition from a society based on castes or caste-like groups to one based on the individual. It plays a liberating role to the extent that it frees the individual from the burdens of arbitrary and artificial distinction perpetuated through sheer social inertia (Beteille, 1983). Dumont's (1970) contribution of *Homo Hierarchicus* is much useful in understanding social discrimination, inequality and equality among castes in the Indian society. Notions of both inequality and equality are built into the ideology and practice of the caste system, and these two are not only closely interrelated but have also undergone changes over a given period of time.

In India, wealth and political power are unequally distributed among castes (Subramanyam, 1997). Inequality is found in the distribution of wealth, earnings and incomes, and in the massive concentration of poverty in both rural and urban India. A gulf exists between the touchable and untouchable (Harijans) castes of rural India. In the caste system the economic and political inequalities are channelled through hereditary groups called castes. Some of the important features of the caste system are that the members of a caste are socially and economically homogeneous, usually pursuing occupations that carry similar prestige and status. Different castes tend to develop separate subcultures and thereby each subcaste becomes a socially exclusive unit. It is therefore clear that by denying the individual the equality of opportunity, the freedom to choose his/her own occupation and by restricting his/her scope to mix freely with the members of other castes, the caste system restrains the individual from being self-reliant, creative and sociable (Samuel, 1990).

Social Exclusion

Buvinic (2005) summarizes the meaning of social exclusion as "the inability of an individual to participate in the basic political, economic and social functioning of society" and goes on to add that it involves "the denial of equal access to opportunities imposed by certain groups in society upon others". This definition captures three distinguishing features of social exclusion between them, and results in deprivation or low income for those excluded (de Haan, 1997; Sen, 2000). Social exclusion leads to various kinds of deprivation. Sen (2002) mentioned that "it leads to the impoverishment of human life through their casual consequences". The consequences of macro-economic policies, such as poverty, unemployment and involuntary migration, exclude some groups from economic, cultural and political activities and thus institutional inequality and discrimination have become pervasive features of our society.

Concisely, social exclusion in its more specific manifestation as discrimination refers to the process through which groups are wholly or partially restricted from full participation in the economic, educational and social institutions that define social membership. Exclusion involves both the act of restricting access and the consequences that follow, i.e., the principal forms of deprivation. In the Indian context, exclusion revolves around the institutions that discriminate, isolate and deprive subordinate groups on the basis of identities like caste, religion and gender. It is mainly based on caste and patriarchy. The salient features of social exclusion on the basis of caste are social stratification, social inequality, hierarchy and hegemony. Patriarchy generates gender inequality. Social exclusion of weaker sections is closely associated with the discrimination and inequality embodied in the institution of caste.

Caste Composition, Inequality and Exclusion in Mandur Village

Mandur village is located in Guntur district of Andhra Pradesh. The village consists of 649 households with a population of 2,635. It is considered as one of the largest villages in Andhra Pradesh. It is a multi-caste and nucleated type of village. There are twenty castes and the principal castes found in the village are Brahmin, Komati (Vaishya), Kamma, Reddy, Kapu, Golla, Goundla, Uppara, Kamsali, Vadrangi, Kummari, Chakali, Mangali, Jangam, Yerukula, Yanadi, Muslim Sunni, Dudekula, Mala and Madiga. Among these castes Kapu is numerically dominant, followed by Brahmin, while the population of each of the remaining castes is less than 50.

All the castes in Mandur are placed in five social categories such as forward castes or general category, OBCs, SCs, STs and religious minorities. The forward castes comprise castes like Brahmin, Komati, Kamma, Reddy and Kapu. About 54.38 per cent of the population in the village belongs to the general category. The OBC category constitutes 17.31 per cent of the total population and consists of castes like Golla, Goundla, Uppara, Kamsali, Vadrangi, Kummari, Chakali, Mangali and Jangam. Malas and Madigas (SCs) constitute 22.9 per cent of the population in the village. The Sunnis and the Dudekula community constituting 3.19 per cent of the population is classified as religious minorities. Yerukula and Yanadi (STs) constitute 2.20 per cent of the population. Majority of the population in the village belongs to forward castes.

In most of the rural areas in India, two categories of castes with specific characteristics are conspicuously found. They are the dominant, landowning castes and the castes engaged in agriculture. The same picture is seen in Mandur village, as the caste system of the village represents different occupational categories like the peasants, agricultural labourers and dominant landowning caste groups. Majority of the castes in the village follow the Hindu religion.

The castes in the village are categorized as high and low according to their social status, but each caste is separate and maintains social distance from other castes on the grounds of purity and pollution, commensality, connubial relations, occupation, wealth and power. The spatial distribution of different castes in the village also shows the existing physical isolation between the highest and lowest castes. The households belonging to the forward castes are situated in the centre of the village, whereas those belonging to the backward classes, Muslims and STs are located on the periphery of the village. The habitats of Madiga and Mala castes are located at the outskirts of the main village. Locally, the habitats of Mala and Madiga castes are referred to as *Malapalle* and *Madigapalle,* respectively. These two hamlets are attached to the Mandur revenue village. Mandur is also a statutory panchayat village. It is noted that the households of each forward caste are located in separate streets (*Veedhi*). Those streets are named after the castes that live there, e.g., *Brahmana Veedhi, Kamma Veedhi, Reddy Veedhi* and *Kapu Veedhi*. Similarly among the backward classes, Chakali and Uppara castes live in separate streets, whereas the households of Yerukula and Yanadi tribes are situated near the village tank bund which is adjacent to *Uppara Veedhi*. Only one locality is found to be multi-caste, where Golla, Goundla, Kamsali, Kummari, Vadrangi, Mangali, Jangam, Dudekula and Muslim Sunni groups inhabit. Artisan and service castes reside side by side in the northern corners of the village settlement. The settlement pattern of the village shows the existing social distance between the different castes. It is noted that members belonging to a specific caste prefer to live by the side of their kith and kin.

Based on the distribution of different castes in the village settlement, one can say that a lot of social gulf and physical isolation exist between the Dalits and other social categories. Even among the Dalits social discrimination and inequality prevail. The habitat of the Madiga caste is located in the north-eastern side and the habitat of the Mala caste is located in the southwestern side of the main village. Each Dalit caste has its own place of worship, water points and burial ground within the vicinity of its respective habitat. A separate primary school is located in Malapalle and the children belong to Madigapalle attend this school instead of the school situated in the centre of the village where the higher and dominant castes inhabit. The Dalits have their own religious and social functionaries such as priest, chakali and mangali who render their services to them. The village Brahmin priests, barbers and washermen do not provide their services to the Dalits on the ground of untouchability.

The Caste Hierarchy: Social Discrimination and Inequality

The basic principle of the caste system is hierarchy. The essence of hierarchy is the presence of social inequality between castes. The *Varna* model of the five-fold divisions such as Brahmin, Kshatriya, Vaishya, Sudra and untouchables is an important reference to identify the local hierarchy very easily within the local patterns. In the village the lower castes tend to imitate the dominant or higher castes to upgrade their social positions, but the latter do not allow them to reach their stage.

The hierarchical order in the village is very clear with the Brahmins in the village at the top and enjoying the highest social status and the Malas and Madigas placed at the bottom. These two are the untouchable castes, as their habitations are at the outskirts of the main village. Among these, the Malas claim superiority over the Madigas on the basis of occupation. They differentiate themselves from the Madigas stating that their traditional occupation in the past had been weaving and since it is less defiling than working with cattle hide they claim that they are cleaner than the Madigas. It is noted that equality and inequality exist in between the castes of the same category in different contexts. For instance, the peasant castes enjoy the same social status in the village, but economic and political inequality prevails among the Kamma, Reddy and Kapu castes. Today the physical isolation very much prevails between the touchable and untouchable castes of the village. The social stigma of untouchability is a barrier for the social mobility of the Mala and Madiga castes in the village. Social distance is perceived and practised between the touchable and untouchable castes. Commensal restrictions are still present in between the pure and impure castes and are severe between the touchable and untouchable castes.

Occupational Discrimination and Economic Inequality

In Mandur, the caste structure is inextricably intertwined with the village economy. Occupational criterion is very strong and it determines the economic status of each and every caste group in the village. It is interesting to note that every caste is identified by a local name. There are mainly three peasant castes in the village, viz., Kamma, Reddy and Kapu. In Mandur, some families of other castes also practice agriculture, but they do not treat it as primary occupation. Some of the caste groups have completely changed their traditional occupations and have taken up other professions. Not only among these castes but some members of other castes have also changed their occupations. Even in castes that follow their traditional occupation, all the members do not confine to their hereditary occupations. The traditional peasant castes in the village enjoy high economic status compared with that of other castes. The other castes including the Brahmins are dependent on the peasant castes. The peasants' occupation of agriculture is monetary when compared to that of the occupations of other castes in the village. On the basis of occupational criteria the castes are classified into advantaged and disadvantaged groups. Brahmin, Komati, Kamma, Reddy and Kapu castes fall under the advantaged category and the rest of the castes are treated as disadvantaged groups.

Agriculture is the main economic activity in the village. People from different castes are directly or indirectly involved in agriculture as self-cultivators, share croppers, tenants and agricultural labourers. Land is the basic means of production in the village. Cultivators produce food items by using both traditional and modern technology. The village carpenters and blacksmiths supply the required agricultural implements to the cultivators, while the Malas and Madigas provide their manual services to the agriculturists of the village. Most of the caste groups in the village interact with each other in agricultural production and exchange of goods and services. With the help of other castes, the peasants cultivate their lands and produce some quantity of food items, out of which a large share is taken by the landowning peasants and a very small share is given to people belonging to other castes in the form of wages. Agricultural production in the village usually develops a matrix of economic relations between the peasants and non-peasants.

The economic relations include the relationship of Jajman and Kamin, master and servant, land owner and tenant and creditor and debtor. Srinivas (1959) called all these four categories of relations as patron and client relations. The traditional peasants are considered to be the patrons of the people belonging to OBCs and untouchable castes in the village. Currently, the Jajmani system is not functioning fully, but some of the families among the washerman, barber, carpenter and potter castes are still providing their services on fixed payment called *Mera*. All the service castes in the village consider the peasants as Jajmans. Wiser (1936) said that "land ownership is clearly the single most important determinant of power in the Jajmani system". Landless and other occupational groups forcefully depend on the traditional landowning communities for their livelihood.

A total of 19 households belonging to Golla, Dudekula, Uppara, Mala, Madiga, Mangali and Yanadi castes are given land on lease by the big farmers belonging to peasant castes. They are the tenant cultivators. According to the terms of tenancy, a fixed rent system is paid in kind only and the tenancy agreement is for 1–3 years. A rich landlord does not personally cultivate, as his tenant manages the agricultural work. The relationship between the land owner and the tenant is quite intimate and it prevails even between the rich peasants and the landless low castes. The practice of share cropping in the village also strengthens the economic relationship between the landlords and landless poor belonging to lower castes and Dalits.

Land Distribution Pattern

The cultivable land in the village is unequally distributed among different castes. Landholding is an important variable in determining the economic status of an individual or a household in the village. Families with large landholdings are found among the Kapu, Reddy and Kamma castes. A few landlords are also found among the Uppara, Komati, Kummari, Chakali, Brahmin, Mangali, Muslim Sunni, Jangam, Yerukula, Yanadi, Mala and Madiga castes. There is no single landowning family among the Golla, Kamsali, Vadrangi and Dudekula castes. It is observed that most of the medium and large farmers in the village belong to the Kamma caste. Since the majority of the land is held by the Kamma caste group, they are economically dominant in the village.

Discrimination in the Political Sphere of the Village

There is still an informal traditional panchayat (village council) operating in the village. The traditional village council consists of five members who are nominated by the members of the village. The village Munsiff (headman) is from the Reddy caste and the other members are from the Kamma and Kapu peasant castes (two each). They still continue to perform leadership function in the political and economic matters of the village and settle minor disputes. Inter-caste and intra-village disputes are usually settled by the village council. There is no representative from the weaker sections in the village traditional panchayat. It clearly shows that the dominant peasant caste plays a key role in the village politics and other castes have no voice in the political arena of the village. However, other castes have their own traditional caste council or caste head.

The Uppara caste has its own caste panchayat, and the Golla, Kummari, Chakali, Mangali, Yanadi, Mala, Madiga and Dudekula Muslim castes have their own traditional caste heads that fulfil their traditional roles for their respective castes. They advise on social and family matters. Serious breaches of norms and traditions of the caste as well as important intra-caste disputes are settled by the caste panchayats and caste heads.

The village statutory panchayat, through which the village is linked to the mandal and district for development purposes, has assumed great importance. It consists of all elected members with reserved seats for women and SCs (three each). The Sarpanch (President) is the key person. He belongs to the Kamma caste. According to the villagers, this post has always been held by a man from one of the peasant castes. The role of other castes in the statutory panchayat is very minimal. It is also noted that the political rivalry exists only among the three peasant castes. A few among these castes are influential with contacts with the state political bodies and administrative units. Therefore, most of the political gains are enjoyed by the dominant peasant castes. The tenant cultivators, agricultural labourers of lower castes and the service and artisan castes are economically dependent on the peasant castes. By virtue of their dependence on the dominant caste, they have to support or accept the leadership of the dominant caste. The politicization of caste is a dominant feature in the Indian society.

Political relations are associated with social and economic factors. These relationships are considered to be the projections of social relationships. Social and economic dominance is the means to attain political power. This political power is being enjoyed only by the so-called economically dominant castes in the village. Politics is an instrument wielded by a particular stratum in society to consolidate or raise its position. In rural India, even today, the caste system is strong and hence there is close relationship between caste, politics and economy. In the democratic set-up of the Indian society, all are given equal opportunities to participate in the elections. But only the high and dominant castes are occupying key political positions at local, regional, state and centre levels.

Generally, horizontal solidarity exists between the families belonging to the same caste and vertical solidarity is found between different castes on socio-religious occasions, such as celebrations of village deity festivals and communal feasts. The economic relations between different castes, such as Jajman and Kamin, master and servant, landowner and tenant, landowner and agricultural labourer, creditor and debtor, reveal the existence of vertical solidarity in the village. Wealthy families usually look down on the poor of their own castes. Marital alliances quite commonly occur only between the families of the same caste which have equal status. Practice of endogamy at caste level results in the continuation of caste system in villages, which is considered as the root cause for the existence of social discrimination and inequality in social, economic and political spheres of Mandur.

Contextual Exclusion and Inclusion

The Dalits and low Hindu castes are found to be excluded from participating in social, economic, political and religious activities as the high and dominant castes in certain situations and contexts. The entry of Dalits into the houses of high castes is prohibited. Close interaction between the people belonging to high castes and Dalits is restricted in public places, meetings and congregational conventions within the village. The entry of Dalits into the Brahmin locality is prohibited and the Brahmins also avoid entering into the habitats of Dalits. The Brahmins are very meticulous in observance of rules of purity and pollution. The entry of Dalits into the village temples is also forbidden. Commensal and connubial restrictions exist between the high and low castes in the village. The high and dominant castes do not accept *Katcha* food items from the impure occupational groups like washermen, barbers, toddy tappers, earth workers, siren herders, potters and leather workers. The Brahmins accept only uncooked food items from the pure castes but nothing from the Dalits. Commensal relations exist between the castes that stand in the same ranking order of the village and enjoy equal social status.

In Mandur, each caste has its own gossiping centre, from where information gets disseminated. Communication gap also prevails between the highest and the lowest castes. People belonging to weaker sections do not have access to information pertaining to village administration matters. Seating arrangements in panchayat meetings and public meetings are also based on local hierarchy; for instance, the high and dominant caste people sit in the front row whereas the Dalits sit or stand in the last row. Women participation in the panchayat and public meetings is prohibited.

In Mandur, the procession carrying the village deity during the annual village festival is a night-long affair. The image of the deity is carried throughout the village and each caste worships it with fruit and flower in its ward (*Veedhi*). The procession reaches the Dalit houses last. However, the image of the deity does not enter the SC area, but stops at the entrance, even though the drum beaters leading the procession are usually the members of SCs (Madigas). They worship earlier in the day at the shrine in the street before taking part in the village festivals.

Discrimination continues to be practiced against the untouchables (Dalits). For instance, food and beverages are served to them in different vessels in tea shops. Landowners are forced to visit the areas inhabited by lower castes including Dalits when they are in need of labour. In the field, people belonging to both the touchable and untouchable castes collectively work together and touch each other. But a similar situation cannot be seen at the household of a dominant caste peasant. The landowner smokes, drinks and eats together with the Dalits and low caste agricultural labour at his farm when he is involved in the agricultural activities of transplantation weeding, harvesting and thrashing. The norm of purity and pollution is not strictly followed in such contexts.

In the past, the Jajmani system facilitated the integration of all the castes into the village economy through the exchange relationships between peasants and other occupational groups. Until recently, Jajmani relations persisted to some extent, despite the changes in the economy. Many village studies indicate that the Jajmani system is extinct across the country. This is due to several social, economic and political reasons. The fall in Jajmani relationships has accelerated the process of association of castes and traditional occupations, forcing the specialist castes to look to new avenues for earning a livelihood. Such dissociation was further accelerated by other developments like industrialization, spread of education, urbanization and the emergence of new occupations. Industrialization attracted not only many specialists from castes that lost their livelihood due to the decline in patronage for their traditional occupations (carpenters, weavers, potters and blacksmiths for instance), but also many young men who would otherwise have continued to pursue the same. Industrialization also replaced many products which the village artisans were producing for their erstwhile patrons.

Rural economy based on caste specialization and the Jajmani system could not meet the costs of new technology, thereby forcing the specialists from certain castes to take up new occupations. Market system and cash economy also brought several changes in the reciprocal relations between the different castes. Efforts of the lower castes to carry over their urban status into their villages have often resulted in inter-caste violence. Every year many incidents of such inter-caste violence are reported in newspapers and discussed in the State Assembly. Such outbursts of violence have generally resulted in mass killings. Physical assault and rape and the economic and social boycott of the upwardly mobile lower castes by the dominant castes is a regular feature. In the past several such instances took place at Padari Kuppam, Karamchedu, Neerukonda Chundur Vempeta and Pottilanka in Andhra Pradesh.

The levels of social exclusion vary from one caste to another even amongst the weaker sections, which reflect the ranking order (local hierarchy) of each and every caste. The criteria for ranking of the castes are endogamy, purity and pollution, occupation, power and health. The artisan castes enjoy better status when compared to that of service castes. The position of service castes is better than that of the untouchable castes. Amongst the weaker sections, Golla, Goundla and Uppara castes stand in the same ranking order and claim to be superior to other caste groups such as artisan, servicing, STs, Muslims and Dalits. Beef eating practice of Muslims and Dalits is taken as an indicator to assign inferior status to them.

Conclusion

The study reveals that the caste system in Mandur village is very rigid, as it is clearly reflected in the discriminatory practices and inequality that exists between the highest and lowest castes. Weaker sections are the socially excluded groups in the village as they still depend on the dominant peasants for their livelihood. Contextual social exclusion and inclusion are common features of the village caste system. Advantaged groups (high and dominant castes) include the disadvantaged groups (weaker sections) in the village economy for their own benefits. The leaders from the dominant castes are the decision-makers in village matters and they dictate terms to others. Social discrimination and inequality are understood as perennial problems not only in this village, but in many parts of rural India.

Intense poverty prevails among the lowest (SCs) castes in the village. Equal opportunities have to be provided to the people belonging to the lowest ladder of the society in the political, economic and social spheres of the village. In India, attempts to foster equality have extended beyond the constitutional or legislative measures and economic planning has been viewed as a major instrument for ensuring equality. The percentage of reservation for weaker sections in education, employment, political fields should be raised in proportion to their population. New strategies should be adopted to eliminate disparities and discrimination between the rich and the poor as well as between the highest and the lowest castes. The power holders and extension agents must provide their services and adopt stringent measures to implement the welfare programmes for the upliftment of weaker sections in order to make an egalitarian society.

References

Beteille, Andre (ed.) 1983. *Equality and Inequality: Theory and Practice*, Oxford University Press, New Delhi.

Buvinic, Mayra. 2005. 'Social Inclusion in Latin America', in Mayra Buvinic and Jacqueline Mazza (eds.), *Social Exclusion and Economic Development*, Johns Hopkins University Press, Baltimore, pp. 3–32.

de Haan, Arjan. 1997. 'Poverty and Social Exclusion: A Comparison of Debates on Deprivation', Poverty Research Unit, Working Paper No. 2, University of Sussex, Brighton.

Dumont, Lewis. 1970. *Homo-Hierarchicus*, Paladin, Granda Publications Ltd., London.

Samuel, C.J. 1990. 'Development and Social Justice', paper submitted for Seminar on Development and Social Justice, organized by the United States Educational Foundation of India, 14–17, September Pune (Mimeo).

Sen Amartya. 2000. *Development as Freedom*, Anchor Books, Random House, New York.

——. 2002. *Rationality and Freedom*, Harvard Belknap Press, Harvard.

Sharma, K.L. 1997. *Social Stratification in India: Issues and Themes*, Sage Publications, New Delhi.

Srinivas, M.N. 1959. 'The Dominant Caste in Rampur', *American Anthropologist* 61: 1–16.

Subramanyam, V. 1997. 'Caste and Power Structure in Andhra Pradesh: A Case Study of Mandur Village, PILC', *Journal of Dravidic Studies*, 7(1): 95–105.

Wiser, W.H. 1936. *Hindu Jajmani System: A Socio-Economic System Inter-Relating Members of Hindu Village Community in Service*, Lucknow Publishing House, Lucknow.

2

Social Exclusion and Inclusive Policy

An Overview

V. Subramanyam

Exclusion as a social phenomenon is expressed in different forms all over the world. In India, unique forms of exclusion are observed, where certain groups like the Dalits, backward classes, women and religious minorities experience systemic exclusion in regard to accruing the advantages of development, and institutional inequality and discrimination have been pervasive features of the society. The study of different aspects of social exclusion and framing inclusive policies has emerged as a new area of research in social sciences.

According to Sen (1997), social exclusion emphasizes the role of relational features in deprivation. Narayan (1999) calls it the norm and process that prevents certain groups from equal and effective participation in the social, economic, cultural and political lives of societies. It is clearly both a process and a product which involves at least four factors: the excluded, the institutions from which they are excluded, the agents whose actions result in the exclusion and the process through which exclusion occurs (ibid.). Power holds the key in the process of exclusion and those with power are implicated and those without it are affected (ibid.). In course of exclusion power asymmetries are observed resulting in the exclusion of certain groups and individuals.

Social exclusion of deprived communities can lead to economic poverty, as social exclusion and poverty are deeply interconnected. However, they are not to be mistaken as the same thing.

Discrimination, inequality and isolation – the main features of social exclusion – have an intense negative impact on quality of life. There are two aspects of this relationship. First, poverty can lead to social stigmatization, marginalization and exclusion from institutions, which further lead to greater poverty. Second, while social exclusion does not always lead to economic poverty, it is always linked to exclusion from institutions of society and leads to a poorer sense of well-being.

The inability of an individual to participate in the basic political, economic and social functioning of society involves the denial of equal access to opportunities imposed by certain groups in society upon others (Buvinic, 2005). This definition captures three distinguishing features of social exclusion between them, and results in deprivation or low income for those excluded (de Haan, 1997; Sen, 2000). Hence, social exclusion leads to various kinds of deprivation. Sen (2002) mentioned that "it leads to the impoverishment of human life through their casual consequences". The consequences of macro-economic policies such as poverty, unemployment and involuntary migration exclude the victims from economic, cultural and political activities.

In short, social exclusion in its more specific manifestation as discrimination refers to the process through which different groups are wholly or partially restricted from full participation in the economic, educational and social institutions that define social membership. It involves both the act of restricting access to resources and the consequences that follow. In the Indian context, exclusion revolves around institutions that discriminate, isolate, share and deprive subordinate groups on the basis of identities such as caste, religion and gender. It is mainly based on caste and patriarchy. The salient features of social exclusion on the basis of caste are social stratification, social inequality, hierarchy and hegemony. Patriarchy breeds gender inequality, and social exclusion of weaker sections is closely associated with the discriminatory practices and inequality embedded in the institution by caste.

According to Bradley (1994), there are five main mechanisms of exclusion in order of increasing severity: geography, entry barriers, corruption, intimidation and physical violence.

Geography

Social exclusion can be a function of geography, and direct correlations between rural isolation and poverty are often found (Ravallion, 1995). In general, the poor live in the most marginal areas, which compound the cycles of poverty and exclusion. In India, most of the tribes inhabit in hills and forests and are thus excluded from mainstream population.

Barriers to Entry

Transaction costs and documentation requirements are the two most common barriers to entry (Ravallion, 1995). Transaction costs are those costs that are involved in acquiring a good or service above and beyond its actual price. Barriers to entry involving the state bureaucracy are mostly related to documentation requirements. The state, which is often inflexible in helping the excluded, denies them access to resources. Documentation is also held responsible for the inability of the poor to gain access to resources. Documentation requirements represent only a part of the barrier. Other barriers to entry include hostility and unfairness confronted by excluded people while dealing with bureaucracy. Documentation therefore allows the state to humiliate and deny services to the excluded.

Corruption

Corruption as a social evil is a common problem in all parts of the world. In general, the poor people emphasize the importance of connections in obtaining goods and services such as social security, pensions, jobs, healthcare, admission to higher educational institutions and business licences. Corruption not only makes access harder for the poor in financial terms, but also destroys the trust that a society needs to function effectively. Corruption makes equal access and fair treatment from the state impossible for the poor and the excluded and accelerates their disengagement from wider society. Thus, corruption has become a central reason, because of which societies grow more insecure. Insecurity leads to depending social cleavages, increasing social exclusion and further societal fragmentation.

Intimidation

Verbal abuse is not an uncommon means of isolating individuals and groups. In general, those with power use the threat of harm to maintain their dominance over those without power. Intimidation is observed at every level by society. As a mechanism of social exclusion, it is often used to reinforce social stereotypes and power relations. For instance, in India, there is still deeply entrenched caste exclusion. The threat of violence is reported to be the major form of control by men over women.

Physical Violence

Social exclusion can result in physical violence. Fear of repercussion imposes a pall of silence around the subject of violence and the violence perpetuated by the state, community, group and individuals. Violence against women in the household is the direct consequence of patriarchy. Violence against Dalits and service castes is a common feature in many rural areas of India. Domestic violence is rooted in the norms of the gender inequality and identity and is often linked to alcohol and drug abuse.

Who Are Excluded?

In almost all human societies, certain groups are excluded and deprived of some opportunities. While the way in which each of these groups is excluded is context-specific, certain social differences continue to serve as grounds for exclusion. These differences include belonging to a particular ethnic, gender, caste, religion or age group; living in a particular geographic area; or having certain physical disabilities. While we present excluded groups in discrete categories, it is difficult to generalize which groups are most likely to be excluded in which society, and the domains from which they are excluded. Various forms of social differences overlap and intersect in complex ways over time. Some of the most common categories of excluded groups are described below:

Women

In most traditional societies even today we find that women are considered as subordinates to men. Women's identity within the household is traditionally centred on their roles as mother and wife. Women speak of their "obligation to feed the family and care for the children, both materially and emotionally, regardless of the contribution of their husbands". In many cases, the role of a wife and mother is reported to be so inflexible that the women who fall outside this category are ostracized by individuals and discriminated against by the state and other institutions. The increasing role of women in low-paid formal and informal job markets has brought new opportunities as well as burdens to women. New sources of income for women do not lead to a clear shift in their authority within their households or in the communities. Due to these inequalities and social constraints some women walk out of abusive homes and assert their rights in overt and covert ways.

Children

Children are among the most disempowered groups in society. They have little or no power or influence over the social processes that govern their lives and they can seldom protect themselves from abuse. Customary law considers children as property of their respective families and gives them no individual rights. The widespread acceptance of highly exploitative labour practices and the practice of genital mutilation of girls are among the most extreme examples of the vulnerability of children. Certain children are excluded from school for both economic and social reasons. This obviously results in child labour. For poor families, the need to get additional income takes precedence over education. Children not only work, but are often forced into the most risky forms of employment. Child prostitution is reported in many underdeveloped and developing countries. In rural areas, especially in the drought-prone areas, bonded child labour is still found.

The Poor

While social exclusion and poverty are distinct concepts, they are inextricably connected. Poor people remain poor, because they are denied access to resources, opportunities and information. For poor people in developing countries this translates into intergenerational poverty. In addition, poverty is socially stigmatized, making it even harder for poor people to gain access to the networks and resources which they need for survival. This vicious cycle is difficult to break in India. Around 40 per cent of the population stands below the poverty line, struggling to eke out a livelihood.

The Elderly

The treatment of elderly people is culture-specific. In Asia (including India) the elderly are treated with deference and respect. Aged people psychologically feel insecure with the collapse of social safety nets over the years. Their vulnerability is compounded by the rapid collapse of support systems that provided them security in their retired lives. With increasing economic stress and breakdown of family solidarity, the elderly are emerging as a new category of excluded poor in many countries across the globe.

Ethnic Groups

Social exclusion due to ethnic differences is a common feature across the globe. In India, exclusion on the grounds of ethnicity is perpetuated by the rigidities of the caste system. The practice of untouchability is seen in most villages of India. Some forms of marginalization are geographical in nature. The best example for such exclusion is the native Adivasi population. It has been pushed into the degraded forests, eroded hill slopes, scrubland and rocky soil by caste settlers. They were forced to become sources of agricultural labour for the non-tribes who encroached on the former's resources. Social exclusion on the grounds of ethnicity is a key to the understanding of the problem of loss of ownership of land by the tribes.

People with HIV/AIDS

Myths and stereotypes that surround HIV/AIDS have caused enormous suffering to the infected. They are excluded from social network, the critical asset of survival for the poor. Stereotypes against HIV/AIDS sufferers are highly culture-specific. A key problem for those with HIV/AIDS is shame denial, social isolation and losing access to social network, which they need in order to cope with the psychological and material consequences of the illness. The major fear associated with HIV/AIDS is the fear of social isolation that would befall on a household or individual if the infection is disclosed. This causes many to hide the fact, thereby hampering efforts to bring the issue into the open to further the spread of awareness. HIV/AIDS have consequences beyond the control of the infected individual. In some cases the entire household may face isolation.

The Disabled

Disabled children are not seen as normal/healthy human beings; they are isolated at home and in many cases, they are not sent to schools due to their disability. Disability is frequently reported as one of the important reasons cited for exclusion. Social exclusion can still continue even when the basic economic concerns of disabled people are fulfilled.

Widows

In many parts of India, widows are considered as an excluded group. Even before the funeral of the diseased husband, some widows are ill-treated by the in-laws who take all the property, including their children. The widows are excluded from attending certain social ceremonies and rituals at both family and community levels. The combination of social prejudices, kinship, customs and lack of accountability on the part of the state explains why widows face great risk of social exclusion and poverty. In India, widows are assumed to be an economic burden on the household: they are wholly dependent on their family for care and support as they do not have any earnings of their own. Socially they are often neglected and considered a burden to the family. The general perception is that they do not make any significant economic contribution to the family as they do not possess any kind of skills.

Inclusive Policy

Social inclusion of certain social groups is also to be understood as contextual and situational. In consonance of the idea of social upliftment through directive principles, the government formulates an inclusive policy. Constitutional safeguards and provisions extended to weaker sections by the government are also considered as inclusive policy in this context. Development policies and programmes are another kind of measurement in order to achieve inclusive growth among the excluded social categories of India. The Indian Constitution provides equality to all citizens, irrespective of caste, creed, religion and gender. It also directs the state to take various measures to remove the different forms of discrimination and inequality and thereby helps to eradicate social exclusion. The state should ensure social justice to all the deprived communities such as SCs, STs, OBCs, religious minorities, women and the disabled.

Conclusions

Ethnicity-based social exclusion is a common feature in many societies, including India. This disintegration of social order is compounded by the fact that for many the old coping mechanisms based on traditional networks are fast disappearing. The poor speak of a loss of community, which was once a partial substitute for the lack of assistance from distant state regimes the poor feel powerless to change. Community solidarity has indeed increased in some places as a form of self-protection but it is unable to confront – much less change – corrupted state institutions that become aligned with criminality and justice and police protection that can be bought and sold. In this type of environment, moving out of poverty is beyond personal control, beyond personal effort. Hence, many poor people see few benefits to increased investment in human capital.

For many vulnerable groups – such as the elderly, those with HIV/AIDS, widows and in many contexts, women – changes over the last decade have eroded important social safety networks and practices. Caught in cycles of poverty and exclusion the poor struggle to survive while opportunities to access to information, jobs, education, healthcare, markets, pensions and other resources exclude them. The way the state is organized often exacerbates existing social tensions and cleavages, leading to even greater inequality between the rich and the poor. Social justice to weaker sections through legal framework is an essential requisite for the upliftment of these vulnerable groups in India. Developmental planning for poverty alleviation among the weaker sections is another form of inclusive growth measure and policy of the government to eliminate disparities between the rich and the poor as well as between the highest and lowest castes and is the immediate intervention strategy to be implemented.

References

Bradley, Christine. 1994. 'Why Male Violence against Women Is a Development Issue: Reflections from Papua New Guinea', in Miranda Davies (ed.), *Women and Violence: Realities and Responses Worldwide*, Zed Books, London.

Buvinic, Mayra. 2005. 'Social Inclusion in Latin America', in Mayra Buvinic and Jacqueline Mazza (eds.), *Social Exclusion and Economic Development*, Johns Hopkins University Press, Baltimore, pp. 3–32.

de Haan, Arjan. 1997. 'Poverty and Social Exclusion: A Comparison of Debates on Deprivation', Poverty Research Unit, Working Paper No. 2, University of Sussex, Brighton.

Narayan, Deepa. 1999. 'Bonds and Bridges: Social Capital and Poverty', Policy Research Working Paper 2167, Policy Research Department, World Bank, Washington, DC.

Narayan, Deepa, Raj Patel, Kai Schafft, Anne Rademacher and Sarah Koch-Schutte. 2000. *Voices of the Poor: Can Anyone Hear Us?* Oxford University Press, New York.

Ravallion, Martin. 1995. 'China's Lagging Poor Areas', *American Economic Review* (Papers and Procedures), 89: 301–305.

Sen, Amartya. 1997. *On Economic Inequality* (2nd ed.), Clarendon Press, Oxford.

——. 2000. *Development as Freedom,* Anchor Books, Random House, New York.

——. 2002. *Rationality and Freedom,* Harvard Belknap Press, Harvard.

Thorat, S. and Katherine S. Newman. 2007. 'Caste and Economic Discrimination: Causes, Consequences and Remedies', *Economic and Political Weekly* (special issue), 13 October, pp. 4121–24.

3

Social Exclusion and the Dalits in India

Y. Chinna Rao

The term 'social exclusion' is so evocative, ambiguous, multidimensional and expansive that it can be defined in many different ways. Yet the difficulty of defining exclusion and the fact that it is interpreted differently in different contexts at different times can be seen as a theoretical opportunity (Gallie, 1956). Rather than putting forward a single definition of exclusion, it is interesting to understand the disputes surrounding the term 'exclusion' and its usage in different contexts, by tracing the history of the idea and decoding the multiple meanings of the term in a variety of national contexts.

In Europe, the term 'social exclusion' emerged in the late twentieth century as a key concept among analysts and policy makers seeking to understand and formulate directives of approaches to alleviate some of the negative social effects of economic restructuring. Thus, the term has an evident appeal for politicians and policy analysts. In Western Europe, those meanings are embedded in the emergence of the term in French political rhetoric and the specific institutional history of the European Union. The term 'social exclusion' was originally coined in France in 1974 to refer to various categories of people who were unprotected by social insurance at the time but labelled as 'social problems' identified as "mentally and physically handicapped, suicidal people, aged invalids, abused children, substance abusers, delinquents, single parents, multi-problem households, marginal, asocial persons and other social misfits" (Silver, 1994). However, in the 1980s, this stigmatizing and narrow view of social exclusion was superseded as the term became central to French debates about the nature of the neo poverty associated with technological change and economic restructuring (Gore et al., 1995). Social exclusion in this context was not simply equated with poverty, but was broadened to refer to a process of social disintegration, in the sense of a progressive rupture of the relationship between the individual and society, which was occurring due to increasing long-term unemployment, particularly focused on unskilled workers and immigrants, the inability of young people to enter the labour market, greater family instability and isolated single-member households, increasing numbers of homeless people and rising tensions and periodic violence in the low-cost housing settlements on the periphery of cities (*banlieues*). This dissipation of the social fabric of society seemed to be a consequence of the long-term process of transformations in the structure and organization of economic life.

Addressing social exclusion requires a holistic approach which promotes involvement of excluded populations in community life, ensures access to all basic services, promotes behaviour change, increases income and addresses other key elements of exclusion (Jenkins and Barr, 2006). Discrimination is clearly a particular kind of exclusion and it can take on either an active or a passive form. Active exclusion through discrimination will see agents systematically refusing to hire or accept the participation of members of a social group despite their formal qualifications (or even overqualification), while routinely favouring members of groups who are equally or even less qualified. The consequences of discrimination can lead to deprivation, indirectly through passive discrimination in which discouragement and lower self-confidence result in poor performance or directly through routes that limit access to income or education that is mobility-enhancing.

In social sciences literature there is general agreement on the core features of social exclusion, its principal indicators and the way it relates to poverty and inequality. Social exclusion is the denial of equal opportunities imposed by certain groups of society upon others, which leads to the inability of an individual to participate in the basic political, economic and social functioning of the society. The developments in social sciences literature indeed enable us to comprehend the meanings and manifestations of the concept of social exclusion and its applicability to caste-and ethnicity-based exclusion in India. The manner in which it has been developed in social sciences literature, the concept of social exclusion, thus, essentially refers to the processes through which groups are wholly, or partially, excluded from full participation in the society in which they live. It emphasizes two crucial dimensions involving the notion of exclusion, namely, the 'societal institutions' (of exclusion) and their 'outcome' (in terms of deprivation). In order to understand the dimensions of exclusion, it is necessary to explore the societal interrelations and institutions, which lead to exclusion of certain groups and deprivation in multiple spheres – civil, cultural, political and economic. Thus, for a broader understanding of the concept of exclusion, the insights into the societal process and the institutions of exclusions are as important as the outcome in terms of deprivation for certain groups. Sen (2000) therefore refers to various meanings and manifestations of social exclusion, particularly with respect to the causes or the processes of discrimination and deprivation in a given society. Exclusion could occur through direct exclusion, violating fair norms of exclusion (that is unfavourable exclusion), or through inclusion, but under unfavourable conditions, again violating fair norms of inclusion (that is unfavourable inclusion), or through deliberate government policies (that is active exclusion), or through unintended attempts and circumstances (passive exclusion) or exclusion caused through inability of some persons to relate to other persons (constitutive relevance). Mainstream economists have further elaborated the concept of discrimination that operates particularly through markets. Social exclusion can indeed arise in a variety of ways, and it is important to recognize the versatility of the idea and its reach.

Social Exclusion in Indian Context

In India, exclusion is embedded in societal interrelations and institutions that exclude, discriminate, isolate and deprive some groups on the basis of the groups' identities such as caste and ethnicity. The nature of exclusion revolving around the caste system particularly needs to be understood and conceptualized. The caste system's fundamental characteristics of fixed civil, cultural and economic rights for each caste, with restrictions for change, imply 'forced exclusion' of one caste from the rights of other castes, or from undertaking the occupations of other castes (Ambedkar, 1987). Exclusion and discrimination in civil, cultural and particularly economic spheres such as occupation and labour employment is, therefore, internal to the system and a necessary outcome of its governing principles. In the market economy framework, the occupational immobility would operate through restrictions in various markets such as land, labour, credit, other inputs and services necessary for any economic activity. Labour being an integral part of the production process of any economic activity would obviously become a part of market discrimination (Thorat, 2003).

In the light of the above, caste- and untouchability-based exclusion and discrimination can be categorized in the economic, civil, cultural and political spheres, as the exclusion and the denial of equal opportunity in economic spheres would necessarily operate through market and non-market transactions and exchange. Firstly, exclusion can be practised through the denial in labour market in hiring for jobs; in capital market through the denial of access to capital; in agriculture land market through the denial in sale and purchase or leasing of land; in input market through the denial in sale and purchase of factor inputs; and in consumer market through the denial in sale and purchase of commodities and consumer goods (Thorat, 2001). Secondly, discrimination can occur through what Amartya Sen would describe as 'unfavourable inclusion', namely, through differential treatment in terms and conditions of contract, one of them would reflect indiscrimination in the prices charged and received by discriminated groups. This can be inclusive of the price of factor inputs and consumer goods, price of factors of production such as wages for labour, price of land or rent on land, interest on capital, rent on residential houses and charges or fees on services such as water and electricity. Discriminated groups can get lower prices for the goods that they sell, and could pay higher prices for the goods that they buy, as compared with the market price or the price paid by other groups. Thirdly, exclusion and discrimination can occur in terms of access to social needs supplied by the government or public institutions, or by private institutions in education, housing and health, including common property resources like water bodies, grazing land and other land of common use. Lastly, a group (particularly the untouchables) may face discrimination from participation in certain categories of jobs (the sweeper being excluded from inside household jobs), because of the notions of purity and pollution of occupations and engagements in so-called unclean occupations:

1. In the civil and cultural spheres, the untouchables may face discrimination and exclusion in the use of public services such as

public roads, temples, water bodies and institutions delivering services like education, health and other public services.

2. In the political spheres, the untouchables can face discrimination in the use of political rights, and in a participation in decision-making process.
3. Due to the physical (or residential) segregation, and social exclusion on account of the notion of untouchability (or touch-me-not-sum), they can suffer from a general societal exclusion.
4. Since there is societal mechanism to regulate and enforce the customary norms and rules of the caste system, the untouchables generally can face opposition in the form of social and economic boycott and violence, which act as a general deterrent to their right to development.

Social Exclusion and Human Rights Situation

Reviewing the effectiveness of policies and programmes in addressing social exclusion relates to the discussion on human development and human rights. Put simply, development approaches from the 1950s to the 1980s primarily focused on social and economic development as an outcome of the development process and were less concerned with civil and political rights. During this period, government policy and the development community were also less concerned with the quality of the process by which the outcomes were achieved (Jonsson, 2003). In contrast, the human rights-based approach to development recognizes both the achievement of a desirable outcome and the establishment of an adequate process to achieve and sustain that outcome. "Participation, local ownership, empowerment, and sustainability are essential characteristics of a high-quality process. A rights perspective is based on principles that emphasize accountability of those with obligations to realize the rights of children; the universality of rights; the indivisibility and interdependence of rights; and also the principle of the best interests of the child and taking into account the views of the child. The state and the other 'duty-bearers' (e.g., parents and teachers) have obligations to fulfill these rights. As rights-holders, children are entitled to demand that the duty-bearers meet their respective obligation to respect, protect and fulfill their rights" (ibid.).

This approach necessitates a broader perspective in addressing the issue of social exclusion, and also highlights the importance of focusing on both achieving the desired outcome (i.e., all children in school) and following an inclusive and participatory process. Similar to the broader recognition that poverty is not merely a lack of income but rather a condition of living in various forms of deprivation, social exclusion is not only a development issue, but also a human rights issue and therefore requires a more comprehensive and process-oriented response.

Historically, the caste system classified people by their occupation and status. Shah et al. (2006) argue that each caste had a specific place in the hierarchy of social status. However, since the nineteenth century, the link between caste and occupation has become less rigid as it became easier for people to change occupations. This change has accelerated with the economic boom which has taken place in India since the early 1990s. In the recent past, the European Parliament had taken a resolution on the human rights situation of the Dalits in India. It mentioned that the National Human Rights Commission of India has reported that the implementation of the Scheduled Castes and Scheduled Tribes (SCs and STs) (Prevention of Atrocities) Act remains very unsatisfactory, and it has even published numerous recommendations to address this problem.

Untouchability is prohibited under the Constitution of India. To give effect to this Article, the Parliament enacted the Untouchability (Offences) Act, 1955, based on Article 17, Abolition of Untouchability. It has scope over the entire country and its provisions are implemented by the respective State Governments and the Union Territories and coordinated by the Government of India. The Act provides penalties for enforcing untouchability or any disability arising thereof – preventing a person from entering a place of public worship and offering prayers or taking water from a sacred tank, well or spring. To make the provisions of this Act more stringent, the Act was amended in 1976 and was also renamed the Protection of Civil Rights Act, 1955 (PCR Act). Under the Act, the Government of India also notified the PCR Rules, 1977, to carry out the provisions of this Act. As cases of atrocities on SCs and STs were not covered under the provisions of the PCR Act, 1955, the parliament passed another Act in 1989 to take measures to prevent the atrocities committed against them. This act, known as the Scheduled Castes and Scheduled Tribes (Prevention of Atrocities) Act, 1989, became effective from 30, January, 1990. For carrying out the provisions of this Act the Government of India notified the SCs and STs (Prevention of Atrocities) Rules, 1995, on 31 March, 1995. Based on the provisions of the SCs and STs (Prevention of Atrocities) Act, 1989, caste-based atrocities committed against the members of the SC and the ST is an offence punishable under the law. Offences under the PCR Act are cognizable as well as non-compoundable. The number of cases registered under the PCR Act is an indication of the continued perpetuation of untouchability, violation of human rights and committing of atrocity and discrimination.

A recent study on untouchability in rural India by Shah et al. (2006), covering 560 villages in eleven states, found that public health workers refused to visit Dalit homes in 33 per cent of villages, Dalits were prevented from entering police stations in 28 per cent of villages, Dalit children had to sit separately while eating in 38 per cent of government schools, Dalits did not get mail delivered to their homes in 24 per cent of villages and Dalits were denied access to water sources in 48 per cent of villages because of segregation and untouchability practices. Another record shows that twenty-seven officially registered atrocities are being committed against Dalits every day; police often prevent Dalits from entering police stations, refuse the registration of cases by Dalits and regularly resort to the practice of torture against Dalits with impunity. And despite the fact that many Dalits do not report crimes for fear of reprisals by the dominant castes, official police statistics averaged over the past five years show that thirteen Dalits are murdered every week, five Dalits' homes or possessions are burnt every week, six Dalits are kidnapped or abducted every week, three Dalit women are raped every day, eleven Dalits are beaten every day and a crime is committed against a Dalit every 18 minutes (Crime in India, 2005).

Untouchability in schools has contributed to far higher dropout and illiteracy levels for Dalit children than those of the general population. This 'gap of illiteracy' between Dalits and non-Dalits has hardly changed since India's independence and literacy rates for Dalit women has remained as low as 38 per cent in rural India. About half of India's Dalit children are undernourished, 21 per cent are 'severely underweight' and 12 per cent die before their fifth birthday (Ministry of Health and Family Welfare, 1998–1999).

It is seen that Andhra Pradesh tops the list in terms of reported cases, while Uttar Pradesh and Bihar, where one-third of the country's Dalits live, report very little. The data need to be taken with much caution since many of these practices are considered part of the existing social rules and norms and are accepted even by the Dalit community as owing to their 'lower' social and economic status. Cases also go unreported owing to the dependency of Dalit communities for their livelihood and the fear of backlash by the perpetrators as they hold social, economic and institutional power in the area. Dalit victims also do not receive any support from the police or administration to register human rights violations against them. From its review with various state governments, the SC and ST Commission viewed that "a large number of cases of atrocities go unregistered, mainly because of reluctance on the part of police officers to register the cases ..." (National Commission for Scheduled Castes and Scheduled Tribes, 2002).

In addition to the PCR Act, crimes against Dalits are also registered under the SCs and STs (Prevention of Atrocities) Act, 1989, and other sections of the Indian Penal Code (IPC). At the all-India level, there were 25,093 cases of crime in 1999, 25,455 in 2000 and 33,501 in 2001. This is an annual average of 28,016 crimes. Approximately three Dalit persons per hundred thousand were subjected to atrocities and violence during this period. It is inferred from the data that during the period 1999–2001, the most intolerant states as far as crimes against the Dalits are concerned were Uttar Pradesh, followed by Rajasthan, Madhya Pradesh and Andhra Pradesh, respectively. It is strange that Uttar Pradesh and Rajasthan show a very small record of cases registered under the PCR Act in the same years. West Bengal consistently claims that there is no practice of untouchability in the state.

The ActionAid Study explored Dalits' access to basic public services that may not be directly related to the state. As is evident from the study, by far the most prevalent practice of untouchability in this realm was related to the denial of access to water resources – a little less than half (48.4%) of the villages surveyed reported the presence of this practice in some form or the other.

The notions of purity and pollution have been particularly resilient in relation to drinking water sources. The study also confirmed the fact and found that persistent conflicts were reported with regard to drinking water. While complete denial of access to a particular water source (well, tank, tubewell and so on) designated as upper caste was quite common, what was even more common was the imposition of differential behaviour on Dalits. In over one-third (about 36%) of the villages surveyed, the Dalits were denied entry into village shops. This usually meant that the Dalits were not allowed to come up to the counter like other customers, but were made to wait outside or at some distance from the shop. In about one thirds of the villages, the teashops discriminated against the Dalits by asking them to be seated separately and there was widespread practice of the two-glass system. The social status of the castes providing services such as those of washermen and barbers is dependent on their denying the services to Dalits. Such denial of services to Dalits is always demanded by non-Dalits. Discrimination by washermen and barbers was found to be present in as many as 47 per cent of the villages.

These can be seen in times of emergency and disaster response as was reported in the time of the Tsunami. Dalits were forced to huddle in a corner and be invisible when relief and aid came and were not allowed to use the water tanks or toilets provided by aid agencies. In many places, dominant castes actively prevented Dalits from accessing food brought by organizations and would serve spoilt and leftover rice the next day after fresh supplies reached them.

One could see the parallel and simultaneous debate on human rights in the Universal Declaration of Human Rights with a commitment to a new world order. Despite India taking a leading role in the formation of the League of Nations and the UN, the anti-caste and anti-untouchability movements within the country did not find any mention in this historical global document as a 'source of discrimination' nor 'Dalits' as the 'victims of discrimination'. It is further surprising to note that India brought up the issue of the discrimination against 'people of India' origin in South Africa. Dalits' topic did not come into the purview or debate or discourse of building universal human rights mechanisms. Caste is not listed in the UN treaties such as International Convention on the Elimination of All Forms of Racial Discrimination (ICERD), International Covenant on Civil and Political Rights (ICCPR), Convention on the Elimination of all forms of Discrimination against Women (CEDAW) or Convention on the Rights of the Child (CRC), and the specificity of caste dimension affecting over 200 million people in Asia was often overshadowed by other dimensions of discrimination and the Dalit concerns did not inform UN Human Rights discourse for many decades. It is the responsibilities of both the state and the society to see that the Dalits and tribes, like the rest of the population, lead their lives with dignity and without fear. Dalit human rights will remain a dream as long as their material conditions are not improved. They continue to be, unambiguously, at the disadvantaged level as a group.

Social Exclusion and Higher Education

The Government of India set up an interim University Grants Commission (UGC) by a resolution and began to function from the last week of December 1953; it came into existence formally through an Act of Parliament only in November 1956. India became Republic in 1950 by adopting a new constitution, in which reservations for SCs and STs were incorporated. Therefore, the government should have directed and the UGC should have adopted the reservation policy at least from 1956, if not from 1953. On the contrary, the UGC went on reiterating that no reservations should be made available to SCs and STs for appointments particularly to the posts of teachers in universities and its affiliated colleges (Namala, 2006). However, for the first time after more than two decades of its existence, in 1975, it agreed, in principle, to provide reservations to SCs and STs for recruitments only at the level of lecturer with a condition that not to operate reservation on a roster system and also not to carry forward reserved posts (Sharma, 2003).

In 1975 the Committee of Vice Chancellors of Central Universities recommended for implementation of reservations, which were not in consonance with the spirit of reservation policy. However, the UGC accepted the same and insisted not to operate a roster system and not to carry forward the reserved posts on a year-to-year basis. By doing so, the UGC almost gave a free hand to the universities to implement the reservations the way they wanted. It gave indirect encouragement to implement the reservations detrimentally. We shall see in the next section how these institutions responded in the process of fulfilling the constitutional mandatory and their apathy towards social justice.

There are three types of universities in India, i.e., Central Universities, State Universities and Deemed (to be) Universities. Out of the twenty Central Universities, 18 get both development (plan) and maintenance (non-plan) assistance from the UGC. And, the remaining two universities, Indira Gandhi National Open University, New Delhi, and Central Agricultural University, Imphal, are directly funded by the Ministry of Human Resource Development and the Ministry of Agriculture, Government of India, respectively. Let us have a look at the manner in which these 18 Central Universities are working in the process of appointments and delivering their institutional responsibilities.

In these 18 Central Universities the total sanctioned teaching posts are 8,765 consisting of 1,430 Professors, 2,592 Readers and 4,189 Lecturers. However, the existing strength of faculty members is only 6,588, leaving 1,177 total posts lying vacant. Out of the present strength of 6,588, Professors are 1,276, Readers 1,935 and Lecturers 2,272. Thus, presently 154, 657 and 1,917 posts of Professors, Readers and Lecturers, respectively, are lying vacant in Central Universities. When thousands and thousands of youth armed with degrees are in search of jobs and many are already in service waiting for promotions, it is quite disturbing to see posts lying vacant in such large numbers. There might be academic and even non-academic constraints of universities, but non-filling of vacancies is likely to adversely affect the national agenda of empowerment of disprivileged sections of the society, particularly the SC and ST communities.

Kale (2006) gives details about the representation of SCs and STs in teaching posts in Central Universities. Out of the sanctioned 1,430 posts for Professors, 1,248 have been occupied by the general category faculty members. However, there are only 11 and 17 posts for Professors belonging to the SCs and STs, respectively. Numerically it comes to be less than one Professor each for SC and ST per university. Only five universities have a Professor(s) who belongs to the SC community. In other words, no Professor who belongs to the SC community is on the rolls of 13 universities. The universities without an SC Professor include Banaras Hindu University, Pondicherry University, Jamia Millia Islamia, North Eastern Hill University and Allahabad University. The University of Delhi, one of the oldest with a faculty strength of 1,086, has just one Professor from the SC category. Vishwa Bharati University with a total 655 teachers also has one Professor belonging to the SC category. The other universities such as University of Hyderabad, Jawaharlal Nehru University and Assam University have two, three and four SC Professors respectively.

In case of STs, their percentage of representation in posts of Professors is also quite low (1.18%). It will not be out of place to point that out of 17 Professors who belong to the ST category, 12 are placed in two universities, that too from north-eastern regions of the country. From the remaining five Professors of ST, three are in Jawaharlal Nehru University and one each in Delhi University and Vishwa Bharati University. Surprisingly, 13 Central Universities do not have even a single Professor from the ST community. Same is the case with Readers.

Until recently, there was no provision of reservations at the level of Professor and Reader in Central Universities, unlike the State Universities. This fact is always used to justify the lower representation of SCs and STs at the level of Professor and Reader. It means whenever and wherever the reservation is applicable, SCs and STs are given due representation as prescribed in the guidelines of the government. Since the reservation in teaching positions in Central Universities is given only at the level of Lecturer, it will be interesting to see its implementation in recruitment at the Lecturer level. Indeed, it is quite disappointing to note that only 4.58 per cent of SC and 3.53 per cent of ST posts have been filled so far, whereas the constitutional mandatory is 15 per cent and 7.5 per cent, respectively. In other words, there should have been 629 and 314 Lecturers of SC and ST category, respectively. Instead, only 192 SCs and 148 STs have been appointed till March 2003. On the other hand, 1,932 posts of Lecturers have been occupied by the general category candidates and 1,917 posts are lying vacant. There are four Central Universities that do not have any Lecturer belonging to the SC category, and three universities have no Lecturer belonging to the ST category.

Conclusion

The question remains as to why the SCs and STs have poor access to all resources that directly and indirectly determine the level of income and capabilities to secure other sources of income. Why the ownership of agricultural land and non-land capital assets is low compared with non-SCs/STs? Why are the unemployment rates high particularly among the SCs compared with non-SCs/STs? Why are the daily wage earnings of SCs/STs in non-farm activities low compared with non-SCs/STs? Why the literacy rate and education level are much lower when compared with non-SCs/STs?

Given the complexity and crucial relevance of these issues to large groups of people, the discipline we are presently considering assumes great significance. The establishment of these social exclusion programmes of study in various institutions holds promise of more specialized knowledge to overcome the challenges posed to government, especially in the post-colonial era. Even if government action is tardy, as it often is, such knowledge matters, because exclusion from the domain of knowledge has got the means of preserving exclusion.

References

Ambedkar, B.R. 1987. 'The Hindu Social Order: Its Essential Features', in Vasant Moon (ed.), *Dr Babasaheb Ambedkar Writings and Speeches*, Vol. 3, Government of Maharashtra, Bombay.

Census of India. 2001. Registrar General of India, New Delhi.

Crime in India. 2005. National Crime Records Bureau, Ministry of Home Affairs, New Delhi.

Gallie, G.B. 1956. Essentially Contested Concepts in Aristotelian Society Proceedings (No. 56) cited in Hillary Silver, 'Reconceptualizing Social Disadvantage: Three Paradigms of Social Exclusion', in Gerry Rodgers, Charles Gore and Jose B. Figueiredo (eds.), *Social Exclusion: Rhetoric, Reality, Responses*, International Institute for Labour Studies, Geneva.

Gore. C., Gerry Rodgers and Jose B. Figueiredo. 1995. 'Introduction: Markets Citizenship and Social Exclusion', in Gerry Rodgers, Charles Gore and Jose B. Figueiredo (eds.), *Social Exclusion: Rhetoric, Reality, Responses*, International Institute for Labour Studies, Geneva.

Jenkins, Robert and Eimar Barr. 2006. *Social Exclusion of Scheduled Caste from Primary Education in India*, UNICEF, New Delhi.

Jonsson, Urban. 2003. *Human Rights Approach to Development Planning*, UNICEF, Eastern and Southern Africa Regional Office, Nairobi.

Kale, R.K. 2006. 'Reservation for SC and ST in Central Universities: Is It a Failure of Will or Efforts?' *University News*, Vol. 44, No. 48.

Namala, Annie. 2006. Dismantling Caste-based Discrimination, Report on Descent-based Discrimination and Access to Rights, New Delhi.

National Commission for Scheduled Castes and Scheduled Tribes. 2002. Sixth Report.

Ministry of Health and Family Welfare. 1998–1999. National Family Health Survey, Government of India, New Delhi.

Sen, Amartya. 2000. *Social Exclusion: Concept, Application and Security*, Asian Development Bank, Manila.

Shah, Ghanshyam, Harsh Mander, Sukhadeo Thorat, Satish Despande and Amita Baviskar. 2006. *Untouchability in Rural India*, Sage Publications, New Delhi.

Sharma, Kavita A. 2003. *50 Years of University Grants Commission*, University Grants Commission, New Delhi.

Silver, H. 1995, Reconceptualising Social Disadvantage: Three Paradigms of Social Exclusion in G. Rodgers, C. Gore and J. Figueivedo (eds) *Social Exclusion: Rhetoric, Reality, Responses,* International Institute of Labour Studies, Geneva.

Thorat, Sukhadeo. 2001. 'Caste Untouchability and Economic and Market Discrimination: Theory, Concept and Consequences', *Artha Vighyan*, Vol. XLII, Nos. 1–2.

——. 2003. *Caste Ethnicity and Religion: An Overview Paper on Exclusion/Discrimination and Deprivation*, DFID, New Delhi.

4

Socio-cultural Anthropology and Social Exclusion

From Simple Description to Complex Process

Rajesh Patnaik

In this research paper, an attempt is made to throw light on certain customs and traditions of the Kolam of Satmala Plateau, which can be considered as the heartland of the Kolam tribals. The traditions and customs here seem to have been significantly well preserved from outside influence. As a part of the Kolam annual 'Ayak' ritual, the clan symbol is carried to the banks of River Godavari, which involves travelling through a number of caste villages. In recent decades the newly politicized village panchayats of these villages have forcibly stopped the Kolam from using their traditional route, thus excluding them from their own ancestral socio-cultural spatial zone. This simple fact has a complex set of ramifications of 'social exclusion' for an entire community.

It would be pertinent to say at the beginning of this paper that the word 'simple description' in the title does not imply that socio-cultural anthropology relies only on description, which is only a qualitative recording of a culture. In fact, one of the major theoretical underpinnings of anthropology in recent decades can be attributed to 'thick description' (Geertz, 1973), wherein the description itself makes a clearer attempt to achieve a deeper interpretation of socio-cultural systems in contrast to a presumed simple description. Writing 'thick description', interpreting cultural meaning as symbolized by members' behaviour, is a complex process; it is scientific, embodying objectivity and capable of being refuted. It is complex, because the structures of meaning underlying any one social situation are multiple, partial and tangled together. We shall return to this argument later in this chapter.

Conceptualization

'Social exclusion' as of now is, at least at the definitional level, being advocated as a multidimensional concept that attempts to highlight the process of exclusion of an individual, ethnic group, community or any other identifiable entity of the larger society. This exclusion puts them at a disadvantage of not being able to participate in various development/improvement living standards. In the last few years a general agreement has emerged, despite the continuing vagueness of the term 'social exclusion', that its main value lies in drawing attention to issues of dynamics and multidimensionality (Berghman 1996; Room, 1999; Sen, 2000).

There are however some issues in the social exclusion literature between an emphasis on a heterogeneity of trajectories and on accumulation of disadvantages, apparently leading to an unsettled focus of the literature (Paugam, 1996). This aspect is stressed in discussions on the social exclusion literature (Room, 1999: 171). As socio-cultural anthropologists, we would only partly agree with Whelan and Whelan (1996: 29) who argued that uncritical insistence on multidimensionality could have the effect of obscuring the processes involved in generating social exclusion. For the present chapter we would like to adhere to social exclusion as a multidimensional concept. Social exclusion arises from a variety of processes: a focus on 'spatial exclusion' and 'environmental exclusion' with ramifications of socio-cultural and religious nature is presented here. Further, this can also be viewed in a secular way and can be conceived as deprivation, a negation of an intrinsic capability of an entire community.

Ethnography can be understood as a particular way of 'inscribing' culture, as a special kind of 'thick' writing. What anthropological analysis amounts to, in a word, is a venture in 'thick description'. Ethnography is the approach to research most closely associated with social and cultural anthropology. Ethnography entails the close and prolonged observation of a particular social group. Geertz characterizes this as recognizing the difference between a twitch and a wink. A wink and a twitch may look the same as a physical movement.

However, the wink is governed by a social convention, and is therefore meaningful. As Geertz puts it, "That's all there is to it: a speak of behaviour, a fleck of culture, and – a gesture" (1973: 6).

An ethnographer is not concerned just with isolated gestures, although a crucial part of the ethnographer's task is to record in detail particular events and actions from the everyday life ultimately concerned to explicate the whole gamut of norms, values and rules that govern and give meaning to behaviour within the group. The central problem confronting the ethnographer is then that of overcoming the barriers that exist to understanding and interpretation. The concept of ethnographic description is vital to extrapolate the deeper meaning of socio-cultural behaviour in given context. The ethnographic description of this nature is termed as 'thick description'. Thick description is a concept introduced into anthropology by Geertz. It is theorized in "Thick Description: Toward and Interpretive Theory of Culture", and perhaps best exemplified in "Deep Play: Notes on the Balinese Cockfight" (both essays appearing in *The Interpretation of Cultures*; Geertz, 1973). The essays remain two of the central texts of what became known as 'interpretive anthropology', and figure as part of a widespread refocusing of anthropological interest.

The term 'thick description' is contrasted with overt and observable behaviour, observation and superficial description, which can be said to be 'thin'. One can move from this 'thin' description to 'thick' description; it could be thought of as stratified layers of significance, which can be described increasingly 'thickly'. And this, Geertz advises, is the main objective of ethnography: to get beneath the surface of behaviour to the piled-up levels of inference and implication, the hierarchy of structures of meaning, in terms of which behaviour is produced, perceived and interpreted.

Thick description is characterized by a complex specificity and a circumstantiality, and this in turn must originate in largely qualitative research a is participatory and long-term, and carried out in small-scale, even confined, contexts. This is not to say that anthropological study does not extend to large-scale canvases – whole villages or cities, whole societies or civilizations – but that large conclusions are characteristically drawn from small, densely textured facts, and broad abstractions grounded in narrow particulars. And as study builds on study, anthropological analysis delves more and more deep and finely into the underlying conceptual structures, which give meaning to the symbolic usage within a socio-cultural milieu. In explicating thick description, Geertz places particular and special emphasis on the notions 'culture' and 'symbol'. Culture is to be understood as an accumulated totality of symbol systems (religion, ideology, common sense, economics, sports, etc.) in terms of which people make sense of themselves and to others. Members of a culture use its symbols as a language through which to read and interpret to express and share meaning. And since the imposition of meaning on life is the major and primary condition of human existence, this reading of culture is constant.

Writing thick description, interpreting cultural meaning as symbolized by members' behaviour, is a complex process; nevertheless, it is scientific embodying objectivity and capable of being refuted. We have seen that it is complex because the structures of meaning underlying any one social situation are multiple, partial and tangled together.

The religious practices of various tribal groups have been well recorded by a number of British administrators, Christian Missionaries and early Indian anthropologists. Most of their practices have been faithfully recorded; of course many of these accounts would bear some ethnocentric bias, but one has to consider the situation under which these were recorded. Some of these records were not meant for analysis by social scientists. The Ayak of Kolam, which is their main clan god, has been described as a part of other ethnography by the renowned anthropologist Furer-Haimendorf (1945, 1948, 1952, 1979). We would be further clear if we understand the nature of ethnography in the context of Geertz's elucidation of thick description in conjunction with an expanded understanding of ethnography.

Kolam

One of the lesser-investigated groups of tribals is the Kolam of South Central India. The Kolam or more appropriately the Kolvar are found mainly in Adilabad district of Andhra Pradesh and the adjoining districts of Maharashtra and Madhya Pradesh states. The recent works on Kolam have brought out only certain aspects of their ethnography (Hazra, 1983; Mohan Rao, 1990). Identification of their precise geographical distribution is at present not an easy task. They are not found in contagious areas, especially in Maharashtra and Madhya Pradesh where they live in isolated regions and in multi-tribal and even in some caste villages.

Environment

In the heart of the Deccan, just south of central India, the Satmala Hill Range runs for about 280 km approximately parallel to the River Godavari, north of its right bank. The Satmala Hill Range reaches a maximum elevation of about 2,300 feet. The southern edge of the hill range is characterized by the presence of a well-defined plateau. This roughly rectangular land is bounded on the north by River Pen Ganga and on the south by the mighty River Godavari. The part of this plateau forms a part of erstwhile Utnoor taluk of Adilabad district. The plateau consists of low hills and some flat lands. The soils vary from rich black cotton to sandy loams. The climate of this region is characterized by hot summers and cool winters, and the monsoon brings varied amounts of rainfall into this area. The major peninsular seasonal fluctuations are well represented in this area. The area is well used for dryland agriculture. Earlier, shifting cultivation was practiced on the hill slopes. The rest of the land on the plateau is covered with thickly wooded teak forest.

The main concentration of Kolam in Andhra Pradesh is found in the Satmala Plateau in the district of Adilabad where they live in exclusive settlements. The Kolam found elsewhere appear to have been in greater contact with plains people, and their language and customs seem to have been more or less modified. Among the Kolam of Adilabad one finds that contact with plains people is limited. The reason for this can be basically attributed to a geographical dimension of accessibility, and the other reason is that the Kolam of Adilabad have been living in the shadow of Gonds for a very long time. Kolam seem to have been living in the Satmala Plateau from an early stage of the populating of Satmala Plateau. It is likely that Gonds migrated to this region after the Kolam. Gonds, who were at one time a very powerful tribe with a fully developed 'state', acted as a buffer between the Kolam and the plains people to some extent. The interaction between Gonds and Kolam was based on the principle of rulers and ruled.

Society

The Kolam are Dravidian-speaking people. Their language has been classified as an independent member of the Dravidian family distinct from the Gondi group of languages (Emeneau, 1995; Zvelebil, 1970). Kolami is known as Kolavi to the tribesmen. The partial influence of Telugu on Kolavi is apparent here, because in the language of Kalavi counting is limited to numerical one and two, the remaining counting is done in Telugu. This can be attributed to the long-standing trading links of the Kolam of this region with that of Telugu-speaking shavakars (traders) living in Janaram (Telugu-speaking area) region. The Yeotmal and Chandrapur districts of Maharashtra have been influenced by Marathi and Hindi. One can assume that the Kolavi spoken by the people of Satmala Plateau is the least influenced by other languages. The Kolam of Satmala Plateau are multilingual – they speak Gondi and Telugu also.

Kolam live in settlements known as gudem. In Satmala plateau the Kolam gudem usually form hamlets of revenue villages; the huts are constructed on a rectangular ground with a common central courtyard. All the gudem in the region belonging to the Kolam reflect this pattern. At present, Kolam are settled cultivators, while some 40 years ago they were shifting cultivators with greater dependence on forest produce. The customs and traditions of Kolam have their most powerful expression in the field of ancestor worship and life cycle rituals. Before we can go into the details, an understanding of Kolam social organization would be essential since in a tribal society based on kinship ties the ritual and social aspects are intertwined in a seamless fashion. The Kolam's basic organizational unit consists of territorial clans. At one time the whole of the Satmala Plateau was divided into a number of clan territories. These units were represented by the presence of a gudem in each territory. A Kolam clan is the primary exogamous unit. Each clan has a name, which descends in the male line. While clans are exogamous, a number of clans are prohibited to exchange woman. It is believed that all these clans are related, and are actually brotherly clans. Thus, the whole of the Kolam society is separated into two major divisions, each consisting of a number of brotherly clans. In the Satmala Plateau both these major divisions are found. The entire plateau is a socio-geographical unit in itself and almost no marriages are conducted beyond this region. Each Kolam gudem has two important functionaries. The duties of these two people are clearly demarcated, the Dela is the ritual head and the Naikon is the secular head. The Dela and his wife Delabai are required at the Ayak's rituals. Each clan has an Ayak, which all the clan members worship (Patnaik, 1992).

Ayak

The Kolam believe in a number of supernatural beings. Some of them are supposed to be benevolent and others malevolent; both these types of supernatural beings need to be appeased. The nature and intensity of displeasure of these supernatural beings depends on the causative mistakes done by an individual, a family or sometimes by the entire gudem. The nature of worship and propagation of the Ayak is intertwined in deep-rooted traditional ancestor worship belief. The rituals of Ayak illustrate not only the Kolam belief in ancestor worship, but also the transmigration of spirits. An engraved square-sectioned wooden post measuring about a metre long represents the Ayak. The head of this wooden post is decorated with peacock feathers. The post is engraved with the symbols of the moon, sun and stars. The foot of the post has an iron spike to facilitate its easy standing on the ground.

The annual Ayak rituals are mainly an occasion to appease and in part also to fulfil, certain vows taken during the year for the Ayak concerned. The Ayak rituals revolve around the offerings of fowls, goats or bulls as sacrifices; these offerings would have to be accepted by the Ayak. The acceptance of these sacrifices is believed to be conveyed by the Ayak through the sacrificial animals. The Dela has a significant role of communicating the acceptance or refusal of the offerings by the Ayak. If an offer is refused, further vows are taken, forgiveness is requested and the quantum of the offering is also increased at times.

The annual rituals and rites of the Ayak are performed during the month of December or January. A group of clan members trek down the hills to the shores of River Godavari, which flows about 15 km south of the Satmala Plateau. After bathing and resting for a day or two they come back carrying a small amount of Godavari water. In the olden days they used to carry the Ayak in a procession to the River Godavari for the ceremonial bath. Subsequently, with the increase of the population en route to the river, objections to the carrying of the Ayak increased. Due to objections from caste people initially the Kolam used to hide the Ayak in a basket en route to River Godavari, but now this practice has also stopped. People only go to the River Godavari and bring back the holy water which is sprinkled on the Ayak, symbolizing a ceremonial bath.

On New Moon night the actual ritual of the Ayak is performed in the central courtyard of the gudem. The wooden symbol of the Ayak is first anointed with vermilion and oil is applied to it. The Supari, who is the actual performer, is the central figure. After it is pitch dark the animals and the fowls are kept behind the Ayak. A huge pile of jowar (millets) is placed next to the Ayak. A number of small horses made of clay are also placed by the side of the Ayak. The Ayak is kept facing the East. All the people of the gudem, including children, men and women, assemble in a semi-circle; each one of them is given a handful of rice. To the music of drums the Supari chants praises and requests the Ayak to accept their offerings. All the people in the semi-circle kneel down. After they stand again, the rice is collected by the Supari and placed in front of the Ayak.

Now the actual offering or the sacrifice of animals is carried out. Different people who have brought fowls and at times goats take turns. Before this, the jointly purchased goat by the gudem people is offered. The goat is first washed and anointed with turmeric paste. It is held by the ears and the request for acceptance is whispered. If the goat shivers. It means the Ayak has accepted the offer and the goat can then be sacrificed. In the case of fowls, a small amount of rice mixed with turmeric and water is placed in front of the Ayak and the request is again whispered. If the fowl starts eating the rice it is believed that the Ayak has accepted it. In the meanwhile, the rhythmic music tempo is built up and people start dancing. Interestingly, some of the people, usually three or four, start gyrating very intensively. It is believed that these people have come under the direct influence of the Ayak and have been possessed. Using large fibre whips, these people are repeatedly beaten. If they are actually possessed they are not expected to feel the pain. Sometimes certain old women also get possessed; they are also beaten by the onlookers.

The persons who use the whips are supposed to hit as hard as possible, otherwise they have to face the wrath of Ayak. While all this is going on no one sits on cots or on any raised platform. The food is then cooked in a central place. The meat of the sacrificed animals is separately cooked and eaten by all. The day after the Ayak rituals is spent relaxing and the entire gudem abstains from any work. The performance of the Ayak rituals in its most traditional form is represented here, and customs and beliefs attached reflect the ancient and long-standing practice of clan gods: the most powerful form of tribal religion.

Social Exclusion

It is believed that if the Ayak is displeased it is likely to cause destruction to cattle and life by taking a form of a tiger. In fact, among the Kolam any cattle killed by tiger is attributed to Ayak's displeasure, the cause of which is a human mistake. It is believed that all the anger caused to Ayak is in one way or the other because of non-adherence of the pollution restrictions. It is the women who during their menses are the primary source of pollution. Death and birth pollution are also the cause of Ayak's displeasure. Certain behavioural norms when not strictly observed may also be the reason of Ayak's anger, for example, in the Kolam society the younger brother's wife is to be strictly avoided; she is also supposed to follow certain restrictions. In the presence of her husband's elder brother she is not supposed to climb a ladder or sit on a cot. Sometimes pollution may be caused by the entire gudem itself and no one person can be singled out. It is assumed that the Ayak being the clan god of a particular clan has a territorial jurisdiction and any polluting activity within this area by anyone aggravates (aggrieved) him. The opposite number in the female supernatural line is the Pollakama. She is equally powerful as the Ayak but she has no clan affiliations. Her role is more closely related to women's activity. Interestingly, pollution plays a less role in warranting her displeasure. Ayak is a clan god descendant.

The Ayak is also known as Bhem Deo. More often this name is referred to by Gonds than by Kolam. The names of the Ayak are also very interesting. The names given are Guntaly Ayya, Pedda Guntala Ayya, etc. These names are public or sabha names. The fact is that each Ayak other than a sabha name has a secret name, which is a closely guarded secret. Only the clan members know the actual name. The names are shrouded in mystery because a part of the ritual act involves whispering of the Ayak name.

The objection of the caste people to the Ayak being carried through their villages is due to the fear of its powers, which are only amplified by the growing sanskritization and formation of elected village panchayats. In the past the caste village elders en route never objected to the passage of the Ayak In fact, they used to show deference in the form of offering a fowl, which was given to the Kolam men who carried the Ayak. The newly evolved objection is not based on any rationale as the Ayak is powerful in its territory and seeks proper adherence and appeasement only from the Kolam. This fact is attested by the older generation of the caste village elders. This form of objection is to exclude the Kolam from a socio-spatial sphere of their traditional route, thus depriving them of their traditional rights.

Conclusion

From the narration of the Kolam, we can understand that these people could practice all the rituals connected with Ayak and they continued practice until the early 1960s. The important aspect of it is giving sabha names: this can be attributed to the fact that by calling it as Bhem Deo they would want it to be respected in the eyes of non-Kolam, especially the Hindus and Gonds (who are also increasingly being Hinduized here). What is most important is the stopping of the carrying of the Ayak to the River Godavari through their villages, which is a socio-geographically exclusion. Until the commence of the Panchayat Raj the villages were controlled by traditional leaders who from ancient times respected the Kolam's Ayak and paid some sort of reverence. But after the elected Panchayats came in, with it came the political parties and these new leaderships never gave any respect to traditional reciprocal statuses and obligations. They started objecting to the carrying of the Ayak through their villages and the sanskritizated religious understanding always viewed these deities as dangerous.

By stopping the carrying of the Ayak to the shores of River Godavari they excluded Kolam from performing one of the most important rituals to Ayak, which is bathing it in the holy waters. The thick description as postulated by Geertz is more complex and processual than the simpler description achieved by social exclusion. The analysis of social exclusion is adequate to formulate a policy to direct the wayside village panchayats to permit the transportation of Ayak. The thick description is useful for a much deeper understanding of the issues and the socio-psychological understanding of the illegal ban.

References

Berghman, J. 1996. 'Social Exclusion in Europe: Policy Context and Analytical Framework', in G. Room (ed.), *Beyond the Threshold: The Measurement and Analysis of Social Exclusion*, Policy Press, Bristol.

Census of India. 1965. Laindiguda, Vol. 2, Andhra Pradesh, Village Survey Monograph, New Delhi.

Emeneau, M.B. 1955. *Kolami, a Dravidian Language* (University of California Publication in Linguistics, Vol. 2), University of California Press, Berkeley.

Furer-Haimendorf, C. Von. 1945. *Tribal Hyderabad*, Hyderabad Revenue Department, Government of H.E.H. The Nizam.

——. 1948. *The Raj Gonds of Adilabad: The Aboriginal Tribes of Hyderabad*, Vol. III, Macmillan, London.

——. 1952. 'The Cult of Ayak among the Kolams of Hyderabad', *Wiener Bietrage zur Kulturgeschichtee und Lingustik*, Vol. XI.

——. 1979. *Gonds of Andhra Pradesh*, George Allen & Unwin, London.

Geertz, Clifford. 1973. *The Interpretation of Cultures: Selected Essays*, Basic Books, New York.

Hazra, D. 1983. 'The Kolam Yeotmal', Anthropological Survey of India, Memoir No. 49, Calcutta.

Mohan Rao, K. 1990. *The Kolams: A Primitive Tribe in Transition*, Book Links Corporation, Hyderabad.

Patnaik, Rajesh. 1992. Kolam of Satmala Highlands, unpublished manuscript, UGC NET Fellowship Report.

Paugam, S. 1996. 'The Spiral of Precariousness: A Multidimensional Approach to the Process of Social Disqualification in France', in G. Room (ed.), *Beyond the Threshold: The Measurement and Analysis of Social Exclusion*, Policy Press, Bristol.

Room, G. 1999. 'Social Exclusion, Solidarity and the Challenge of Globalisation', *International Journal of Social Welfare*, 8(3): 166–74.

Sen, Amartya. 2000. *Social Exclusion: Concept, Application and Scrutiny*, Social Development Paper No. 1, Office of Environment and Social Development, Asian Development Bank, Manila.

Whelan, B. and C.T. Whelan. 1996. 'What Way Is Poverty Multidimensional', in G. Room (ed.), *Beyond the Threshold*, Policy Press, Bristol.

Zvelebil, Kamal. 1970. *Comparative Dravidian Phonology*, Mouton, The Hague.

5

From Culture of Reservations to Culture of Representations

Phule–Ambedkarite Agenda for Social Inclusion in India

P.D. Satya Pal

Social exclusion has been broadly defined as the process through which individuals or groups are wholly or partially excluded from full participation in the society within which they live (Jalal, 1998; Sen, 2000). Two important factors involved in this process are: (a) the institutions governing societal relations that cause exclusion, and (b) consequential deprivations and denial of equal rights in several spheres of life. Exclusion based on race, gender, ethnicity and class exists in many nations. However, caste-based exclusion in combination with other forms of exclusion in India have resulted in the most severe and intensely discriminative form of deprivation. The caste system, also known as the Brahmanical system, has regulated the life of the people of India over centuries, in which the organizational scheme is based on the division of people into endogamous caste groups and the civil, economic, political and religious rights of each individual caste are ascribed inequally by birth and made hereditary. The system implies forced exclusion of one caste from the rights of other castes in all spheres of life, and a regulatory mechanism to enforce several instruments of social ostracism is built in (Thorat, 2008). This hierarchical and systemic exclusion assigns absolute rights to few *leisure* castes and denies equal privileges and basic human rights to the majority *labour* castes.

Mahatma Jotirao Phule (1827–1890) from Maharashtra launched the movement of social revolution in modern India against the trammels of physical and mental slavery of the majority of the population, i.e., the Bahujans, and Dr Ambedkar (1891–1956) is regarded as the heir of that movement, who went on to achieve constitutional rights to the excluded majority. From Phule to Ambedkar we find a continuum of ideological movements led by Sahu Maharaj of Kolhapur, Narayan Guru and Ayyankali of Kerala, Iyothee Thass and Periyar of Tamil Nadu – all who fought against the structural exclusion of the Brahmanical system, referred to as Phule–Ambedkarite movement. When we couch their analysis of the societal process in terms of exclusion and inclusion, we find that their insights are very crucial to the understanding of these concepts in the Indian context. It can be seen that Phule and Ambedkar displayed the exclusionary perspective of the Brahmanical system and also strived to replace it with a comprehensive inclusive programme.

Phule and Ambedkar exposed the interface between ideology and social order, which caused social, economic and political exclusion of the Bahujans. The nature of exclusion revolving around the caste system is fundamentally conceived by the Brahmanical ideology and concept of natural inequality. Elements of Brahmanical cosmology proclaim inequalities to be built into the very nature of categories of people, natural objects, foods, occupation and even gods themselves. The Brahmanical metaphysics and ethics rationalize inequality as natural and legitimize the social order. Phule's thesis is that the Arya Brahmins (Bhats) subjugated the original inhabitants (Shudras and Atishudras) and devised many ways to perpetuate their own interests by various means. He maintains that by concocting spurious religion tracts, they dispossessed the common natives of their legitimate rights and assumed for themselves a pre-eminent place in the hierarchy of society (Patil, 1991). Ambedkar (1936) declared that the real enemy behind this deliberate design is not the people who observe caste, but the Shastras that teach them this religion of caste. "They shun social intercourse with fellow human beings not because they are inhuman or wrong headed … but because they are deeply religious. The myriad hierarchies and taboos of caste have the sanctity of the Shastras … people will not change their conduct unless they have ceased to believe in the sanctity of Shastras" (p. 111). He explained that untouchability is only a logical corollary to this understanding of nature, god and human agency bound together by the law of karma. It can be understood from the analysis of Phule and Ambedkar that Brahmanical ideology is an *ideology of exclusion* that moulds a social order based on inequality where no two castes are equal and the divided castes are made to oppose each other.

Forms of Exclusion and Brahmanical System

Sen (2004) presents four forms of exclusion that are distinguishable depending upon the nature and the context of exclusion. They are active and passive exclusion, living mode exclusion, constitutive relevance of exclusion and unfavourable exclusion. The Brahmanical system, as espoused by Phule and Ambedkar, relates to all forms of exclusion. According to Sen, active exclusion is the fostering of exclusion on some groups from equal opportunity through deliberate means. The institution of caste, through ascription of status to an individual at birth, thrusts upon civil, economic and political disabilities to the Bahujans in a most flagrant manner. Ambedkar (1943) points out, "Is there a system anywhere on the surface of the earth, except perhaps among the Hindus, where a man is regarded as so low as not to be touched? Is there any society in the world which has unapproachable, unshadowables and unseenables?" Passive exclusion is explained as the exclusion which results from a set of circumstances. Caste-and untouchability-based exclusion is essentially structural in nature and comprehensive and multiple in coverage. Living mode exclusion reflects the inability of individuals and groups to interact freely and productively with others and take part in full in the economic, social and political lives of a community. "The caste system prevents common activity and by preventing common activity it has prevented the Hindu from becoming a society with a unified life and consciousness of its own being .... The caste system is infested with the spirit of isolation and infact, it makes isolation of one caste from another a matter of virtue" (Ambedkar, 1936: 27). Phule and Ambedkar explained that the Brahmanical system denies the right to existential dignity to the Bahujans and relegates them a subhuman existence. It also denies their right to identity. All the identities that are attached to the Bahujans are not given by themselves, but are given by others. The identities such as Anarya, Pisacha, Shudra, Atishudra, names of individual castes and even the surnames – are all insulting, demeaning identities and are the identities of suppression. The Bahujans are denied the right to choice of occupation and are forced to take up polluting occupations as hereditary occupations. The

Brahmanical system reserves for 'upper' castes clean and respectable jobs and assigns to the untouchables dirty and mean jobs and thereby clothes the 'upper' castes with dignity and heaps ignominy upon the 'lower' castes. "There are many occupations in India which on account of the fact that they are regarded as degraded by the Hindus provoke those who are engaged in it to aversion ... all are slaves of the caste system. But all slaves are not equal in status" (Ambedkar, 1936: 31). They are forbidden to exercise any right to access or claim over resources of the society in which they live. On the whole, the caste system clamps social oppression, economic exploitation and political suppression, which are worse than slavery (Ambedkar, 1916).

Sen (2000) refers to constitutive relevance of exclusion, which arises due to the inability of the excluded to relate to others and to take part in the life of the community, which can directly impoverish the members of these groups. Ambedkar explains the plain survival of the low castes, which as an outcome of exclusion results in poverty and powerlessness. "They are denied the elementary rights due to every human being and refused the benefits of civilization and culture. Without equality of opportunity, theirs is the most degraded condition" (1943: 20). With regard to the condition of untouchables and their economic position, Ambedkar states, "As an economic system it permits exploitation without obligation. Untouchability is not only a system of unmitigated economic exploitation, but it is also a system of uncontrolled economic exploitation" (1945: 196). He argues that the tolerance of tyranny and insults has killed the sense of retort and revolt. Vigour and ambition have completely vanished and the Bahujans have become helpless, unenergetic and pale (Ahir, 1977: 17). Unfavourable inclusion results in a situation where some people are included on deeply unfavourable terms, which results in exploitative conditions of services and unequal terms of social participation, i.e., adverse participation (Thorat, 2008). The Brahmanical system equates everything which is attached to the lower castes as lowly, polluting, mean and subhuman. Ambedkar analyses the isolation of castes as most unfavourable: "What are the consequences of isolation? Isolation means social segregation, social humiliation, social discrimination and social injustice. Isolation means denial of protection, denial of justice, denial of opportunity. Isolation means want of sympathy, want of fellowship and want of, consideration. Nay, isolation means positive hatred and antipathy" (1989: 416).

Levels of Exclusion

The Brahmanical system represents group-based exclusion. The focus of exclusion is the social group, not the individual. The caste system does not recognize the individual and his/her distinctiveness as the centre of social purpose. For the purpose of rights and duties even the family is not regarded as a unit in Hindu society except for purposes of marriage and inheritance. The primary unit is caste, and hence the rights and privileges or lack of them of an individual flow from the membership of a particular caste (Ambedkar, 1989; Thorat, 2008).

The dimension of spatial segregation of residences is a marked exclusion in the caste system. This system maintains spatial distribution of households belonging to a particular caste corresponding to the status position in the hierarchy. The households of the untouchables are invariably kept away from the main village. Physical segregation of households belonging to a particular caste inside the village also follows the social gradation.

Phule and Ambedkar demonstrated that the Brahmanical ideology and its social order resulted in *Alpajan Sukhaya* and *Alpajan Hitaya*, which were beneficial for few. This *culture of reservation* kept 100 per cent reservations to the so-called upper castes in literacy, power and economy. The theory of karma provided immunity to the offenders and converted the victims as culprits and willful vassals.

Agenda Inclusion

Phule and Ambedkar sought to reconstitute the society by establishing a new social order based on liberty, equality, fraternity and justice. They strived to bring about awareness among the suffering Bahujans about their physical and mental slavery. Their efforts focused on notional change so as to bring about a structural change in the society. Dispelling the divine origin, caste and caste system are explained as the deception of the Brahmanical sections to keep the masses under the yoke. Ambedkar (1936) explained caste as a devise designed to divide. “Caste is the notion, a state of mind. It is a disease of the mind”. He declared that the structural alternative is to annihilate caste.

Radical Awareness through Education

Phule and Ambedkar realized that by keeping education as the secret code, the Brahmanical sections could colonize the minds of the Bahujans and capture the social order. They strived to provide education to the Bahujans to bring about awareness and consciousness of their victimization. Phule analysed this in his book *Cultivators Whipcord* (1883): "Without knowledge, the mind was lost, without mind, virtue was lost, without virtue, fortune was lost, without fortune, wealth was lost, without wealth the Shudras sank; such was the havoc wrecked by wisdom's lack". Phule established the first school for girls in Pune in 1848 with his wife Savitri Bai as the teacher. He also established schools for the Shudras and Atishudras. In his book *Slavery* (1873), Phule declares, "Let there be schools for the Shudras in every village; but away with all Brahman school-masters". Ambedkar advocated education as the basic requisite for social change. "If you give education to the lower strata of the Indian society which is interested in blowing up the caste system, the caste system will be blown up" (Keer, 1962: 491).

Culture of Representations and Democratic Ideology

The ideology of Phule and Ambedkar was to bring in a culture of representations in order to pave way for an inclusive society built upon democratic foundations. In 1882, Phule advocated before the Hunter Commission for representations to all communities, based on their pro rata of population, in the fields of education, employment, agriculture, industry and bureaucracy of the country. Ambedkar, in his memoranda submitted to the Southborough Committee in 1917, Montague-Chelmsford in 1919, Muddiman Committee in 1923, Simon Commission in 1929 and the Round Table Conferences in 1930 and 1931, sought for representation, i.e., true and adequate representation in education, employment and legislative positions to Depressed Classes, along with other sections.

Phule in his last book (1888), *Saarvajanik Satya Dharma* (*The Universal Religion of Truth*), outlined a concrete plan of action to herald an inclusive society based on fraternity and equality. Ambedkar (1936) identified lack of social endosmosis and organic filaments in the caste society and strived for laying foundations of a unified society. He was the lone speaker at the Constituent Assembly of 1946, which discussed the framework of the future Constitution to underline the need to build up a cohesive society. "Our difficulty is not about the ultimate future; our difficulty is how to make the heterogeneous mass that we have today take a decision in common and march on the way which leads us to unity. Our difficulty is not with regard to the ultimate; our difficulty is with regard to the beginning". In order to establish an inclusive society, Ambedkar looks at democracy, not as a political arrangement, but as "a mode of associated living. The roots of democracy are to be searched in social relationship, in terms of the associated life between the people who form the society" (Keer, 1962: 480). He highlights fraternity as the root of democracy and without fraternity other ideals of democracy like equality and liberty cannot endure. He defined democracy as a "form and method of government where by revolutionary changes in the economic and social life of the people are brought about without bloodshed" (p. 61). Though mindful of the great obstacles to the establishment of a democratic arrangement in the Indian society, Ambedkar was optimistic about a cohesive society. "I am convinced that, given time and circumstances, nothing in the world will prevent this country from becoming one and with all our castes and creeds, I have not the slightest hesitation in saying that we shall in some way be a united people" (p. 388). He exhorted the nation to preserve independence by establishing equality and fraternity in all spheres of life.

Incompatibility of Ideologies and Continuing Contradictions

The cherished aspiration of paving the way for an inclusive society has not yet been realized, for reasons too well known for Ambedkar. The unmitigated contradictions of our society have resulted in a situation in which the laws are on the side of equality, and the customs that people follow in their daily lives are on the side of inequality. This paradox is explained as the incompatibility of ideologies. "Indians today are governed by two different ideologies. Their political ideal set out in the preamble of the Constitution affirms a life of liberty, equality and fraternity. Their social ideal embodied in their religion denies them" (Keer, 1962: 459). Unless the ideology of inclusion, i.e., the democratic spirit, is properly grasped and put to practice, it is difficult to bring in a democratic society. Explaining the three dimensions of democracy – political democracy, social democracy and economic democracy – Ambedkar said that while political democracy provides *one man – one vote*, the soul of democracy lies in *one man-one value*, which is possible only when there is social and economic democracy. He warned that "political democracy cannot succeed where there is no social and economic democracy" (Das, 1978: Vol. I, 30). It is unfortunate that even after six decades of Constitutional policy, democratic ideals are yet to find firm ground among the citizens of India. Owing to illiteracy, poverty and powerlessness, they are not in a position to make democracy work. The Phule–Ambedkarite programme of reservations as representations to provide awareness, access and participation to all citizens in the fields of education and employment is also being distorted. In Articles 15 and 16 of the Constitution, the fundamental rights provided to the socially and educationally backward classes who constitute the majority, i.e., the Bahujans of the country, are being denied to a large extent in the pretext of dubious argument of merit. This equal opportunity legislation quite often drives the society to take emotional polemic positions. The underlying problem is that the method has been confused with the policy; providing representations or fair access or equal opportunity being the policy, the quota mechanism is a method to secure fairness. In the recent discussion on reservations in the private sector in India, similar confusions and deliberate misinterpretations prevailed (Thorat, 2008). In addition, Ambedkar's practical policy of bringing unity among the Socially and Educationally Backward Classes on the basis of their common victimhood (SCs due to untouchability, STs on the basis of isolation and OBCs who are socially and educationally deprived) as the platform of unity has been ignored even by the victims of caste system themselves. It is because they still continue to be influenced by the ideology of exclusion, i.e., Brahmanism which shapes their lives.

So long as the foundations of democratic society are not laid properly, and liberty, equality and fraternity as principles of life are not recognized and practised as a way of life, India would remain an exclusive society. Laws cannot guarantee people their rights when the ethos of the society do not recognize and respect them. Phule and Ambedkar identified that an attitude of respect and equality towards fellow citizens and a social organization free from rigid social barriers along with the observance of constitutional morality are the conditions for the successful working of a democracy: "Society must have either the sanction of law or the sanction of morality to hold it together without either, society is sure to go to pieces" (1950). They felt that democracy is incompatible and inconsistent with isolation and exclusiveness resulting in the distinction between the privileged and the underprivileged. Bringing education within reach of everyone, so as to develop awareness, and inculcating constitutional morality are the ways which Phule and Ambedkar regarded as the minimum prerequisites to develop an inclusive society, replacing the archaic, exclusionist ideology and social order. Ambedkar cautioned about the perils of the euphoria that India being a progressive nation.

"I am of opinion that in believing that we are a nation, we are cherishing a great delusion. How can people divided into several thousands of castes be a nation? The sooner we realize that we are not as yet a nation in the social and psychological sense of the word, the better for us" (Das, 1978: 188). Therefore, it becomes imperative upon the citizens and democrats to develop and inculcate social and moral conscience in order to build a cohesive, inclusive and vibrant society in India.

References

Ahir, D.C. 1977. *Selected Speeches of Dr B.R. Ambedkar, 1927–51*, Blumoon, Delhi.

Ambedkar, B.R. 1916. *Castes in India: Their Mechanism, Genesis and Development, Writings and Speeches*, Vol. I, Government of Maharashtra, Bombay.

——. 1936. *Annihilation of Caste, Writings and Speeches*, Vol. I, Government of Maharashtra, Bombay.

——. 1943. *Ranade, Gandhi and Jinnah, Writings and Speeches*, Vol. I, Government of Maharashtra, Bombay.

——. 1945. *What Congress and Gandhi Have Done to the Untouchables, Writings and Speeches*, Vol. I, Government of Maharashtra, Bombay.

——. 1950. 'Buddha and Future of His Religion', *Mahabodhi Society Journal*, Calcutta.

——. 1989. *Away from the Hindus, Writings and Speeches*, Vol. V, Government of Maharashtra, Bombay.

Das, Bhagwan. 1978. *Thus Spoke Ambedkar*, Vols. I and II, Bheem Patrika Publications, Jullandur.

Jalal, K.F. 1998. Opening and Welcome Remarks, Asian Development Bank Seminar on Inclusion and Exclusion: Social Development Challenges for Asia and Europe, Geneva, 27 April.

Keer, Dhananjay. 1962. *Dr Ambedkar: Life and Mission*, Popular Prakashan, Bombay.

Patil, P.G. 1991. *Introduction to Slavery, Translation, Complete Works of Mahatma Jotirao Phule*, Vol. I, Government of Maharashtra, Bombay.

Sen, Amartya. 2000. 'Social Exclusion: Concept, Application and Scrutiny', Social Development Papers No.1, Office of Environment and Social Development, Asian Development Bank, June.

Thorat, Sukhadeo. 2008. 'On Economic Exclusion and Inclusive Policy', in *Reservation, The Die Is Caste, The Little Magazine*, Vol. VI, Issues 4 and 5, www.littlemag.com.

6

The So-Called Development and Dispossession

An Analysis of Land and Forest Rights of the Socially Excluded Project Affected Tribal People

Deepak Kumar Behera and Nibedita Nath

Dam building is primarily responsible for the generation of electricity, irrigation and water supply and flood control but is associated with a number of negative factors as well. Mega dams destroy not only the environment but also the lives of those people at whose cost they are built. Mohan (2002) writes that these big dams submerge vast land and displace thousands of people from their original habitations in the name of 'national development', without considering the views of the project affected population. Displacement dismantles the production system, disorganizes physical and social aspects of human residence, disrupts natural resources and degenerates community resources. All these are associated with risk factors like landlessness, homelessness, joblessness, marginalization, food insecurity, loss of access to common property resources (CPRs), increased morbidity and social disarticulation which often culminate in material impoverishment and social disintegration of displaced families (Swain and Panigrahi, 1999).

Today, nearly half of the world's rivers have at least one large dam and there are more than 45,000 large dams in the world (Parasuraman, 1996). According to an estimate, each year between 1.2 million and 2.1 million people are displaced worldwide because of new dam construction alone (Cernea, 1991). In India alone, an estimated 25 million were displaced from 1947 to 1997 (Fernandes, 1991). It has been calculated that during the last 40 years about 56,377 families comprising roughly 2.7 lakh people have been displaced due to construction of dams/irrigation projects in Orissa. In other words, on an average 5,000 persons have been displaced in a year (Dalua, 1993).

Majority of the people displaced are usually from the poorest and most vulnerable sections of population. A recent report by the World Commission on Dams (hereafter WCD) estimates that 40–80 million people have been physically displaced by dams worldwide, a disproportionate number of them being tribal people (World Commission on Dams, 2001). A significant point to be noted here is that the tribal communities constitute roughly 8 per cent of the total population of the country, yet over 50 per cent of those displaced belong to this section of our population (Hasnain, 1999).

Objectives and Methodology

The objective of the present study is to explore the impact of the Upper Indravati Hydroelectric Project (hereafter UIHEP) on the poor tribal people in terms of loss of their customary rights on forests and lands. It also makes a critical assessment of the inadequacy of the existing laws in providing justice to the tribal people.

A diachronic approach was adopted to provide a comparative picture of the life of the affected people before and after the displacement. All the heads-of-households (HOHs) were taken as the sample respondents for the study. Qualitative data were collected through observation, focus group discussion (FGD), key informant interview and case study methods. The pre-displacement scenario of the submerged villages was reconstructed by collecting information from the living memory of the displaced indigenous people of the resettlement clusters. Secondary data, especially from the Resettlement and Rehabilitation Unit (RRU), Khatiguda, were collected to supplement our analysis. Data were analysed with the help of computer software packages like Software Packages for Social Sciences (SPSS) and Atlas-ti.

The Sample Area and People

The study covered seven resettlement clusters (villages) of Guturkal Gram Panchayat (undivided) of Thuamul-Rampur block in Kalahandi district, Orissa. Two different categories of resettlement clusters (villages) were selected for the collection of data. They were: (1) isolated resettlement clusters (Purnapadar, Bagbeda, Luthkudi, Dhepoguda and Gutrukhal), and (2) resettlement clusters within traditional villages (Talnagi and Hatisalmurka). The study covered 92 tribal (Pend, Kondh and Jhadia) resettled households of the above-mentioned villages.

The Upper Indravati Hydroelectric Project (UIHEP)

The UIHEP is situated at the tri-junction of Kalahandi, Koraput and Nawarangpur districts of Orissa. It is located between of 82° 55′E longitude and 19° 25′N latitude. The dam was constructed with the objective of providing irrigation water for 1,09,300 hectares (later revised in 1994 to 1,28,000 hectares) of agricultural land in the watershed of the Hati barrage in the adjacent Mahanadi river basin and of generating 600 MW of electric power. The total land acquired by the project was 32,530.87 acres. The catchment area of the project is 2,630 km^2 and the reservoir area is estimated to be about 12,865 hectares.

It was constructed by evicting 18,269 people belonging to 5,988 families. Of these affected families, 43.31 per cent belonged to STs, 16.48 per cent belonged to the SCs and the remaining 40.19 per cent were from other castes (mostly OBCs). In total, the project affected 105 villages – 44 from undivided Koraput and 61 from Kalahandi district. Of these, 73 villages (66 submerged + 7 *tapu*), i.e., 13 villages from Koraput, 18 from Nawarangpur and 42 villages from Kalahandi, were directly affected by the impounding of water. In the remaining 32 villages some agricultural lands were acquired and the habitation was not totally affected. A large number of poor and underprivileged communities have been dispossessed of their livelihoods on the basis of dubious claims of 'common benefit' and 'national interest'. It sold dreams of prosperity to the poor and the marginalized in order to take away from them even their meagre and fragile bases of existence.

The UIHEP and the Loss of Customary Rights of Tribals on Land and Forest

Their economy was multiple loci, mostly revolving round cultivation in both *donger* and plain land, collection of forest produces, hunting wild games and wage earning as agricultural labourers. Land and forest are the important sources of livelihood of the tribal people. They are dependent on *donger* as it is one of the significant means of livelihood for them. Much of their food and other daily needs are met by the forest. Traditionally, around 80 per cent of their food came from shifting cultivation on forest land (Fernandes, 1997: 82). As a result of the forcible acquisition of lands and common property resources, e.g. forests during the construction of UIHEP, the tribal people have been marginalized and further pushed into poverty. For the tribal people, loss of access to the forest and land had resulted in deterioration in their income and standard of living.

Impact of Loss of Rights on Land Resources

Tribal people cultivate on hill slopes and forest lands. They have only customary rights and no legal rights over those lands. They own very little landed property according to the modern legal norms of rules of the Land Acquisitions Act 1894 (amended in 1984). Some tribal people jointly cultivate the field and equally share the produce. Such an arrangement proves to be economically more sustainable than individual holding and it also augments intra-familial cooperation. That is why they are not particular about individual ownership of lands. But the Land Acquisition Act 1894 recognized only individual and not collective or community rights. For the purpose of payment of compensation, the customary rights and collective/community rights are not recognized under the land acquisition acts as they recognize only individual legal rights on land (ORG, 1998; Swain and Panigrahi, 1999). Thus, in case of the UIHEP, the lands of the persons who had only customary rights and the CPRs such as grazing land, forest land, etc., were forcibly acquired under the Land Acquisition Act 1894 for the UIHEP.

The total land acquired for the UIHEP was 32,530.87 acres. A total area of 3,943.53 acres of forest land was submerged due to the construction of the dam. But compensation was given only for the loss of homestead land and agricultural *patta* land. The government did not bother for those who did not possess *patta* land. With the total loss of lands, which they were cultivating since time immemorial, many families became economically non-viable. As many of them were totally dependent on the non-patta land, they were left with no land for cultivation after the construction of the dam. Their losses were not taken into account. The CPRs were not at all compensated by the project officials. For the tribal people, particularly for the landless and assetless, loss of access to the CPRs such as pastures, forest lands, water bodies, burial grounds, quarries, etc., resulted in significant decline in their incomes and subsequently quality of life. The UIHEP uprooted people from their ancestral homes and hearth for a pittance called 'compensation' in the name of national development. But this forced eviction violated the basic right as enshrined in the Indian Constitution, as Article 21 of the constitution guarantees the right to livelihood apart from the right to live with dignity.

Of the total HOHs, 77.2 per cent openly expressed their dissatisfaction on the compensation amount besides the general commensality package; compensation was given only for the *patta* land to be submerged. Further, the project authorities did injustice while giving compensation for such land. The rates were fixed taking into account the land registration rates during the past 10 years within a radius of 10 km. As the registration rates were very low in comparison to the actual price of the land, the poor tribal people were highly dissatisfied with the rates fixed by the project authorities. These people accepted their decision, as they were not aware of the legal procedure nor had enough money to fight their cases in the courts of law. The people were forced to buy infertile land at far off places that too in different patches for reasons like less amount of compensation paid to them in different phases of the resettlement, the sudden hike in the price of fertile agricultural land, the non-availability of suitable fertile land in the nearby localities, etc. A lot of dummy buying and selling also took place to qualify for getting the remaining amount of compensation. Table 6.1 provides a picture of the possession of *patta* land by the sample project affected people before and after displacement.

Table 6.1

Distribution of Households on the Basis of Their Possession of Patta Land

Area of Land (in acres)	*Land Possessed at the Native Village (in acres)*	*Land Possessed at the Resettlement Cluster (in acres)*
0	31(33.69)	31(33.69)
0 to <3	40 (43.47)	57 (61.95)
3 to <36	13 (14.13)	3 (2.17)
6 to <10	2 (2.17)	1 (3.26)
>10	6 (6.52)	0 (0.00)
Total	92	92

Note: Figures in parentheses indicate percentage.

It is significant to note that in many cases the distance between the resettlement cluster and the relocated agricultural land is more than 20 km. Some have already sold away all their lands; lands of some are now either lying vacant or have been leased out; some lands have also been encroached by other people living in that area, while some lands have completely turned into infertile ones with the inflow of sandy soil and boulders from the nearby canals. This clearly indicates that even those who got compensation for land got further marginalized in the process of rehabilitation. Extreme marginalization occurred when families lost a stable source of income and started moving on a 'downward mobility' path.

When the Jhola (plain) lands were lost, people were left only with non-submerged *donger* land to cultivate. The tribal people use tracts of steep hill slopes for longer *chas* (shifting cultivation), which is practiced by them since time immemorial. They cultivate different types of crops and cereals on d*onger* mostly for consumption. The evacuees thereby put great pressure on the *donger* lands. Increased dependence on the remaining non-submerged *dongers* resulted in the reduction of the fertility level of the *donger* land due to shortening of the follow-up period and thereby considerably reduced the agricultural production.

The most important factor that brings down the number of households engaged in *dongerchas* is the non-availability of suitable and fertile *donger* for cultivation. Most of the non-submerged *dongers* have now turned into barren land due to their increasing use by the growing population of the region. The indiscriminate cutting of trees for firewood and building materials have accelerated the pace of deforestation of those *dongers*. The *donger* land has also lost its earlier fertility due to constant removal of the topsoil.

The fast growth of some varieties of weeds and shrubs has further reduced the fertility of the *donger* land. In the barren *dongers*, the weeds grow fast causing problems to the people. The poor tribal people find it extremely difficult to control the growth of these weeds with their simple technology. Sometimes out of frustration, they leave their patch of *donger* land fallow. When the *dongers* were dense and deep, the weeds were never a problem to the people. In the pre-displacement period, they took the help of their close relatives and friends in the village to clear the tract or to remove the weeds. This arrangement of labour exchange was operated on the basis of mutual obligation and reciprocity. In the post-displacement period when kinship matrix broke down, the disappearance of this system was found in our sample village. When a household is too poor to meet the expenses of *dongerchas* at different stages, it stops practicing the same. Also when the family size is too small and the family lacks manpower, it finds it difficult to go for *dongerchas*.

Table 6.2

Distribution of Resettled Households on the Basis of Major Crops Produced (N=92)

Major Crops	*Native Village*		*Resettlement Cluster*	
	No. of Households	*Quantity (in kg)*	*No. of Households*	*Quantity (in kg)*
Paddy	63 (72.41)	78,852.00	59 (68.60)	44,046.00
Mandia	86(98.85)	32,154.00	82(95.35)	21,976.00
Kosla.	79(90.80)	22,065.00	76(88.37)	17,031.00
Kango	52(59.77)	39,60.00	30 (34.88)	1,566.00
Kandul	78 (89.66)	22,122.00	67 (77.91)	12,603.00
Macca	58 (66.67)	18,114.00	50 (58.14)	11,088.00

The increasingly infertile *donger* fails to produce the expected yields. Less number of households is engaged in the production of different crops and small millets, as both shifting and wet cultivation are now less profitable ventures. As a result, the quantity of production of each item, viz., paddy, mandia, kosla, kandul and macca, has gone down so much that many tribal people from the resettlements clusters have switched to non-agricultural occupations.

Impact of Loss of Rights on Forest Resources

The forests, the mainstay of tribal economy, are reserved in the interest of the nation and the tribal people remain at the mercy of the officials from the plains. The forest resources are taken away from the remote areas for the development of the people of more advanced communities (Vyasulu, 1985; Mohanty, 1997). The UIHEP has exerted double impact on the forest of the area, i.e., first through the submergence of the forest by the dam itself, and second by bringing people from the plain areas (mostly as project officials) who liquidated the forest resources.

During the initial phase of the project, a local tender call was made for felling of trees both in the plain and *donger* lands. The local contractors, who got those tenders, took advantage of the remoteness of the area and started felling valuable trees beyond their allotted patches of land. This infused a negative attitude in the minds of the local people towards the state. Tribal people started to feel that *donger* was no longer inseparable from them. They now feel that all the remaining *dongers* also belong to the state. The state and its administration are solely responsible for the changing attitude of the people towards forest resources. With this changing perception, they have now started exploiting forest-based resources as and when opportunity arises. The previous 'constructive dependence' of the tribal people on forest resources is now slowly getting replaced by 'destructive dependence'. As forests have always been an intrinsic part of the economy of the tribal people, their reservation by the state has reduced the self-provisioning ability of local peasants (Baviskar, 1995).

In the pre-displacement period the forest was a rich resource to the tribal people in terms of fulfillment of basic needs and drives in regard to livelihood. It was a source of food, shelter and medicine not only for the tribal people but also for the domesticated animals. In the forest-based economy, activities like cultivation on hill slopes, collection of minor forest produce (MFPs), hunting and trapping are interwoven. They commonly collect local *chhatu* (mushrooms), *sag* (leaves/spinaches), fruits, *alu* (roots), *kardi* (tender bamboo shoots), *aam taku* (mango kernel), *kankada* (crab), etc., during different times in a year. Forests provide the tribal people with soil for making *khapar* (country tile) and raising walls and floors, timber, wood for doors, wooden poles (sargi, bija and phasi), stones, reeds, slates, grass poles, bamboo, canes, rope and rope-like materials such as *giredi* and *danturi.* Forests provide material for shelter not only for people but also for their cattle and goats. People are also dependent on forests for materials for manufacturing their tools and household articles such as wood or bamboo for making *benta* (handle) for *tangi* (axe), *kadki* (hoe) and *ila* (sickle), *dhanu* (bow) and *sar* (arrow), *barchi* (spear), *musal* (wooden pestle), *dala* and *pachia* (flat and hollow bamboo container). Besides, these, different types of leaves such as *kike siali, sargi* and *kusum* are collected for the making of leaf cups and plates.

As wet cultivation in the limited lands and *dongerchas* in the remaining non-submerged forest lands failed to provide the tribal people the required quantity of yield, they started collecting different non-wood forest produces (NWFPs) on a regular basis to sell or exchange them in local markets (*Lamtaguda* on Tuesday and *Benakhamar* on Saturday) for their survival. The NWFPs include flowers, leaves, seeds, roots, bamboo shoots, myrabolans, gum, lac, fibre, honey, wax, barks, hill brooms, nuts, berries, bones, hides, skins, herbs, etc. But complete or partial submergence of many nearby forests due to the construction of UIHEP deteriorated their rich forest-based resources, which is a major source of livelihood for them.

Table 6.3

Some Important Forest Products and Their Tentative Prices in the Post-Displacement Period

Forest Products	*Unit*	*Non-season Price*	*Season Price*
Kusum seed (for oil)	Per kg	Rs. 5	Rs. 4
Tamarind	Per kg	Rs. 4	Rs. 3
Tamarind seed	Per kg	Rs. 4	Rs. 4
Tamarind without seed	Per kg	Rs. 6 to Rs. 7	Rs. 6 to Rs. 7
Dhab piri (used for root making)	No more available		
Siali rope	5 bundles	Rs. 2.50	Rs. 2
Bichal bark (for dhup kathi)	Per kg	Rs. 6 to Rs. 7 (dry)	Rs. 4 (fresh)
Bahada lasa (for soap and gum)	Per kg	Rs. 6 to Rs. 79	
Chilli (for soap)	Per kg	Rs. 10 (dry)	Rs. 6 (fresh)
Kendu leaves	No more sold		
Jhuna	No more available		
Lakha	No more available		
Sargi seed	Per kg	Rs. 3	Rs. 3
Honey	Per kg	Rs. 50 to Rs. 60	Rs. 50 to Rs. 60
Mango kernet	Per kg	Rs. 1.5 to Rs. 2	Rs. 1.5 to Rs. 2
Broom sticks	Per bundle	Rs. 5	Rs. 5

The selling of NWFPs is also no more a profitable venture, as it is becoming risky and time-consuming. There is also an increasing degree of uncertainty involved in such ventures. They have to move to far-off forests in a group for collecting NWFPs. The average distance covered for collection of forest produce has increased from 3 km to 12 km during the past 10 years. Data obtained from tribal areas of Orissa show that the average distance covered for collection of forest produce has increased from 1.7 km to 7 km over the previous 20 years (Fernandes et al., 1988). It has now become a labour-intensive and time-consuming process, as sometimes the tribal people have to cross the reservoir to reach the nearest forest.

Moreover, with the passage of time there is also a fall in the demand for some NWFPs in the local market. Further, they do not get the actual price of NWFPs as they are cheated at the time of barter of their goods with the middlemen in the market. Along with the entry of outsiders due to the UIHEP, modern systems of measurements (e.g., kilograms etc.) were introduced. The businessmen receive produces in the *ada* and give the exchange product weighing in kilograms. As the tribal people are not acquainted with the modern systems of measurement, the businessmen cheat them by giving less quantity of goods in exchange of their products. The tribal people also encounter such situations during barter exchange with the businessmen coming to their villages from outside.

Collection of kendu leaves was an important source of livelihood for the tribal people of this area in the pre-displacement period. Before inundation, an agent was coming to the village Guturkhal to collect kendu leaves for some beedi factories located in the plain areas. However, after the submergence of Guturkhal, the owners of those factories found it difficult to collect the raw materials from the village. As a result, the agent no more collects leaves from the tribal people. In the absence of a government godown in a nearby place, the villagers have now stopped collecting kendu leaves. This is a big loss to their household economy.

Though selling of firewood was prevalent even before displacement, people were less dependent on it as they had enough agricultural yield and NWFPs. However, firewood selling has become an important means of livelihood in recent times. The people of Dhepoguda, Purnapadar, Bagbeda and Hatisalmurka are very much dependent on firewood selling throughout the year. In the absence of sustainable means of livelihood in the post-displacement era, the tribal people of the field area are now forced to sell firewood on a regular basis. In recent times an important means of survival is the selling of firewood. Without this, it is not possible for them even to have two squares of meal.

Table 6.4

Tentative Prices of Firewood, Bamboo, Kaisi and Patia in the Local Market

Items	*Quantity*	*Approximate Cost*
Firewood	2 bundles	Rs. 15 to Rs. 20
	One load of cycle	Rs. 20
Bamboo	Per piece (small)	Rs. 1 to Rs.
	Per piece (big)	Rs. 10 to Rs. 20
Kalsi	Per piece (small)	Rs. 10 to Rs. 20
	Per piece (big)	Rs. 10 to Rs. 15
Patia	Per piece	Rs. 50 to Rs. 70

But collection of firewood is no more an easy task. Our field investigation reveals that due to deforestation, there has been an increase in the distance of forest from our sample resettlement clusters. It is significant to note that the people of the resettlement clusters cover at least double the distance they used to cover in their native villages for fetching different kinds of forest products. As all the nearby *dongers* are now almost barren, they (two to three people make a group) walk for 15–16 km crossing the reservoir to reach the interior forests. They spend the whole day on firewood collection. Sometimes they stay back in the jungle for one night and come back to their respective homes the next day morning.

Earning through illegal felling had never been a practice of the people of this region in the past. The invasion of their natural habitat by outsiders and the mounting pressure of demand for timber from outside is one of the causes for which some people started timber business in the absence of any alternative source of making their livelihood. It is reported that those who are involved in illegal timber business have contacts with some agents in the nearby towns of Mukhiguda, Khatiguda and Jaypatna. Whenever they receive any order from the agents they go to the forest and fell trees of stipulated size and supply those to the agents for a price. But there are also others who in a crisis situation are forced to fell some trees in the forest and take those to the nearby towns for selling. Sometimes people cut trees for wage labour for the middlemen present in and around the villages.

As regards the primary occupation in the pre-displacement period, the highest sample HOHs (51.08%) were primarily dependent on *dongerchas* for their survival, followed by 27.17 per cent for whom wet cultivation was the primary source of livelihood. Only 19.56 per cent HOHs were primarily engaged as wage labourers either in the agricultural sector or the non-agricultural sector in contrast to the above pre-displacement scenario. The highest percentage of HOHs primarily depend on forest collection for their survival, followed by 22.82 per cent who subsist on *dongerchas* (shifting cultivation) and 17.39 per cent who rely on wet cultivation. Only 10.86 per cent of the HOHs depend on wage earning either in agriculture or non-agriculture sector and another 10.86 per cent rely on other sources for their survival. The submergence of vast patches of *jhola* and *donger* land has displaced some of the HOHs from their primary occupations of *dongerchas* and wet cultivation in the post-displacement period. This is a clear reflection of occupational displacement of the tribal in the post-displacement period, which is an indication of the further marginalization of an already marginalized group.

In the pre-displacement period, 40.21 per cent, 26.08 per cent and 23.91 per cent HOHs had their secondary dependence on *dongerchas*, wet cultivation and wage earning, respectively. In contrast, in the post-displacement period 45.65 per cent and 27.17 per cent HOHs had secondary dependence on *dongerchas* and wage earning, respectively. Only 11.95 per cent, 6.52 per cent and 8.69 per cent HOHs depend on wet cultivation, forest collection and other sources of livelihood, respectively.

Table 6.5

Distribution of Resettled Households on the Basis of Their Primary and Secondary Source of Livelihood in Resettlement Cluster (N=92)

Source of Livelihood	*Primary*		*Secondary*	
	Native Village	*Resettlement Cluster*	*Native Village*	*Resettlement Cluster*
Wet cultivation	25 (27.17)	16 (17.39)	24 (26.08)	11 (11.95)
Dongerchas	47 (51.08)	21 (22.82)	37 (40.21)	42 (45.65)
Wage labour	18 (19.56)	10 (10.86)	22 (23.91)	25 (27.17)
Forest collection	1 (1.08)	35 (38.04)	7 (7.60)	6 (6.52)
Others	1 (1.08)	10 (10.86)	2 (2.17)	8 (8.69)
Total	92 (100)	92 (100)	92 (100)	92 (100)

Note: Figures in parentheses indicate percentage.

Conclusion

The real losses and full costs of displacement of tribal people are not assessed properly and hence are not compensated by the project officials of the UIHEP. The construction of this dam has deprived them of their CPRs like forest and *donger* lands on which they had customary rights for centuries together. They have lost substantial parts of their income base as the CPRs were taken away from them. They face different livelihood risks because of the submergence of substantial part of *jhola* land (plain land), *dongers* and forest. Subsequent depletion of the resources due to increasing pressure has further affected their economy. All these have brought a major setback in the economy of the tribal people. They have been experiencing a series of problems related to occupation, infrastructure and social support mechanism in the new resettlement sites. The tribal people bearing the social and environmental costs and risks of this large dam never got water, electricity, services and economic benefits. Thus, the project has utterly failed to provide justice to the tribal people and ignored their inalienable customary rights over their immediate resources of livelihood.

References

Baviskar, Amita. 1995. *In the Belly of the River*, Oxford University Press, New Delhi.

Brochure on Resettlement and Rehabilitation Activities (R and R). 2000. Upper Indravati Hydro-Electric Project, November – December.

Cernea, Michael M. 1991. 'Socio-Economic and Cultural Approaches to Involuntary Population Resettlement', *Guidelines on Lake Management*, Vol. 11, World Bank Reprint Series, 468.

Dalua, A.K. 1993. *Environment Impact of Large Reservoir Projects on Human Settlement*, Ashish Publishing House, New Delhi.

Fernandes, W., G. Menon and P. Viegas. 1988. *Forest, Environment and Tribal Economy: Deforestation, Impoverishment and Marginalization in Orissa*, Indian Social Institute, New Delhi.

Fernandes, Walter. 1991. 'Power and Powerlessness: Development Projects and Displacement of Tribals', *Social Action*, 41(3): 243–270.

——. 1997. 'Displacement of Tribals: Struggles and Implications for Resettlement', in Georg Pfeffer and D.K. Behera (eds.), *Contemporary Society: Tribal Studies*, Vol. 2, Concept Publishing Company, New Delhi.

Hasnain, Nadeem. 1999. *Tribal India*, Palaka Prakashan, Delhi.

Mohan, M. 2002. Development, Displacement and Rehabilitation: A Study on Project Affected Populations of Somasila Irrigation Project, unpublished Ph.D. dissertation, Department of Anthropology, S.V. University, Tirupati.

Mohanty, B.B. 1997. 'State and Tribal Relationship in Orissa', *Indian Anthropology*, 27(1): 1–17.

Operations Research Group (ORG). 1998. *Socio-Economic Survey of DPs of Upper Indravati Project*, report submitted by ORG to UIHEP, Orissa Hydro-Power.

Parasuraman, S. 1996. 'Development Projects, Displacement and Outcomes for Displaced', *Economic and Political Weekly*, 15 June.

Swain, M. and N. Panigrahi. 1999. 'Development, Displacement and Rehabilitation in Orissa', *Man and Life,* 25 (3&4) 163-175.

Vyasulu, V. 1985. 'Under Developing Koraput', *South Asian Anthropologist*, 6(1): 63–71.

World Commission on Dams. 2000/2001. *Dams and Development: A New Framework for Decision Making*, Report of the World Commission on Dams, London and Sterling, VA, Earthscan.

7

Scheduled Tribes and Rights Discourse

V. Subramanyam, J. Srivirajarani and N. Babavali

The Scheduled Tribes (STs) in India with 8.2 per cent of population are different from other communities, in a way that they are considered to be less developed, physically isolated, backward and to have low literacy levels when compared to the caste communities. Also, these communities depend on their natural habitats, laws, customs, beliefs, dialects and socio-economic conditions. Realizing their underdevelopment, the government is continuously striving hard to elevate their condition throughout the country by implementing different welfare measures. The efforts carried out by the state undoubtedly brought substantial development and change for these communities over the years. Given the current developmental scenario in the country, yet there is lot to be done, so as to declare that the STs have come up equally with the rest of the communities.

Taking into consideration their distinct way of life, there were different perspectives on their identity, and their inclusion in mainstream society was debated while preparing the policies for their upliftment. Though there has been political integration, psychological integration has not been fully achieved over these years.

While tracing out the long history of Indian tribes and their significant contribution towards national interest, Fernandes (2002) presents the current situation on how a large number of progressive-minded activists (whose ideology is based on integrated and inclusive society) have been viewing the tribes as communities whose livelihood, i.e., the natural resources, is threatened by modern development which is proposed by the dominant classes as national interest. Thus, while speaking about the tribes, one refers to the communities that are waking up to the reality of their ongoing impoverishment and marginalization, to the communities that are demanding their right to be fully human and to be an integral part of the country. They realize that, together with other impoverished communities, they are paying the price of what is called national development. Not only do these tribes not get the benefits of these developmental activities which are mainly targeted to other population under the guise of national development, they also silently suffer from this situation. In many parts of the country, these communities protest to continue with this situation.

All tribal societies across the country continue to preserve their ethos despite some cultural contacts with the outsiders. The unique feature of these communities is that their life is preoccupied with their cultural systems. Due to sustained efforts by the government and voluntary agencies working in tribal areas, the communities are slowly realizing their place in the general system, and also realizing the loss incurred during these years in the name of developmental projects targeted towards non-tribal communities, where much of their own resources are depleting. In many parts of the country, tribes assert their right to claim their natural resources. They want to participate in the national developmental process but not at their cost of losing their original identity.

Constitutional Rights and Violations

The Indian Constitution concentrates more on the ideals of equality and justice in both the social and political fields. Accordingly, it abolishes any discrimination to any class of persons on the ground of religion, race or place of birth. Austin (1966) reiterates the fact that the makers of the Indian Constitution adopted fundamental rights to safeguard individual liberty and also for ensuring, together with the directive principles, social, economic and political justice for every member of the community.

Unlike other communities, STs are the most isolated and unrepresented communities in India. Provisions of special protective measures for the development of tribal communities was felt necessary since late nineteenth century and were reflected at different points of time in the form of the Scheduled District Acts of

1874, the Indian Education Commission of 1882 and the Government of India Acts of 1919 and 1935, which paid some attention to the special treatment of the communities (Behura and Panigrahi, 2006)

Basu (1990) highlights the outstanding features of Indian Constitution, which distinguish it from other constitutions. It is obligatory for the state to fulfil the basic primary needs of all citizens of all communities including the STs. The Indian Constitution assures people civil, political, economic, education, cultural and health rights, and the tribes are no exception.

Constitutional Safeguards

The Constitution of India provides to all citizens, social economic and political justice and equality of status and opportunity. Article 46 specifically provides that "the State shall promote with special care, the educational and economic interests of the weaker sections of the people and in particular, of the Scheduled Castes and Scheduled Tribes and shall protect them from social justice and all forms of exploitation". For achieving these objectives, various safeguards relating to protection and development of weaker sections, particularly SCs and STs, have been made under the Constitution. The constitutional provisions relating to safeguards for protection and development are as follows:

1. *Safeguards relating to protection:* Protective safeguards are broadly classified into:
   (a) Social safeguards: Articles 17, 23, 24 and 25(2) (b)
   (b) Educational safeguards: Articles 15(4), 29 and 46
   (c) Political safeguards: Articles 164, 320(4), 332, 334, 243 D, 243 T, 371 B, 371C, 371F, 371G and 371H
   (d) Service safeguards: Articles 16(4), 335 and 338
2. *Safeguards relating to development:* Provisions relating to development/economic safeguards are contained under Articles 273(1) and 339(2) of the Constitution.

Protective Provisions

Article 15 prohibits any discrimination on grounds of religion, race, caste, sex or place of birth. But clause 4 of this Article provides an exception to this. It empowers the state to make any special provision for the advancement of socially and educationally backward classes of the citizens or for the SCs and STs. This provision is in accordance with the policy envisaged in Article 46 that the "State should promote with special care, educational and economic interests of the weaker sections of the people and protect them for social injustice". This clause has been especially incorporated to prevent any special provision made by a state for the advancement of socially or educationally backward classes of citizens from being challenged in the law courts on the ground of it being discriminatory.

Special provisions consist of (a) reservation of seats for members of Scheduled Tribes in educational institutions, (b) relaxation of qualifications required for admission into such institutions, (c) provision of housing accommodation to members of weaker sections (including STs), and (d) concessional treatment for them in the matter of settlement of government lands.

Article 16(4): Reservation in posts and services. It is an exception to the right of equality of opportunity in the matters of public employment laid down in clauses 1 and 2 of Article 16.

Article 19(5): Safeguards tribal interest in property. While the rights of free movement and residence throughout the territory of India and of acquisition and disposition of property are guaranteed to every citizen, special restrictions may be imposed by the state for protection of the interests of the members of the STs under Article 19(5).

Article 23: Prohibits traffic in human beings, beggars and other similar forms of forced labour. This is a very significant provision so far as STs are concerned, as many of them are employed as bonded labour.

Article 29: Cultural and educational rights. According to this, a cultural or linguistic minority has right to conserve its language and culture. This Article provides protection to STs to preserve their language, dialects and cultures. The state would not thrust any alien language or culture on any tribe.

Article 46: Provides for promotion of educational and economic interests of SCs STs and other weaker sections.

Article 164: Provides for a minister incharge of tribal welfare in the states of Bihar, Orissa and Madhya Pradesh, which have substantial tribal population. Special provision for a minister to look after tribal welfare is an evidence of the concern of the framers of the Constitution for safeguarding the interests of the STs.

Article 320(4): Provides that the Public Service Commissions need not be consulted as respect to the manner in which any provision referred to in clause 4 of Article 16 may be made or as respect to the manner in which effect may be given to the provisions of Article 335.

Articles 330, 332 and 334: Seats shall be reserved in the House of People for SCs and STs (Article 330); seats shall also be reserved for the SCs and STs in the Legislative Assembly of every state (Article 332). Such reservation shall cease to have effect on the expiration of a period of 40 years from the commencement of the Constitution, i.e., in 1990 (Article 334). It was originally for a period of 10 years from the commencement of the Constitution, but through an amendment of Article 334, it has been extended by another 30 years.

Article 335: Limits of reservation. The claims of members of SCs and STs shall be taken into consideration in the matter of appointment to the services and posts under the Union and the states as far as may be consistent with the maintenance of the efficiency of administration.

Article 338: Special Officer. There shall be a special officer for the SCs and STs to be appointed by the President. It shall be the duty of the special officer to investigate all matters relating to the safeguards provided for the SCs and STs under the Constitution. He shall report to the President upon the working of those safeguards at such intervals as the President may direct. The President shall cause all such reports to be laid before each House of Parliament. Such an officer has been appointed and designated as Commissioner for SCs and STs.

Article 339(1): Appointment of a commission. The President may at any time and shall, at the expiration of 10 years from the commencement of the Constitution, by order appoint a commission to report on the administration of scheduled areas and the welfare of the STs in the states (Article 339(1)). Only one such commission, namely, the Scheduled Castes and Scheduled Tribes Commission, was appointed on 28 April 1960 and it submitted its report in October 1961.

Although the Indian Constitution has made elaborate provisions for safeguarding the interest of STs, the enforcement of the same has not been of the desired level as per the provisions made under Articles 371(A), 371(B) and, 371(C). The Fifth and Sixth Schedules of the Constitution are specifically meant for the declaration of scheduled areas by the President.

Economic Development

Provisions relating to the economic development of STs are mainly contained in Articles 275(1) and 339(2). Briefly, it may be stated that Article 275(1) envisages for grants-in-aid for meeting the cost of such schemes of development as may be undertaken by a state with the approval of the Government of India for the purpose of promoting the welfare of STs or raising the level of administration of the scheduled areas therein to that of the administration of the rest of the areas of the state. In pursuance of this Article, provision of special central assistance has been made to the states having ST population. As per the provision, the grant is to be made against such specific schemes as are necessary for the welfare of STs and are undertaken with the prior approval of the Union Government. But this is actually not followed. The grants are released without specific schemes.

Article 339(2) goes still further and empowers the Union Executive to issue directives to a state for the drawing up and execution of schemes specified in the directives to be essential for the welfare of the STs in the state. Despite poor performance by the state government, the powers vested in these provisions have not been utilized so far, and no directive has been issued.

Violation of Rights towards Adequate Living Standards

Stressing the importance of fundamental rights and privileges for all communities, STs in particular, Pandey (1997) lists the constitutional provisions applicable to these communities. Though the Indian Constitution specifies that the state shall promote the welfare of the people striving to eliminate inequalities in status, facilities and opportunities and improving the standard of living, denial of these rights is manifested in poor health conditions. The fulfilment of standards enshrined in the Indian Constitution and also in the Universal Declaration of Human Rights 1948 and the International Covenant on Economic, Social and Cultural Rights declared in 1966.

Many anthropological studies reveal that the national and international declarations on human rights for a dignified living has not been fully reflected especially in tribal lives as a large majority of the tribes is denied access to electricity for domestic and agricultural use, safe drinking water, roads, public transportation, housing facilities, modern media, primary health care and education. More than 40 per cent of the tribal population stands below the poverty line. It is still worst among the primitive tribes. Most of them are not able to meet both ends, leaving them in a state of scarcity of food resources. A large majority of the interior tribal settlements have inadequate infrastructural facilities.

Violation of human rights in vulnerable communities is underreported in many part of the country. An atrocity on lower caste people by the dominant caste people is a perpetual problem in our country. It is not only on the lower caste communities, we often hear about sporadic incidents taking place in the form of atrocities on tribes, especially on tribal women.

In principle, there are certain constitutional safeguards that protect the fair sex, but violation of gender rights has been categorized under the Indian Constitution, Indian Penal Code, the Convention on the Elimination of All Forms of Discrimination against Women in 1979 and the Declaration of the Elimination of Violence against Women. Tribal women are subjected to physical abuse and ill treatment in many parts of our country. To understand the magnitude of the problem, the recent episode (Vakapalli incident) reflects the violation of human rights, where few tribal women were physically abused and molested by a group of men. An incident like this is once again a wake-up call to the entire nation on how women's rights are being violated everywhere. Also, these incidents reflect the tribes' vulnerability. Low negotiation skills have been exploited, since they cannot represent themselves.

Violation of Land Rights

Verma (2002) explains in detail how tribes fight for their rights on land in different parts of India. The issue of land rights is one of the most crucial and pressing concerns for tribes in many parts of our country. It is also interlinked with the issue of rights over forests. As discussed before, the tribes' traditional homelands being forest lands fall today under the state-imposed system of reserved forests. From the British period to the present day, the tribes have witnessed wide-scale alienation of their lands to the non-tribals and the state. The ramifications are immense for these communities, who are denied a right to culture, religion, livelihood, dignity and life itself. Moreover, given the national and international commitments to recognize and protect the rights of tribals, it leaves us to question the substance of government commitments to securing tribals' land rights. Taking this right, and measuring its enjoyment against the main standard of

SC/ST (Prevention of Atrocities) Act, 1989, U.N. Declaration on Permanent Sovereignty over Natural Resources, 1962, International Conventions, 1957, Indigenous and Tribal Populations, 1989 and the Convention of Biological Diversity, 1992, enquiries were conducted through anthropological research.

Land alienation is not a recent phenomenon, but has been taking place in the tribal areas at least for the past century. However, its continuing pattern is due to the lack of stringent action, and also that the existing Land Acts are not properly implemented. Land alienation was a key issue for tribes. The factors that have contributed to the marginalization of the tribes from their land holdings and assets can be summarized as below:

- Introduction of an alien legal system mainly protecting the interest of the encroachers of tribal land
- Adoption of various methods that weakened the enforcement of protective laws such as keeping controversial government officials, resorting to administrative delay, encouraging legal litigation, etc.
- Considerable influx of migrants attracted by the possibility of 'cheating' tribes from their lands
- Use of force to suppress the mobilization of the tribes fighting for their land rights

Some of the ways used by outsiders to grab tribal land are as follows:

- Benami transfer: The land is held and cultivated by a non-tribal, but the legal title remains with a tribal. In another method, the non-tribal adopted was to keep tribal women as concubines and enjoy the benefits of land in their name.
- Certification ploy: The non-tribals, while migrating to scheduled areas, acquire a tribal status certificate. Non-tribals try to establish connections with the government officials and political leaders. They are 'certified' under STs and enjoy the benefits of development over the disadvantaged minority.
- The encroachment of government land by non-tribals: Non-tribals have already encroached upon a large amount of land. When the government assigns these lands to tribals, the eviction becomes very difficult and, moreover, the litigation process takes considerable time and resources. Justice is sometimes delayed so much that it becomes equivalent to justice denied.

- Land Acquisition Act of 1894: This law has displaced more tribes than any other law. Most of the resources of the country (about 70%) are found in the tribal land, which constitutes about 20 per cent of the country's geographical area. In the process of resource accession and infrastructure development, the tribals are displaced without compensation.

Government's Negligence or Denial of Tribals' Right towards Forest Produce

The introduction of the Forest Department in tribal areas has created conflict with the tribals. Within no time, traditional forest lands have been taken away from the Adivasis and they have been transformed from forest dwellers to 'intruders' and 'encroachers' in the forest. Ignoring the tribals' total dependence on the forest, their ability to extract forest resources in consonance with their socio-cultural principles of conservation and respect for nature, the Forest Department officials have sought to keep the forests within their hold. They exercise almost total control over the forests, denying the Adivasis freedom to enter their own traditional forest homeland. This is in effect contravenes the National Forest Policy 1988, which recognizes the right to firewood and fodder to the tribals.

Land and forest disputes become a regular feature in many tribal areas and create unrest among the tribals. The tribals forcefully encroach into the 'reserved' forest lands basically for their livelihood. In turn, the forest officials file legal cases against them. A number of such cases are pending in the court of law. Most of the tribals have been slowly dispossessed of much of their original lands; some hold a small piece of land, often supplementing their income through agricultural labour, firewood selling, wage labour in construction and road works. There is clear evidence of exploitation of natural resources by various outside agencies and individuals, leading to deprivation of their livelihoods. Despite the tribals' self-sustaining lifestyle, the government fails to protect their right to use the original land and forest resources in a sustainable manner.

Forest officials assume the role of policing and not at conservation and perpetuating. As a result, the tribal's indigenous knowledge about forest, its maintenance and sustainable development does not find a place in the revenue-oriented government policy of forest conservation.

Unfulfilled Rights to Education, Health and Information

Formal education is instrumental for socio-economic development. It is noticed among tribes throughout the country that majority of the tribal communities have low literacy levels, no-enrolment, and high dropouts among tribal children at all levels of schooling. Further, it is witnessed that girl education is deplorably low among these communities. It is felt that to raise the awareness levels about the rights and privileges constituted for them, education is a powerful tool to disseminate these legal provisions provided for them. Hence, tribal people may get to know about their rights and duties specific to land labour life, security and social welfare through education.

This specifically refers to the duty of the government to fulfil its obligation under Article 26, Indigenous and Tribal Population Convention 1957, by which a rights awareness programme appropriate to the social and cultural characteristics of tribal people should be undertaken to ensure that tribals are educated and measures are put in place to protect and promote their rights against exploitative non-tribal groups. A large majority of the interior tribals do not have access to public health services due to geographical and ecological barriers. Even if some one visits the health facility, they are ill-treated by the health personnel.

It is a fact that a large majority of the tribes are not aware of the constitutional provisions and rights provided to them due to their geographical Isolation and illiteracy. Knowing their innocence and ignorance, non-tribals exploit them in numerous ways, especially in the areas of procuring commercial products and labour market.

To conclude, though, there exist different constitutional provisions to safeguard the tribes' rights, identity and welfare for these deprived and vulnerable groups. Negligence and violation of these constitutional obligations are really disheartening. Stringent action plans must be adopted for those who exploit these innocent and voiceless communities. Advocacy and framing more inclusive policies along with the existing ones requires support from different organizations like NGOs working towards welfare of the tribes. Legal awareness campaign with missionary zeal should be taken up by local bodies to percolate into all tribal groups.

References

Austin, Granville. 1966. *The Indian Constitution*, Prentice-Hall, Inc., Englewood Cliffs, NJ.

Basu, Durga Das. 1990. *Introduction to the Constitution of India* (13th ed.), Prentice-Hall, Inc., Englewood Cliffs, NJ.

Behura, N.K. and Nilakantha Panigrahi (eds.). 2006. *Tribals and the Indian Constitution*, Rawat Publications, Jaipur.

Fernandes, Walter. 2002. 'Tribals and Advocacy Efforts in India', in John Samuel (ed.), *Struggles for Survival*, National Centre for Advocacy Studies, Pune.

Pandey, J.N. 1997. *Constitutional Law of India* (32nd ed.), Central Law Agency, Allahabad.

Verma, R.C. 2002. *Indian Tribes through Ages*, Publications Division, Ministry of Information and Broadcasting, Government of India.

8

Tribal Population and Development Policies

A Critical Analysis

J. Srivirajarani and V. Subramanyam

India has a substantial tribal population, next only to Africa. The tribal population is distributed all over the country, except in the states of Punjab and Haryana, with varying levels of concentration. The Census of India enumerates the population data of all the communities including Scheduled Tribes (STs) once in every 10 years and anthropologists make use of the data on tribes as secondary source of information and to follow the sampling procedure in their research endeavours. The data on tribal population is also useful in formulating development policies and programmes.

In this paper, an attempt is made to explain the distribution of tribal population in India and in the state of Andhra Pradesh as per the Census of India (2001). It analyses data pertaining to STs on the basis of age and sex composition, occupation, literacy, growth rate and infrastructural facilities that exist in the tribal settlement (villages). In addition to examining the policies vis-a-vis tribal development, the paper makes suggestions in regard to the collection of valid and reliable data by the Census of India.

The data collected by the Census of India have both academic and research value. The census data on various castes, tribes and ethnic groups provide their demographic profile at national and state levels. It is the only authentic source of information available to us in order to understand the population structure of India. Anthropologists rely on these data to some extent to formulate the research study design, to select the field area as well as to follow the sampling procedure in collection of empirical data on the chosen community (tribe, caste or ethnic group) or respondents for the study.

Tribal Population

India is home for 635 tribes with a population of 8,43,26,240 (8.20%) as per the Census 2001. The state of Andhra Pradesh consists of 33 tribes with a population of 50.24 lakhs (6.59%), distributed among all the 23 districts with varying degrees. Majority of the tribal population in the state is concentrated in the tribal sub plan areas of nine scheduled districts. About 60.66 per cent of the tribal population in the state is concentrated in nine scheduled districts of Srikakulam, Vizianagaram, Visakhapatnam, East Godavari, West Godavari, Khammam, Warangal, Adilabad and Mahaboobnagar. Khammam has the highest concentration of tribes (26.47%), followed by Adilabad (16.74%), Visakhapatnam (14.55%), Warangal (14.10%), Nalgonda (10.55%), Vizianagaram (9.55%), Nellore (9.08%), Mahaboobnagar (7.93%) and Nizamabad (7.07%). In other districts the percentage of tribal population is less than 6 per cent. The tribal population in Andhra Pradesh constitutes 5.96 per cent of the total tribal population of India. In Visakhapatnam district there are 14 major tribes with a population of 5,57,572 (14.55%).

Table 8.1 shows the state-wise ST population in India as per Census 1991 and 2001. From the table it is noted that the north-eastern states like Mizoram, Nagaland, Meghalaya and Sikkim have the highest concentration of tribal population. Similarly, the Union Territories like Lakshadweep and Dadra & Nagar Haveli also have a large tribal population. The differential tribal population growth rate between 1991 and 2001 is 0.12 per cent, while the tribal population growth rate in India between 1991 and 2001 census periods is 24.45 per cent. The growth rate of the ST population in Andhra Pradesh was 16.6 per cent during 1991–2001. The lowest tribal population is found in states like Uttar Pradesh, Goa, Tamil Nadu and Kerala. Likewise, states of Manipur, Chattisgarh, Tripura, Jharkhand, Orissa, Sikkim and Madhya Pradesh have large proportions of tribes. It is observed that a large chunk of tribal population in India is mainly concentrated in the high-altitude forest zones like the Eastern Ghats, Western Ghats, and the North-eastern, Central and Himalayan mountains.

Table 8.1

State-wise ST Population in India (2001 and 1991 Census)

Name of the State or Union Territory	*ST Population (2001 Census)*	*% to Total Population*	*ST Population (1991 Census)*	*% to Total Population*
Andhra Pradesh	5,024,104	6.6	4,199,481	6.31
Arunachal Pradesh	7,05,158	64.2	5,50,351	63.66
Assam	3,308,570	12.4	2,870,441	12.62
Bihar	7,58,351	0.9	6,616,924	7.66
Chattisgarh	6,616,596	31.8	—	—
Goa	566	0.0	878	0.03
Gujarat	7,481,160	14.8	6,161,775	14.02
Haryana	—	—	—	—
Himachal Pradesh	2,44,587	4.0	2,18,349	4.22
Jammu & Kashmir	1,105,979	10.9	N.A	—
Jharkhand	7,087,068	26.3	—	—
Karnataka	3,463,986	6.6	1,91,5691	4.26
Kerala	3,64,189	1.1	3,20,967	1.10
Madhya Pradesh	1,22,33,474	20.3	1,53,99,734	22.27
Maharashtra	8,577,276	8.9	7,318,281	9.27
Manipur	7,41,141	34.2	6,32,173	34.41
Meghalaya	1,992,862	85.9	1,517,927	85.53
Mizoram	8,39,310	94.5	6,53,565	94.75
Nagaland	1,774,026	89.1	1,060,822	87.70
Orissa	8,145,081	22.1	7,032,210	22.21
Punjab	—	—	—	—
Rajasthan	7,097,706	12.6	5,474,891	12.44
Sikkim	1,11,405	20.6	90,901	82.36
Tamil Nadu	6,51,321	1.0	3,74,194	1.03
Tripura	9,93,426	31.1	8,53,345	30.95
Uttar Pradesh	1,07,963	0.1	2,87,901	0.21
Uttaranchal	2,56,129	3.0	—	—
West Bengal	4,406,794	5.5	3,808,760	—
Andaman and Nicobar Island	2,9,469	8.3	2,677,030	—
Chandigarh	—	—	—	—
Dadra & Nagar Haveli	1,37,225	62.2	1,09,380	78.99
Daman & Diu	13,997	8.8	11,724	11.54
Delhi	—	—	—	—
Lakshadweep	5,7,321	94.5	48,163	93.15
Pondicherry	—	—	—	—
India	8,43,26,240	8.2	6,77,58,386	8.08

Source: Census of India 2001 and 1991.

Table 8.2 provides the classification of census data on STs of Andhra Pradesh. It provides details regarding the gender, sex ratio, different categories of workers, literacy rate, work participation, number of tribal villages, number of towns in tribal areas and tribal population distribution in rural and urban areas of Andhra Pradesh.

Table 8.2

Census Data of STs in Andhra Pradesh

Total number of districts			23
Total number of subdistricts			1,125
Total number of villages			28,123
Total number of inhabited villages			26,613
Total number of towns			210
Total number of statutory towns			117
	Persons	Males	Females
ST Population			
Total	5,024,104	2,548,295	2,475,809
Rural	4,646,923	2,353,939	2,292,984
Urban	377,181	194,356	182,825
Population (0–6 years)	862,844	437,649	425195
Literates (7 years and above)	1,541,277	1,005,947	535,330
Total workers	2,705,636	1,418,849	1,286,787
Main workers	2,146,002	1,222,118	923,884
Marginal workers	559,634	196,731	362,903
Cultivators	928,354	550.401	377,953
Agricultural labourers	1,332,950	581,197	751,753
Household industry workers	80,038	35,435	44,603
Other workers	364,294	251,816	112,478
Sex ratio			972
Child sex ratio			972
Literacy rate	37.0	47.7	26.1
Work participation rate	53.9	55.7	52.0
Percentage to total workers			
Main workers	79.3	86.1	71.8
Marginal workers	20.7	13.9	28.2
Categories of total workers			
Cultivators	34.3	38.8	29.4
Agricultural labourer	49.3	41.0	58.4
Household industry workers	3.0	2.5	3.5
Other workers	13.5	17.7	8.7

Table 8.3 explains the distribution of tribal population in 23 districts of Andhra Pradesh. More number of tribal people are found in Khammam and 14 tribes inhabit Visakhapatnam district. In general, hill tribes are mostly concentrated in the agency areas that are characterized by forest environment typical of the Eastern Ghats ecosystem. The plains tribes like Lambada, Yerukula and Yanadi live in the villages and these groups have established symbiotic relationship with the caste communities.

Table 8.3

District-wise Tribal Population Distribution in Andhra Pradesh as per 2001 Census

Name of the District	*Total General Population*	*ST Population*		*Total Males and Females*	*% of ST in Total Population*
		Males	*Females*		
Adilabad	24,88,003	2,09.586	2,06.925	4,16,511	16.74
Nizamabad	23,45,685	83,135	82,600	1,65,735	7.07
Karimnagar	34,91,822	45,807	44,829	90,636	2.60
Medak	26,70,097	68,966	65,567	1,34,587	5.04
Hyderabad	38,29,753	17,862	16,698	34,560	0.90
Rangareddi	35,75,064	75,074	71,003	1,46,057	4.09
Mahaboobnagar	35,13,934	1,43,115	1,35,587	2,78,702	7.93
Nalgonda	32,47,982	1,78,373	1,64,303	3,42,676	10.55
Warangal	32,46,004	2,35,451	2,22,228	4,57,679	14.10
Khammam	25,78,927	I3,44,027	3,38,590	6,82,617	26,47
Srikakulam	25,37,593	75,284	75,965	1,51,249	5.96
Vizianagaram	22,49.254	1,06,079	10,860	2,14,839	9.55
Visakhapatnam	38,32,336	2,78,399	2,79,173	5,57,572	14,55
East Godavari	49,01,420	95,234	96,327	1,91,561	3.91
West Godavari	38,03,517	47,887	48,772	96,659	2.54
Krishna	41,87,841	55,201	52,410	1,07,611	2.57
Guntur	44,65,144	1,06,101	1,02,056	2,08,157	4.66
Prakasam	30,59,423	60,670	57,571	1,81,241	3.86
Nellore	26,68,564	1,23,554	1,18,703	2,42,257	9.08
Kadapa	26,01,797	31,643	29,728	61,371	2.36
Kurnool	35,29,494	36,097	33,538	69,635	1.97
Ananatapoor	36,40,478	65,722	61,439	1,27,161	3.49
Chittor	37,45,875	65,048	63,037	1,28,085	3.42
Total	76,21,007	25,48,295	24,75,809	50,24,104	6.59

Table 8.4 gives details of the population of all tribes in Andhra Pradesh as per Census 2001. Among the 33 tribes, Lambada is numerically dominant, followed by Koya, Yanadi, Yerukula, Gond and Konda Dora. The population of certain tribes like Konda (meaning hill in Telugu), Reddis, Kattunayakan, Rena and Bhil is very less and some of them run into few hundreds. In Visakhapatnam district the Bagata tribe is economically and politically the dominant group as the Gonds in Adilabad district and the Koyas in Khammam district. The existence of hierarchy in tribal communities is noticed. Among the plains tribes the Lambadas claim to be superior to the other two tribes, Yerukula and Yanadi. Among the 33 tribes, 8 tribes have been classified as the most primitive tribes in Andhra Pradesh: (1) Chenchu, (2) Khond, (3) Gadaba, (4) Konda Reddi, (5) Konda Savara, (6) Porja, (7) Kolam, and (8) Thoti. The economy of the tribes is agro-forest-based and largely considered as a subsistence economy.

Table 8.4

ST-wise Population in Andhra Pradesh as per 2001 Census

Name of the Tribe	*Total ST Population*		
	Total	*Males*	*Females*
Andh	9,735	4,920	4,815
Batata	1,33,434	66,920	66,514
Bhil	421	213	208
Chenchus	49,232	24,962	24,270
Gadaba	33,878	17,636	16,242
Gond	2,52,038	1,25,212	1,26,826
Goudu (Agency)	7,749	3,796	3,953
Hill Reddi's	77	37	40
Jatapu	1,18,613	58,021	60,592
Konda Kammara	45,010	22,188	22,822
Kattunayakan	161	85	76
Kolam	45,671	22,863	22,808
Konda Dora	2,06,381	1,03,468	1,02,913
Konda Kapu	11,780	5,820	5,960
Konda Reddi	83,096	41,459	41,637
Khond	85,324	42,530	42,794
Kotia	48,408	23,781	24,627
Koya	568,019	2,83,106	2,84,913
Kulia	368	182	186
Malis	2,513	1,242	1,271
Manne Dora	13,579	6,828	6,751
Mukha Dora	37,983	18,941	19,042

Cont'd

Cont'd

Nayak	14,222	7,104	7,118
Pardhan	23,724	12,029	11,695
Porja	32,669	16,132	16,537
Reddi Dora	1,721	874	847
Rona (Rena)	200	104	96
Savara	1,22,979	61,410	61,569
Sugalis/Lambadu	20,77,947	10,71,589	10,06,358
Thoti	2,074	1,032	1,042
Valmiki	66,814	33,195	33,619
Yanadis	4,62,167	2,36,137	22,60,30
Yerukula	4,37,459	2,20,518	21,69,41
Generic tribes etc.	26,458	13,761	12,697
All STs	50,24,104	25,48,295	24,75,809

Source: Tribal Cultural Research and Training Institute, Tribal Welfare Department, Government of Andhra Pradesh, Hyderabad, March 2004.

Table 8.5 shows the number of scheduled and non-scheduled villages in sub-plan areas (integrated tribal development agencies (ITDAS)) of Andhra Pradesh. From the table it is noted that the sub-plan areas cover an area of 31,485.34 km^2, comprising 5,938 scheduled villages and 809 non-scheduled villages. The Khammam district has an area of 6,899 Km^2, followed by Adilabad (6,138.50 Km^2), Visakhapatnam (5,904.51 Km^2), East Godavari (4,191.65 Km^2) and Warangal (3,122.46 Km^2) districts, respectively. The rest of the sub-plan areas are spread within an area of less than 2,000 km^2.

Table 8.5

Number of Scheduled and Non-Scheduled Villages in Sub-plan areas (ITDAs) of Andhra Pradesh

Name of the ITDA/District (Sub-plan Area)	*Area (Km^2)*	*No. of Scheduled Villages*	*No. of Non-scheduled Villages*
Seethampeta/Srikakulam	1,289.32	108	240
Parvathipuram/Vizianagaram	1,740.98	298	183
Paderu/Visakhapatnam	5,904.51	3,368	96
Rampachodavaram/East Godavari	4,191.65	559	40
Kota Ramachandrapuram/West Godavari	1,006.10	102	1
Bhadrachalam/Khammam	6,899.92	889	8
Eturnagaram/Warangal	3,122.46	177	77
Utnoor/Adilabad	6,138.50	412	164
Mahaboobnagar	1,191.90	25	—
Total	31,485.34	5,938	809

The available data on STs of Andhra Pradesh give details of population distribution of the tribe in the state, district, mandal, rural and urban areas; age and sex composition; decadal population growth rate, density of population, ST population and its proportion to the total population of Andhra Pradesh, sex ratio, child sex ratio (0–6 years), percentage of child population in the age group of 0–6 years, literacy status, male and female literacy, work participation rate (male work participation rate and female work participation rate), main workers, marginal workers, cultivators, agricultural labourers, household industry workers and other workers. The data also show the availability of infrastructure facilities in the tribal villages or habitats.

Table 8.6

Predominant Tribal Groups and Population in Tribal Sub-plan Areas of Andhra Pradesh

Name of the District	*Predominant Tribal Groups*	*Population*		*Total Males and Females*	*Number of STs to Total Population*
		Males	*Females*		
Srikakulam	Savara, Jatapu, Gadaba, Konda Dora	75,284	75,965	15,1249	5.96
Vizianagaram	Savara, Jatapu, Gadaba, Konda Dora, Manne Dora	1,06,079	1,08,760	2,14,839	9.55
Visakhapatnam	Bagata, Gadaba, Konda Kammara, Kotiya, Khond, Mali, Manne Dora, Reddi Dora, Rena, Porja, Konda Kapu, Kulia, Dulia, Nooka Dora	2,78,399	2,79,173	5,57,572	14.55
East Godavari	Koya, Konda Reddy, Konda Kammara, Konda Dora	95,234	96,327	1,91,561	3.91
West Godavari	Koya, Konda Reddy, Yerukula, Yanadi	47,887	48,772	96,659	2.54

Cont'd

Cont'd

Khammam	Koya, Konda Reddy, Sugali or Lambada	3,44,027	3,38,590	6,82,617	26.47
Warangal	Koya, Lambada	2,35,451	2,22,228	4,57,679	14.10
Adilabad	Gond, Kolam, Andh, Pardhan, Thoti, Lambada, Naikpod	2,09,586	2,06,925	4,16,511	16.74
Mahaboobnagar	Lambada, Chenchu, Yerukula	1,43,115	1,35,587	2,78,702	7.93
Total		15,35,062	15,12,327	30,47,389	10.45

Tribes and Development

More than 45 per cent of the tribal population in India stands below poverty line and faces problems like food insecurity, illiteracy, indebtedness, land alienation, exploitation, malnutrition, morbidity and early deaths. The Government of India has taken a number of measures that include constitutional safeguards and poverty alleviation programmes for the upliftment of tribal communities. The successive five-year plans have allocated considerable funds for the development of these autochthonous groups.

Constitutional Provisions for Scheduled Tribes

The British policy of isolation and the sporadic tribal uprisings in different parts of the country has been duly taken note of by the policy makers in the formulation of policy for tribal welfare and development. Soon after independence, a sub-committee was appointed with A.V. Thakkar Bapa as chairman for suggesting measures for the welfare and development of tribes living in the excluded and partially excluded areas. Based on the recommendations of the committee, the Constitution of India has incorporated provisions for the welfare and upliftment of the tribal people.

There are as many as 20 Articles and two schedules in the Constitution of India concerning the welfare of the tribals. The most important one is Article 46, which states that "the State shall promote with special care the educational and economic interests of the weaker sections of the people and in particular of the Scheduled Castes and Scheduled Tribes, and shall protect them from social injustice and all forms of exploitation". In pursuance of the spirit of this Article, several enactments were made to protect the interests of the tribes, though their efficacy is debatable.

Article 244 of the Indian Constitution empowers the president of India to declare any area where there is a substantial tribal population as a scheduled area and to include or exclude a tribe in the list of STs in the V Schedule on the recommendations of the state government concerned and with due approval of the Governor of the state. The scheduled areas have been constituted with two major objectives. One is to protect and facilitate the tribals in enjoying their rights, and secondly to develop the scheduled areas to promote economic, educational and social progress of the STs.

Similarly, Article 275 for assistance to the states for the implementation of the provisions of the Constitution and grants-in-aid from the consolidated fund of India to states for implementation of tribal development programmes. Articles 330, 332 and 334 provide for reservation of seats for STs in the Lok Sabha and the State Legislative Assemblies. Article 385 provides for reservation in the services and Articles 15, 16 and 19 ensure equality.

Development Policies and Programmes

Two diametrically opposite views are expressed in regard to the policy formulation for the development of STs. On one hand, it is suggested that since the tribal identity and heritage should not be disturbed they ought to be left alone with minimal interventions (policy of segregation), while the other viewpoint calls for their integration into the mainstream of the national life (policy of assimilation/integration). Verrier Elwin was the votary of the former approach and Ghurye of the latter. Elwin pleaded for the protection of their cultural identity and heritage from the impact of change so that the tribal communities are not forced into a state of 'loss of nerve'.

Ultimately, a middle path has been adopted in consonance with the views expressed by Nehru. He observed: "We cannot allow matters to drift in the tribal areas. In the world of today that is not possible or desirable. At the same time we should avoid over administration in these areas .... It is between these two extreme positions that we have to function". He desired that people should be allowed to develop along the lines of their own genius. Govind Ballabh Pant concurred with the views of Nehru and stated that the tribes should develop their own culture and make contribution to the cultural richness of the country. The present policy is to bring the tribals into mainstream and make them to participate in the development process while making efforts for preserving their identity and heritage.

A number of commissions and committees were formed to look into the problems of development in the tribal areas of the country. They have recommended several measures to remove the socio-economic imbalances and also to break down the age-old psychological barriers of the tribal communities hindering their progress. The inputs from the recommendations of these committees have formed the basis for periodical review in formulating and reformulating tribal development polices and programmes. For example, the Dhebar Commission (1961) recommended an integrated approach based on the minimum essential needs such as food, drinking water, education, employment, health and village roads. The Task Force on Development of Tribal Areas (1972) suggested that the ecological, occupational and social parameters of the tribal population should be properly assessed for formulation of the policy and its implementation, so that a steady flow of benefits could be assured. The Dube Committee (1978) suggested that the problem of tribal development should be defined at the national level and national efforts are required for tackling it. It also recommended for an integrated area development approach in line with the genius and aspirations of the tribal people.

As a result of the above recommendations, strategies and approaches such as Multi-Purpose Tribal Development Blocks, Modified Area Development Approach (MADA) Tribal Development Block, Girijan Development Agencies and Tribal Sub-plan Approach with a focus on integral area development have been adopted.

Tribal Sub-plan Approach

The Fifth Five-Year Plan marked a significant change in the process of tribal development. The plurality of occupations marked variations in the levels of development, and varied geo-ethnic milieu of various tribes gave rise to a plethora of problems, which are not amenable to uniform approach for their development. Therefore, area-specific strategy has been evolved based on the recommendations of an expert committee set up by the Ministry of Education and Social Welfare in 1972 under the chairmanship of Prof. S.C. Dube for the rapid socio-economic development of tribal people inhabiting the scheduled areas where more than 60 per cent of the tribal population is living. The main objectives of the tribal sub-plan are:

1. Socio-economic development of STs
2. Protection of tribes against exploitation

The salient features of the tribal sub-plan are:

1. It falls within the ambit of state plan meant for the welfare and development of tribes. Such a plan is a part of the overall plan of a state and is therefore called a sub-plan. The benefits given to the tribes and tribal areas of a state from the TSP are in addition to what percolates from the overall plans of the state.
2. The sub-plans:
   (a) Identify the resources for TSP areas
   (b) Prepare a broad policy framework for the development
   (c) Define a suitable administrative strategy for its implementation
3. The most significant aspect of this strategy is to ensure flow of funds for TSP areas at least in equal proportion to the ST population of the state.
4. The recent initiative of the ministry with regard to the TSP component of various departments/sectors of the states is to put the TSP fund of the state plan in a different demand head in the budget of the Tribal Development Departments of the state. In Andhra Pradesh, the tribal sub-plan area covers the scheduled areas as well as the adjoining non-scheduled villages in which 50 per cent of the population is tribal. These villages are in the districts of Adilabad, Warangal, Khammam, West Godavari, East Godavari, Visakhapatnam, Vizianagaram and Srikakulam.

Modified Area Development Approach (MADA) and Clusters

After removal of area restriction as per the provisions of SC & ST Orders (Amendment) Act, 1976, the Yerukula, Yanadi and Lambada living in Telangana region became STs. This change necessitated extending developmental activities on a large scale to tribes living in plain areas.

Three criteria have been laid down for identification of the tribal pockets under the Modified Area Development Approach (MADA):

1. there should be a minimum population of 10,000;
2. 50 per cent of the population in the pockets should belong to STs; and
3. the villages in the pockets should be contiguous.

In accordance with the above guidelines 41 MADA pockets were identified and sanctioned. The working group on development of STs during the Seventh Five-Year Plan (1985–90) suggested the relaxation of the present norm of a population not less than 10,000, of which not less than 50 per cent should be STs. Accordingly, 17 clusters having a total population of at least 5,000 and above with an ST concentration of 50 per cent or more were identified.

Primitive Tribal Groups

Various tribal groups of our country are at different stages of economy starting from the stage of food collection to settled agriculture. The most disadvantaged groups who are at food gathering, hunting and fishing stages are facing multifarious problems in modern times in their own habitats.

The question of tackling the problems of more backward communities drew the attention of various commissions and study teams connected with tribal welfare. The Scheduled Castes and Scheduled Tribes Commission (1961), popularly known as the Dhebar Commission, classified the STs into four different groups: (i) those that are living in the remotest corners and for that reason are almost in a primitive stage, (ii) those in the 'jhuming' (shifting) cultivation stage, (iii) those who have taken to regular agriculture, and (iv) those who have been already been assimilated. The Study Team on Tribal Development Programmes (1969) (Shilu AO team) observed an imbalanced development among the tribal communities, with a large number of tribal communities continuing to be extremely backward, some of them still in the primitive food gathering stage. They reiterated the view of the Dhebar Commission that the 'lowest' layer needed utmost attention and should be made the special concern of the state government. They suggested that state governments and administrations of union territories should make an objective study of the extent to which each of the tribal development programme has been implemented. Further, separate schemes for imparting education and economic upliftment should be designed and treated as central schemes, including special provision in the plan for the purpose.

At the time of review of tribal development programmes on the eve of the Fifth Five-Year Plan, it was recognized that special programmes for the extremely backward tribal groups known as primitive groups should be taken up on the basis of proper identification on the lines suggested by the Shilu AO team. It was also envisaged that the programmes would be financed entirely by the Ministry of Home Affairs. The important guidelines for identification of primitive tribal groups are:

1. pre-agricultural level of technology
2. low level of literacy
3. a stagnant or diminishing population

The Government of India has identified 75 tribes as the most primitive groups in our country which are still at the pre-agricultural stage of economy. In Andhra Pradesh, the Government of India had identified three communities, namely, Chenchu of Ranga Reddy, Kurnool, Mahaboobnagar, Nalgonda, Prakasam and Guntur districts in the year 1975–76 and Kolam of Adilabad and Konda Reddis of East Godavari, West Godavari and Khammam districts in the year 1980. In the year 1982–83 the Government of India had also recognized the following five communities as primitive tribal groups: (1) Thoti, (2) Khond, (3) Porja, (4) Gadaba, and (5) Konda Savara.

The central sector scheme for the development of primitive tribal groups is implemented through ITDAs in Andhra Pradesh. In general, the population growth rate in primitive tribal groups is very low when compared with that of other tribes. Some of the primitive tribal groups like Jarwa, Shompen and Onge are on the edge of extinction. Hence, some primitive tribal groups are exempted from family planning. However, some of the primitive tribals are also found adopting birth control measures due to poverty and to get incentives of family planning programmes.

Conclusion and Suggestions

- Some methodological errors specific to the collection of data at household level by using of the questionnaire or schedule tool are observed. Proper care should be taken to select right respondents (actual) in collection of valid data for the household level by employing well-trained personnel.
- Collected data should be analysed quickly and made available within a span of one or two years.
- Abstract tables should be prepared for each category, viz., tribe-wise population, literacy, occupation, age and sex composition, marital status, etc.
- It is high time the census undertakes the collection of data caste-wise and tribe-wise.
- Classification of poverty levels of each tribe needs to be done.
- During the field visits to some tribal areas of Visakhapatnam and Vizianagaram districts in 2005, it was noticed that some villages were not included in revenue records. Nor were they included in

any district records. These villages are inaccessible and hence the revenue as well as health workers are not visiting these villages. The Census of India therefore should carry on the enumeration in a meticulous manner, so that exclusion of some sections can be avoided.

References

Census of India. 2001. Andhra Pradesh: A Profile of the State, Director of Census Operations, Andhra Pradesh.

Prasad, O.S.D. et al., 2004. *Tribes and Tribal Areas of Andhra Pradesh*, Tribal Cultural Research and Training Institute, Tribal Welfare Department, Government of Andhra Pradesh, Hyderabad.

9

Interactive Model for Inclusive Education

Benefits for Tribal and Non-Tribal Students

K.R. Rama Mohan

India being a welfare country is wedded to the directive principles of upliftment and overall development of all the deprived and isolated communities. For a long time, tribal communities across the country managed to live in isolation, away from the mainstream society, and maintained their cultural uniqueness. But, owing to the advancement in many spheres of life such as transportation, communication and rapid technological development, it had increasingly become difficult for these tribal communities to isolate themselves any longer and avoid cultural contacts.

Social scientists have observed that culture contacts without proper education and preparation have been harmful to the tribes and created many adjustment problems. The numerous tribal groups in India, who are vastly different from each other in culture and language and are at different levels in the ladder of development, are to be integrated with the mainstream society. Though politically it has already been done, the social, economic and psychological integration has yet to be fully achieved so that they can identify themselves as citizens of India without giving up their ethnicity. Nehru (1955) expressed that "the greatest problem of India is not so much political as psychological integration and consolidation". Proper care should be taken for the tribes to be integrated into the rest of India, without disintegration of their unique cultural patterns.

Admitting that a full-fledged integration of the different tribal groups into the mainstream was very essential, the question was how to achieve this. Education was found to be helpful in facilitating the integration of the tribes into the national democratic set-up. The Government of India has been implementing special packages and programmes for the socio-economic development of different tribal groups. The basic aim of these programmes has been to involve them in the developmental process and enable them to secure for themselves an equitable and rightful place in the national system.

There were many areas like health, employment/livelihoods, basic infrastructure and education where tribes were totally neglected. Education is the most vital ingredient of development which is grossly neglected. Realizing the importance to develop the tribal communities across the country, the government came out with special provisions and privileges intended for their development and to enable them to fully participate in nation building. Education being instrumental in developmental process related to the tribes had become an important challenging area for educationists and educational planners.

The policy makers in the post-independence era felt that there should be no institution, school or college exclusively for tribes, as such segregation leads to sectarianism and clannishness in the minds of the pupils, especially during the formative years of life. However, after reviewing many reports and studies the government decided to educate tribes in their own socio-economic and cultural milieu.

Within the gamut of the national curriculum, the tribes are being educated, though they are geographically isolated within the mainstream society. In order to raise the literacy levels of tribal boys and girls by increasing their enrolment and lowering dropout rates, the government has provided additional facilities and privileges to prevail on the parents to provide formal education to their children. Since then there have been several schemes and educational programmes targeting the tribes.

Educational Policies in India

The National Policy on Education (NPE), 1986, with modification in 1992, the Comprehensive Education Programme called Sarva Shiksha Abhiyan (SSA) in 2001–02 and prior programmes like DPEP, Shiksha Karmi, Lok Jumbish have all geared towards making primary education successful. It is also encouraging in the case of tribal groups with certain disparities in literacy rates (NCERT, 2006–07).

With these different educational programmes, India has made tremendous progress in the development of education. This can be seen in terms of a phenomenal increase in institutions, teachers and students at the elementary level. Enrolment has also increased in remote tribal areas, thus addressing the problem of access to schooling. All tribal habitations have a primary school in their vicinity. Further, the dropout rate among boys and girls have been significantly minimized due to sustained efforts in the form of bridge courses, residential camps, drop-in-centres, summer camps and remedial schools. It is interesting to note that the participation of girls in education has increased significantly over the years.

Given the pace of unprecedented technological changes which the country is experiencing, there is a need to uncover human potential across all societies, more so in tribal communities, to meet the demands of the changing times. Hence provision of quality education to bring out these hidden talents from these people is the need of the hour. Further, artificial social barriers created between communities will be minimized.

The question that arises at this juncture is that what place do the tribes occupy in our country when the nation is boasting of becoming an economic superpower in the recent times. Chalam (2007) argues that even after 60 years of India's independence, why has the government failed to achieve universalization of education? He further questions that who are the people or groups or castes that are deprived of education and what is required to be done to bring them into the mainstream (inclusive growth)? These are some of the important questions that need to be raised and answered to achieve inclusive education.

At the global scenario, many Western countries have a policy to include ethnic minority learners in the mainstream education system to attain inclusive growth. Even the students at mainstream have special programme like "School Year Abroad" which provides the students to explore and learn different cultures in a host country. The basic aim of these programmes is to make the students encounter human challenges they have never experienced.

At this backdrop of student exchange programme for innovative learning in different cultures, this paper is intended to raise certain issues to help policy makers, teachers, educationists and the school administrators to understand the concept of inclusive school (education) and how children of different tribal communities can be made integral participants in the education process without upsetting the present educational framework. This could be an opportunity to study an extended curriculum in non-tribal schools in rural and urban areas to learn the culture and new frontiers of knowledge.

Learning from Tribal and Non-Tribal Students: A Model for Inclusive Education

In recent years, the paradigm shift of inclusive education has risen to significance on the international education agenda. while this rise has been rapid, it is, however, essential to trace a set of long-term historical developments of which inclusion is simply the latest manifestation. "Inclusive education is concerned with removing all barriers to learning, and with the participation of all learners vulnerable to exclusion and marginalization. It is a strategic approach designed to facilitate learning success for all children. It addresses the common goals of decreasing and overcoming all exclusion from the human right to education, at least at the elementary level, and enhancing access, participation and learning success in quality basic education for all" (UNESCAP, 1998).

It has been suggested that inclusion has arisen from two interrelated but distinct processes. The first process is a reconstruction of notions of socially excluded groups and disability. Such notions related to conceptions of human rights and social justice. The second process involves social, economic and educational developments that are not tied specifically to disability and socially excluded groups but are much concerned with the role of education in building the contemporary societies. Thus, inclusive education is a developmental approach to the learning needs of all children, youth and adults, especially those who are vulnerable to marginalization and exclusion.

Sayed (2003) feels that 'special schools' or 'special education' for the STs and the disabled are seen as simply reinforcing problematic inequalities which lead to further exclusion. He further elaborates that for the Scheduled Tribes and the marginalized groups, inclusion of their special interests and needs with the mainstream education is a political priority. Inclusion is a means to redress power imbalances and to secure a greater share of resources, representation and involvement in the society.

Advantages from Inclusive Education

Inclusion in education involves the process of increasing the participation of students and reducing their exclusion from the cultures, curricula and communities of local schools (Puri and Abraham, 2004). The core aspect of this inclusive education is to see diversity As a rich resource, and hence it should not be perceived as a problem. Further, it facilitates learning through participation of all students who are vulnerable to exclusionary pressures. Lastly, inclusive education should not be dealt in isolation since it is a part and parcel of inclusive society. In recent years scholars have argued about inclusive education from a political strategy perspective. It is based on human rights and democratic principles that confront all forms of discrimination, a part of a concern to develop an inclusive society and to ensure that some students receive additional resources and are not ignored or neglected (ibid.).

Further, the inclusive idea can highlight the concept of togetherness (enabling all to participate together in society from the beginning, contributing to social harmony and stimulating the building of relationships among individuals, groups and nations) which will facilitate a true understanding in the educational process. The strengths of inclusive education can be visualized in the form of breaking barriers, an familiarity and tolerance reduce fear, prejudice and for instance rejection.

Using 'inclusive model' is a way to reach out to all these children as well and to create a generation of adults who are well adjusted, confident and well informed to be the leaders of a progressive India. We have been fortunate to be 'included' in the 'mainstream' from our early childhood. Mostly in all aspects of life, inclusion is not another fancy concept; it is a way of life.

India's rich socio-cultural, religious, linguistic and geographical diversifications, give a wonderful opportunity for the children to learn about diversity in the classroom. We need to question whether the present tribal schools really reflect these finer aspects. Inclusive learning with different children will have an opportunity to grow up recognizing, experiencing, respecting and accommodating this diversity. It is repeatedly said that the core aspect of education is all about growing up knowing the environment in which we live in all its dimensions.

Segregation vs Integration

There has been a debate on segregation vs integration among the academia, which involved questions like "Should tribal children completely give way to integration?" In this case, it is wise to ask for reasons for this shift in attitude. The first possible reason is that Tribal

Welfare (Ashram) Schools with the same curriculum are excluding the children not only academically but also socially. These 'special' residential schools deny the children their right to acquiring knowledge through interaction with their peers in the mainstream education system.

This isolation also contradicts the fact that knowledge is formed socially, where children can acquire knowledge and skills in mainstream schools. Moreover, children also gain knowledge and discipline through their peers in mainstream school compounds and on the way from home to school.

In addition to this, although the special residential schools for the tribes and other disadvantaged children have a concentration of huge resources and more expertise, they are accommodating limited number of children. However, the above-mentioned expensive special materials and specialists would be able to serve the needs of children in the regular schools.

Integration vs Isolation

Similar to the debate of segregation vs integration, there was another debate on integration vs isolation. Through time, educators began to indicate or point the limitations of integration (mainstreaming). Since integration is an attempt to change the learner or to support the child, it hardly responded to the special needs of the learners in the regular schools, especially disabled children. Therefore, integration or mainstreaming remained stagnant and unchanged for many years.

The paternalistic nature of the special residential schools approach and the charitable discourses may be taken up for serious discussions. The reason is that such discourses were demeaning, casting students who are socially excluded into the role of dependents on the rest of the society. It can also be used to legitimate the maintenance of social arrangements that systematically marginalize and disadvantage such students due to their geographical and socio-cultural constraints.

Challenges to the Individual and Tribal Growth

Inclusion creates opportunities for cultural exchange between tribal and non-tribal children in school for their own mutual benefits. The advantage of inclusion is that it introduces the tribal child to the mainstream of life. The child is literally thrown into the shallow end of the stream where he or she learns the art of living in a friendly pace, recognizing and appreciating expectations, responsibilities, challenges and the opportunities of life. The environment is friendly but competitive; the bar is constantly raised and each person or child is continuously challenged to perform at higher levels. Teaching, training and grooming in the school are directed at enhancing skills, abilities and techniques to actualize this challenge.

In this process, certainly there will be a change in attitude towards different children by forming the basis for a just and non-discriminatory society, which encourages people to live and learn together. As pointed out by Mishra (2004), lack of social mobility and the problem of intercultural communication are the major retarding factors in the present mode of tribal education throughout the country. This can be countered with inclusive education, where they have good social mobility and intercultural dialogue. To enhance mixed participation of tribal schoolchildren with non-tribal schoolchildren, Mishra suggests that there should be a mix of these students in every school activity.

Interactive Exposure as a Means of Inclusive Education for Tribal and Non-Tribal Students and Teachers

Introduction to the concept/model: There are many educational programmes designed and implemented for non-tribal and other disabled students, like school excursion programmes in the form of historical/sight-seeing tours for both groups form a non-curriculum-based approach. But these excursions/study tours are highly limited to just visiting certain monuments and places.

The proposed study exchange programmes will provide extra benefits for both groups of students in the form of extended curriculum by learning different aspects. As the educational planners give less importance into bringing out innovative educational programmes for the tribal children, this exchange programme is highly beneficial to the tribal students than the non-tribal students. Keeping this in view, there is a need to introduce a system where tribal and non-tribal students get to learn from each other for mutual benefit, leading to inclusive education for all secluded tribal students. In the same manner, non-tribal (mainstream) students must be exposed to certain tribal (school) areas.

Areas wherein both tribal and non-tribal students can be benefited through this interactive exposure to enrich the present curriculum are listed in the following table:

	Tribal Students	*Non-Tribal Students*
Environmental science	Urban landscape	Flora, fauna, wildlife, different natural resources
Science/technology/media	Learn about modern scientific aspects, media	Indigenous technology, artefacts
Psychological aspects	Achievement motivation, competitiveness, high levels of aspiration	Cooperativeness, attitude of simple life, native coping mechanisms, adjustability
Physical aspects	Understand the racial differences	Understand the racial differences
Socio-cultural aspects	Learn about the cosmopolitan urban way of life, different religions, languages	Learn about the different tribe customs, folkways, languages, festivals, food habits, division of labour
Extra-mural aspects	Learn about different forms of entertainment, games and sports	Learn about local forms of entertainment like songs, dance and arts

It is not only that both groups of students benefit in this process, teachers also equip themselves with certain important aspects in their teaching methodologies. Teachers being very influential in imparting, skills to students also make a huge impact on students' personalties, and hence should also experience the different aspects of the teaching-learning process in different settings. To support this, teachers need to have a broad understanding of every student's needs, and hence need some 'cultural therapy'. Spindler (1963) suggested that teachers must go through sensitization process to teach a diversified students.

Teachers working in tribal and non-tribal areas must exchange their teaching strategies, problems encountered in delivery, tackling truancy and, dealing with slow learners and dropouts. While both tribal and few non-tribal teachers working in tribal areas will learn new modern pedagogical methods applied in fast-paced urban settings, non-tribal teachers will learn the ways and means of teaching methods in nature-based settings. Apart from these, teachers working in these different settings will also exchange some concerns and views regarding their well-being, and professional hazards faced in their tenure.

The Execution Process

As this is a new programme which is being suggested, it should be launched between the government schools operating both in tribal and non-tribal areas. For the urban corporate schools, NGOs and other agents working in tribal areas should facilitate the exchange programme between tribal and urban corporate schools.

Modalities of Implementation, Logistics, Issues and Challenges

Ideally, students should be split into two groups: 6–8 grades, and 9–10 grades. The student exchange programme can be stretched for a weekday, planned during the school vacation. Interactive learning in inclusive education also challenges the prevailing systems in terms of physical structures, human resources, curriculum, teaching and communicative media and methodologies, teaching and learning materials, attitude, etc.

It also involves restructuring cultures, policies and practices to respond to the diversity of students in their locality.

Interactive learning in inclusive education provides an opportunity for planners, designers, policy makers, administrators and implementers to work on and develop the concept of universal design. This could well be the nursery of a civil society that provides for all its members without exception. Education must not only provide the child learning and vocational skills, but also nurture an intellect and a psychology that reflect and demonstrate confidence, a positive attitude and a passion for life. A combination of skills and belief in one's own self would be the essence of inspiration for these socially excluded children.

Despite the fact that many government schools in both tribal and non-tribal areas are short of infrastructural facilities, both students and teachers should take it as a constraint to support this kind of creative programmes which will certainly bring qualitative changes in students, especially in the tribal students.

Necessary infrastructure and arrangements should be planned in advance for students' accommodation in the form of home stay or school stay. The state agency must allocate some funds to support these programmes. However, there are some issues and challenges to execute this programme in terms of taking care of students' health when they stay in a new environment. Another major issue could be parents' non-acceptability to send their wards away from home as they may experience home sickness. As far as tribal parents are concerned, they may view it as losing their children's support in agricultural activities and non-timber forest produce collection as well as in household chores in the case of girls.

Suggestions

Though excursion tours are conducted by some schools for tribal and non-tribal students, these should be replaced by the "teaching and learning exchange programme" for both teachers and students. This is a new educational programme, with a novel approach, from which everyone can benefit. There may be some issues and challenges in implementing this programme, but one must give a thought to the benefits that may be reaped out of these programmes. Further, it needs micro-level planning to take it on for a long-term basis. Lastly, it is important to note that the pyramid of higher education delicately hinges upon the base of primary education. Consequently, the soundness of the base decides the fate of the upper structure. As India is aiming at global leadership, there should not be any disparity or development targeted to only certain groups. Keeping in view the holistic approach of the development of the country at large, where the tribal youth especially will benefit to a great extent by these exchange programmes. This in turn will enable the socially and geographically isolated educated youth to join the highly skilled human resource pool in the coming years.

References

Annual Report 2006–2007. NCERT, New Delhi.

Chalam, K.S. 2007. 'Inclusive Education and Eleventh Plan', *South Indian Journal of Social Sciences*, V(2): 1–5.

Mishra, Bibuthi. 2004. 'Reorienting Tribal Education', *The Hindu*, 23 July.

Nehru, Jawaharlal. 1955. *'The Tribal Folk': The Adivasis*, The Publication Division, Ministry of Information and Broadcasting, Government of India.

Puri, Madhumita and George Abraham (eds.), 2004. *Handbook of Inclusive Education for Educators, Administrators and Planners*, Sage Publications, New Delhi.

Sayed, Yusuf. 2003. 'One Size Fits All? Approaches to Inclusive Education', *IDS Bulletin*, Vol. 34.

Spindler, George D. 1963. *Education and Anthropology*, Stanford University Press, California.

United Nations Economic and Social Commission for Asia and the Pacific (UNESCAP). 1998. Report No. 32.

10

Role of SHGs in the Empowerment of Weaker Sections

Strategies for the Upliftment through Inclusive Policies

R. Ramakrishna, Jayasheela Prakash and D. Tata Rao

Poverty being an outcome of multiple deprivations, empowerment of the poor is considered a critical factor in accelerating poverty reduction. In contemporary development economics, people's participation is the central theme for poverty reduction initiatives. This paradigm shift calls for considerable efforts to mobilize human energies and building up community-based economic leadership at grassroots. In this context, the Self-Help Group (SHG) methodology has been found very effective to realize the goal of comprehensive empowerment of low-income households. Accordingly, NABARD initiated a project to link SHGs with banks in the year 1992. Experimentation with SHGs has shown positive signs, gaining satisfaction of all concerned. Andhra Pradesh has the largest formation of SHGs in the country and more than 4,00,000 groups are functioning in the state. The state has also been in the forefront under The SHG-Bank Linkage Programme by effecting linkage for 2,00,000 groups. Both governmental and non-governmental agencies have played an active role providing synergy in group formation and bank linkage.

Puhazhendi and Satyasai (2000), Chavan and Ramakumar (2002), Ramakrishna (2001, 2004 a,b, 2005), Ramakrishna and Rao (2008 a,b) and Sirivardana (2001) have systematically analysed the empowerment of weaker sections. The present study endeavours to examine the incidence of poverty among sample households. An attempt is also made to study inclusive growth in Andhra Pradesh through the SHG-Bank Linkage Programme that aimed at poverty reduction.

Objectives

1. To analyse the effect of the SHG-Bank Linkage Programme on incidence of poverty among sample households.
2. To study the impact of the SHG-Bank Linkage Programme on socio-economic empowerment and nutritional development among households.
3. To suggest strategies for the sustainability of SHGs for the upliftment of weaker sections.

Methodology

A multi-stage sampling technique was used in the selection of units in the study area. Accordingly, in the first stage of sampling, Visakhapatnam district, one of the backward districts in north coastal Andhra Pradesh, was selected purposively. In the second stage of sampling, out of the 42 mandals, Subbavaram mandalam was selected for the study. Selection of the mandal was done keeping in view that it should satisfy the two criteria: (a) cover the maximum number of poor households, and (b) cover the maximum coverage of SHG households. The third stage of sampling covered the selection of villages. The fourth stage of sampling involved the selection of households. In all, 300 households were selected for the study by using random sampling technique. While 200 of these households were the members of SHGs, the remaining 100 were non-SHGs (NSHGs). These two groups of sample households have been chosen keeping in view the probability proportion to their actual number in the total number of poor households in the study area. A survey was conducted during the period of 1 November 2007 to 31 December 2007.

Socio-economic Profile of the Respondents

The socio-economic profile of the sample households shows that a majority of the heads of households of the SHG households were in the age group of 20–30. For a majority of the SHG households the family size was four and below. In the literacy levels of the heads of the households, the SHG households had more literates than the NSHG households. The percentage of earners to the total family members in the SHG households was higher than that in the NSHG households and the dependency ratio was lower in the SHG households than in the NSHG households. These differences may have been due to the empowerment of the poor through the SHG-Bank Linkage Programme (see Tables 10.1–10.4).

Table 10.1

Distribution of Heads of Households by Age Composition

Groups of Households	*Age Composition (Years)*					*Total*
	Below 20	*21–30*	*32–40*	*41–50*	*Above 50*	
SHG	5.50	35.50	31.00	19.00	9.00	100.00 (200)
NSHG	2.00	28.00	39.00	22.00	9.00	100.00 (100)

Note: Figures are in percentages. SHG households, 200; NSHG households, 100.

Table 10.2

Distribution of Households by Size of the Family

Groups of Households	*Family Size*			*Total*
	4 and below	*5 and 6*	*7 and above*	
SHG	61.50	34.50	7.00	100.00 (200)
NSHG	52.00	40.00	8.00	100.00 (100)

Note: Figures are in percentages.

Table 10.3

Distribution of Heads of Households by Literacy Level

Groups of Households	*Literacy Level*				*Total*
	Illiterates	*Primary*	*Secondary*	*Higher*	
SHG	45.50	18.50	28.50	7.50	100.00 (200)
NSHG	49.00	27.00	21.00	3.00	100.00 (100)

Note: Figures are in percentages.

Table 10.4

Distribution of the Family Members by Earning Status

Groups of Households	Earners				Non-earners				Total	Dependency Ratio
	Male	Female	Children	Total	Male	Female	Children	Total		
SHG	28.28	17.42	0.79	46.49	14.59	11.31	27.60	53.51	100.00 (884)	1.15
NSHG	28.73	14.25	1.11	44.10	20.27	12.92	22.72	55.90	100.0 (449)	1.27

Note: Figures are in percentages

Incidence of Poverty among Rural Poor

The studies on poverty conducted by individual researchers tried to estimate poverty by using different methods. The Planning Commission takes into consideration the monthly per capita expenditure norm to estimate the poverty. Having wide methodological differences in the methodology used for fixing the norm to identify the poverty line, all the estimates showed that the incidence of poverty is on a decline in India. In this study monthly per capita expenditure as a measure of standard of living is also used for the analysis of poverty. The official poverty line is adjusted to the year 2000–01 by using the Consumer Price Index for rural labourers. Accordingly, the estimated poverty line of Rs. 264.36 is taken for the rural areas in this study. The three measures of poverty, head count ratio, poverty gap ratio and modified Sen's index of poverty, were used to estimate poverty for the two groups of households.

Head Count Ratio

For the SHGs as a whole, about 41.5 per cent of the total households were found to be below the poverty line, while this picture is accounted for by 67 per cent in case of the NSHGs. Based on the above facts, it can be concluded that the incidence of poverty among the NSHG households was comparatively higher than that among the SHG households (see Table 10.5).

Table 10.5

Group-wise Estimates of Three Poverty Measures

Groups of Households	Head Count Ratio	Poverty Gap Ratio	Modified Sen's Index of Poverty
SHG	41.5	11.80	0.0044
NSHG	67	15.72	0.0118

Note: Head count ratio and poverty gap ratio are expressed as percentages.

The Poverty Gap Ratio

From Table 10.5, the estimates of the poverty gap ratio clearly indicate the poverty, as a fraction of total expenditure needed to support everyone in the population at the poverty line. Thus, the larger the estimate, the larger is the requirement of resources to guarantee the entire population an expenditure equivalent to the poverty line. Moreover, its smaller empirical results, when analysed, helped us in deriving the following inferences. The results of this poverty measure show that the poverty gap ratio was found to be higher in the NSHG households.

Modified Sen's Index of Poverty

As mentioned earlier, Sen's modified poverty measure overcomes the limitation of the earlier measure, viz., the poverty gap ratio. The latter measure suffers from the limitation of being insensitive to the redistribution of income among the poor. The modified Sen's index of poverty overcomes this drawback. The modified measure of poverty lies between zero and unity. It assumes a value of zero when everyone's income is above the poverty line and becomes unity when everyone has zero income. Thereby we may infer that the lower the value of this measure, the closer is the distribution of the poor to the poverty line and vice versa. The measure of Sen's index of poverty assumed values close to 0 in both the SHG and the NSHG groups (0.0044 for the SHGs and 0.0118 for the NSHGs) (see Table 10.5). This indicates that the distribution of the poor is closer to the poverty line.

The empirical results show that the incidence of poverty is less in the SHG households compared with the NSHG households. A lower poverty gap ratio was found in the SHG households compared with the NSHG households. The modified Sen's index of poverty indicates that the distribution of the poor is closer to the poverty line in both the groups of households. To sum up, according to all the three measures of poverty, the SHG households are in a better position than the NSHG households.

Socio-economic Empowerment and Nutritional Development of the Respondents

Strengthening of people's institutions like the Panchayat Raj Institutions (PRIs), Village Organizations (VOs) and Community-Based

Organizations (CBOs); enhancing the quality of governance through decentralization of development process; and earmarking larger allocations for social development have been the key elements of the strategy for achieving the Plan objective of growth with social justice. These institutions are expected to improve the quality of delivery of development goods and in the process make governments more responsive and responsible. The Ninth Five-Year Plan has made a qualitative shift in its approach from 'welfare' to 'empowerment' for ensuring the well-being of the disadvantaged. Economic independence and self-reliance through employment and income-generating activities and group action have been the main planks. Therefore, it can be inferred that the ingredients essential for the social mobilization process for empowerment and poverty reduction, viz., creation of an enabling environment, building up the capacities of facilitating agencies, creation of opportunities for social and economic development and social protection measures, are well articulated in the Plan documents.

Social Empowerment

Education

Women's education is the most important indicator for social empowerment. Women need education in order to improve their knowledge in various fields such as political, economic, social and other areas. If a woman is educated in the family, she will be able to play a successful role in her family. Above all, education is the means to improve the status and position of women in general. The details of households regarding female literacy is presented in Tables 10.6 A, B and C. The data presented in the Table 10.6 reveal that the majority (66%) of the literates were in the SHG households. It was observed that almost half (47%) of the women were illiterates in the NSHG households may be due to lack of empowerment. Table 10.6B shows that the majority (55%) of the SHG households were in the literacy level of 6th to 10th standard when compared with the NSHG house holds. (50%). Table 10.6C shows that almost all the female members in the NSHG group were studying in government schools, whereas in the SHG group around 15 per cent of the female members were studying in private schools.

Table 10.6A

Female Literates in the Households

Literacy Status	*SHG*	*NSHG*
Illiterates	33.69	47.13
Literates	66.31	52.87
Total	100.00 (377)	100.00 (174)

Note: Figures are in percentages.

Table 10.6B

Female Literacy Level

Literacy Status	*SHG*	*NSHG*
Upto 5	32.4	38.04
6–10	55.6	50.00
11 and above	11.6	11.95
Total	100.0 (250)	100.00 (92)

Note: Figures are in percentages.

Table 10.6C

Place of Schooling among Females

Place of School	*SHG*				*NSHG*			
	Upto 5	*6–10*	*11 and above*	*All*	*Upto 5*	*6–10*	*11 and above*	*All*
Balwadi	1.21	—	—	1	—	—	—	—
Government School	80.49	88.48	75.86	211	94.28	93.47	100.0	87
Private School	18.29	11.51	24.13	38	5.71	6.52	—	5
Total	100.00 (82)	100.0 (139)	100.0 (29)	250	100.0 (35)	100.0 (46)	100.0 (11)	92

Note: Figures are in percentages.

Economic Empowerment

Savings

Savings supplement family income and improve the standard of living. The distributions of households by monthly savings are presented in Table 10.7. The data show that the majority (85%) of the households are in the monthly savings range of Rs. 50–100 in the SHG households. However, no single NSHG household reported savings. The distribution of households by utilization of additional income generated in their family is presented in Table 10.8. It shows that the majority of households (33%) used their income for better health care and education for their children, followed by 20 per cent towards loan repayment and 17 per cent for social functions.

Table 10.7

Distribution of Households by Monthly Savings

Monthly Savings (in rupees)	*SHG*	*NSHG*
Nil	—	100.0
Less than 50	5.0	—
50–100	85.0	—
100–150	10.0	—
150 and above	—	—
Total	100.0 (200)	100.0 (100)

Note: Figures are in percentages.

Table 10.8

Distribution of the Households by Utilization of Additional Income Generated

Items	*SHG*
Nutritious food for the family	6.8
Purchase of household durables	4.0
Towards loan repayment	20.0
Minor repairs to house	4.4
Better health care	18.0
Better clothing	4.0
Better education for children	15.2
Social functions	17.2
Purchase of household durables + purchase of house site	10.4
Total	100

Decision-making

Our main concerns are to examine women's empowerment and to identify the factors associated with variation in the indicators of women's empowerment in the household. Under what conditions do women feel more empowered and under what conditions do women feel less empowered? This was examined and is presented in Table 10.9. The results show the wife to be the most important decision-maker in the SHG households and the husband in the NSHG households with regard to their children's schooling as well as other issues.

Table 10.9
Who Makes Decisions in the Households

Decision-making	*SHG*				*NSHG*			
	Wife	*Husband*	*Both*	*Elderly People*	*Wife*	*Husband*	*Both*	*Elderly People*
Whether the boy should go to school	60.5	12.5	6.5	41 (20.5)	47 (47.0)	51 (51.0)	—	2 (2.0)
Whether the girl should go to school	44.5	29.5	7.5	37 (18.5)	19 (19.0)	34 (34.0)	9 (9.0)	38 (38.0)
Whether the female member should work	36.5	34.5	18.5	21 (10.5)	15 (15.0)	39 (39.0)	5 (5.0)	41 (41.0)
Regarding loans	18.0	25.5	48.4	17 (8.5)	10 (10.0	44 (44.0)	34 (34.0)	12 (12.0)
Regarding purchase of household items	30.0	13.5	49.0	15 (7.5)	32 (32.0)	39 (39.0)	29 (29.0)	—

Note: Figures are in percentages.

Nutritional Empowerment

Health Status

The national statistics on health shows that majority of family members suffer from malnutrition resulting in health problems. Table 10.10 shows the health problems of family members in the study area. More than 50 per cent of the family members suffer from health problems in NSHG households. Whereas in the case of SHG, only 33 per cent of the members suffer from health problems. Among the health problems, the family members reporting improper eyesight are high (14%) followed by 'fatigue', 'growth failure' and 'oedema' in both the households.

Table 10.10

Distribution of Family Members Suffering from Health Problems

Nature of Health Problem	*SHG*	*NSHG*
Oedema	4.52	8.68
Growth failure	2.82	8.46
Fatigue	12.44	18.93
Improper eyesight	13.34	14.25
Nil	66.85	49.66
Total	100.0 (884)	100.0 (449)

Note: Figures are in percentages.

Nutritional Status

Among the various indicators, the nutritional status of family members acquires greater importance. Table 10.11A shows that children suffering from nutritional deficiency are more in NSHG households (60%) than in SHG households (53%). The data in Table 10.11B show that adults suffering from nutritional deficiency are relatively more in NSHG households (55%) than in SHG households (43%).

Table 10.11A

Distribution of Children Suffering from Nutritional Deficiency

Nutritional deficiency	*SHG*	*N-SHG*
Anaemia	24.30	21.49
B-complex deficiency	14.34	17.75
Vitamin A deficiency	13.94	20.56
Nil	41.03	40.18
Total	100.0 (251)	100.0 (107)

Note : Figures are in percentages.

Table 10.11B

Distribution of Adults Suffering from Nutritional Deficiency

Nutritional deficiency	*SHG*	*NSHG*
Anaemia	15.08	17.25
B-complex deficiency	14.17	15.20
Vitamin A deficiency	13.72	21.63
Nil	57.01	45.90
Total	100.0 (633)	100.0 (342)

Note: Figures are in percentages.

SHG Members' Views on Social, Economic and Nutritional Empowerment

It is observed from Table 10.12 that as compared with NSHG households, those covered under SHG fared better with respect to socio-economic empowerment and nutritional development. If the SHGs are allowed to develop links with bank branches, the access to credit for the poor would improve.

Table 10.12

Distribution of Members' Views on Socio-economic and Nutritional Empowerment

Items	*SHG*	*NSHG*
Adoption of small family norm	84.0	64.0
Access to information about government programmes	86.8	48.8
Improvement in children's education	94.8	62.4
Improvement in education of girl child	72.8	53.6
Improvement in sanitation	76.4	52.0
Discontinuation of child labour employment	63.2	29.6
Access to markets	87.2	40.0
Increase in bargaining power	84.8	38.4
Increase in self-confidence	65.2	28.8
Increase in self-employment potential	78.0	37.6
Increase in marketing and communication skills	80.4	36.0
Improvement in decision making	86.8	72.8
Early marriage discontinued	84.4	60.8
Improvement in nutritional status	84.0	64.0
Able to sign	85.2	36.8
Improved banking habits	85.2	38.4
Improvement in credit worthiness	69.2	26.4
Better productive skills	82.0	53.6
Mobility	74.8	51.2
Better awareness of health	84.0	73.6

Note: SHG households, 200; NSHG households, 100. Figures are in percentages.

Application of ICT Devices for Sustainability of SHGs

Through the application of modern information technology the sustainability of SHGs is possible individually and collectively. Information and Communication Technology (ICT) will facilitate the articulation of women at the grassroots of their experiences, concerns and perceptions. It provides necessary information and insight into transforming them into active, conscious and confident participants in the sustainability of SHGs. Several methodologies like one-way audio, teleconferencing network, videoconferencing with cameras at two or three locations, multimedia using text, sound, images, animations and video utilized (to inform or entertain) from the village level to the district level will be effective in the management of SHGs. Implementation of ICT devices at group level, bank level and NGO level would contribute to the healthy growth of women in the rural areas (see Table 10.13).

Table 10.13

Application of ICT Devices for Sustainability of SHGs

Interventions for Improving SHGs	*Strategies for Sustainability of SHGs through ICT Devices*
Tackling gender bias	Organizing gender training and sensitization in the banking system
Specific policies for women's requirements	Live interactive sessions with the expert panel and participants at community level
Long-term plans on the credit flow to women entrepreneurs	Online networking with groups, bankers, experts, etc.
Loans on liberal terms at a low rate of interest	Loan availability at door step without obstacles
Simplification of procedures for project proposals and project reports	Interactive session with the bankers
Banks' initiative for reaching out to women for their credit requirements	Teleconferencing with groups and bankers
Expansion of Mahila rural co-operative bank in remote villages	Bankers' and experts' discussions and interviews for the expansion of bank services
Separate branches/counters for women for credit disbursement	Online and ATM disbursement for speedy credit
Entrepreneurship development programme/training facilities for women for acquiring skills	Teleconferencing, multimedia using text between groups and management experts

Cont'd

Cont'd

Free technical training for the needy	Face-to-face training and capacity building
Marketing facilities	Improved methods and techniques on marketing skills by expert panel
Separate women's cells for counselling on self-employment opportunities	Online net working with the SHGs by experts through teleconference
Free counselling and reconciliation for economic empowerment	Interactive and participatory sessions with SHG members and experts on telecounselling – face-to-face training
Publicity campaign/awareness programmes	Online regional level networking, exchange of views, etc.
Strong database	Getting information through separate web sites useful for development policy
Role of NGOs and SHGs	Common platforms to NGOs and other agencies for networking and sharing knowledge and experience
Mobilization of masses for effective involvement in group activity	Exhibitions relating to role plays on women's agitations and interactive and participatory sessions

Summary and Recommendations

Our study has clearly brought to the fore that the SHG experiment has reduced the intensity of poverty among sample households. It is further observed that as compared with NSHG households, those who covered under SHG fared better with respect to socio-economic empowerment and nutritional development. The growth of SHGs in the country demonstrates the willingness of the poor to pay for the credit and other financial services rendered by NGOs and credit institutions without depending on any kind of subsidy from the government agencies. In a market-oriented economy, this is a healthy attitude. There is an apprehension that the launching of various government programmes, under which the SHGs are to be promoted as well as subsidized by DRDA, may hamper the development of the micro-credit system as it promotes a subsidy culture, which goes against the philosophy of micro-credit. This aspect needs to be examined in the light of the feedback obtained, and if warranted the modalities may have to be redefined as to provide a conducive environment for the growth of the SHG-Bank Linkage Programme in India. There is a need to have a broad and inclusive growth to benefit all sections of the society. It is more challenging for the state to achieve inclusive growth than getting an 8–9 per cent growth in the gross state domestic product.

References

Chavan, Pallavi and R. Ramakumar. 2002. 'Micro-Credit and Rural Poverty: An Analysis of Empirical Evidence', *Economic and Political Weekly*, 9 March.

Puhazhendi, V. and K.J.S. Satyasai. 2000. *Micro-Credit for the Rural People: An Impact Evaluation*, Study Report, National Bank for Agriculture and Rural Development, Mumbai.

Ramakrishna. R. 2001. 'Credit Needs of the Rural Poor and the Role of SHGs', *Indian Journal of Agricultural Economics*, 56(3), July-Sept.

——. 2004a. 'Developing Grass Root Organisations for Sustainability of Self-Help Groups', in M. Indira Devi (ed.), *Strategies for Sustainability of Self-Help Groups*, A.U. Press and Publications, Visakhapatnam, pp. 71–76.

——. 2004b. 'Empowering Rural Women through Self-Help Groups', in M. Indira Devi (ed.), *Strategies for Sustainability of Self-Help Groups*, A.U. Press and Publications, Visakhapatnam, pp. 163–70.

——. 2005. 'Empowerment of Women through Sustainability of Micro-Finance: Co-operative Perspective', *Journal of Co-operative Management*, 39(4), January–March, pp. 1–8.

Ramakrishna, R. and D. Tata Rao. 2008a. 'Social Mobilization, Empowerment and Poverty Reduction', in K. Vijaykumar (ed.), *Empowerment of Weaker Sections: Future Planning and Strategies for Rural Development in Andhra Pradesh*, Seminar Volume, Department of Sociology, Andhra University, Visakhapatnam.

——. 2008b. 'Urban Poverty Alleviation through Self-Help Groups and Micro-Credit', in B. Vijayalakshmi and R. Swami Das (eds.), *SHGs and Role of Social Work Profession*, Seminar Volume, Department of Social Work, Andhra University, Visakhapatnam.

Susil, Sirivardana. 2001. *The Core Methodology of Social Mobilisation in Women's Empowerment as a Transformative Strategy for Poverty Eradication*, SAPNA Regional Centre, New Delhi.

11

Are the Current Educational Policies Inclusive of Tribals?

N. Indira Rani, S. Haranath and B. Devi Prasad

What is Social Exclusion?

In India, even after fifty years of democratic governance and development planning, the inequalities still remain, and certain categories of people continue to live miserable lives mired in poverty. A majority of the population has neither socially nor economically taken advantage of the programmes and policies. Investigations into the persistence of poverty and inequality in spite of economic growth have thrown light on a different form of disadvantage, termed as social exclusion, which was not fully captured by conventional economic measures and approaches. There is a considerable debate about the precise meaning of this term. According to Duffy (1995), social exclusion is concerned with the "inability to participate effectively in economic, social, and cultural life and, in some characteristics, alienation and distance from mainstream society". However, as pointed out by Kleinman (1998), "the term [social exclusion] is rapidly becoming a cliché to cover almost any kind of social ill". Beall and Clert (2000) point out that the reason for this wide and less than rigorous application is that "in its colloquial and political usage, the concept of social exclusion has tremendous resonance and is very compelling".

Buvinic (2005) summarizes the meaning of social exclusion as "the inability of an individual to participate in the basic political, economic and social functioning of society" which involves "the denial of equal access to opportunities imposed by certain groups in society upon others". Thus, social exclusion is multiple disadvantages experienced as a group phenomenon rather than an individual one. It reflects the multiple and overlapping nature of the disadvantages experienced by certain groups and categories of the population, with social identity as the central axis of their exclusion. The multiple disadvantages affecting these groups of people could be cultural devaluation, discrimination, internalization of inferiority and so on. Such processes can have profound effects on the sense of self-worth of the members of these groups.

According to Kabeer (2000), social exclusion revolves around social identities of people or groups and reflects the cultural devaluation of people based on *who they are* or *who they are perceived to be*. Caste, ethnicity, religion and gender are examples of such group identities. Thus, social exclusion is more than an economic phenomenon. It refers to the alienation of or 'leaving out' certain people within a society, which has consequences on social and cultural dimensions. It is argued that social exclusion based on identities is a process independent of income characteristics or the merit of individuals. In brief, social exclusion reflects the multiple and overlapping nature of the disadvantages experienced by certain groups and categories of the population, with social identity as the central axis of their exclusion. It is thus a group or collective phenomenon rather than an individual one. It gives rise to what Stewart calls a 'horizontal' model of inequality, one that draws attention to disparities within different income or asset strata rather than simply across them. In particular, it draws attention to the concentration of socially excluded groups among the poorer and most disadvantaged sections of a population (Kabeer, 2006).

Social exclusion is a unique feature of the Indian society, particularly that of Hindu society. Social exclusion involves "the process through which individuals or groups are wholly or partially excluded from full participation in the society within which they live on the basis of group characteristics like social origin, ethnicity and religions. Concern about exclusion and discrimination thus arises from the fact that exclusion generates adverse consequences in terms of human rights violation, deprivation and poverty that it particularly brings to the excluded groups. From the human rights perspective, it essentially means denial of basic human rights, economic, civil and others. In India exclusion involves social processes that exclude, discriminate, isolate and deprive some groups on the basis of caste, ethnicity and religion. These excluded groups include former untouchables (or dalits), adivasis and some religious minorities. Although these social groups experienced exclusion and isolation that caused deprivation and poverty, there are differences in sources and process of deprivation" (Thorat, 2006a).

The word 'exclusion' suggests that there is a core and a periphery, and that 'excluded' people are those who are actively blocked access to the core. The importance of these perspectives is that poverty is not perceived to be a mere attribute of certain categories of people. Instead, it is seen as something that is actively *done* to people. It is not what they are, but what they have been made (Mander and Kumaran, 2008). According to Thorat, "It is necessary to recognize the exclusionary and discriminatory character of our society and economy, a creation largely of differences arising from identities. But to design appropriate remedial policies, an understanding of contemporary forms of discrimination in multiple spheres and their consequences is very necessary".

In Indian context, one particular form of social exclusion is caste, which is ascriptive rather than an achieved characteristic. As it is not a consequence of individual agency, it cannot be altered. While caste had been much-studied topic, the issues of social exclusion based on economic, cultural and religious discrimination were not given much focus. Alternatively, the identities may also relate to *categories* of people who share some characteristics such as an illness, an age category, a way of life or a common predicament. Such members do not necessarily know each other and may share very little in common, aside from the nature of the discrimination they face. In this sense, social exclusion also applies to the disabled, minority groups, refugees, the mentally ill, street children, the elderly and to people with leprosy or AIDS. Thus, ageism is also a form of social exclusion.

Room (1995) adds a new dimension to the discussion by couching the issue of social exclusion in a rights-based language when he talks about social exclusion as the "denial or non-realization of civil, political, and social rights of citizenship". Such a rights-based approach to the problem of social exclusion has much to recommend. It has great affinity with the capability approach developed by Amartya Sen, which calls for efforts to ensure that people have equal access to basic capabilities such as the ability to be healthy, well-fed, housed, integrated into the community, participate in community and public life and enjoy social bases of self-respect (Sen, 1992, 1999).

However, the approach to social exclusion starts by looking at relational forms of deprivation, which is its major strength. Exclusion necessarily involves two sides: one that defines who or which is excluded and the other excludes. Studies of exclusion attempt further to identify the processes of exclusion. The approach therefore has to examine real-life situations, throwing live questions and challenges for policy makers to solve and tackle. In other words, the concept helps in pinning down the frequently anonymous 'improvization' and 'marginalization' processes, sheds light on how these exclusion processes actually occur due to social dynamics of discrimination and stigma and rescues policy prescriptions from safe 'techno-managerial' solutions (Mander and Kumaran, 2008).

It is very appropriate to talk about social inclusion, another concept closely linked to social exclusion. Social inclusion, on the contrary, is an affirmative action or positive discrimination to change the circumstances and practices that lead to or are leading to social exclusion. It is a strategy to combat social exclusion, which may include compensating for the past disadvantages suffered by the groups and adopting remedial policies against the discrimination in the present. A range of policies can be mentioned aiming at social inclusion. Some of them are reservations given to indigenous people, dalits, women and backward communities in education, employment, political representation and so on. The notion of social inclusion can vary according to the type of strategies organizations adopt. Changing public perceptions through education system, media and public campaigns, equalizing educational and employment opportunities, improving access to health and other public services, providing protection to the excluded groups and encouraging more inclusive governance are some of the inclusive practices. It is in this background we wish to examine one of the socially excluded groups, the tribals. The tribal communities continue to lag behind the general population in terms of education, and on other development indicators, in spite of the constitutional guarantees and efforts of government and NGOs.

Social Exclusion in Relation to Tribal Communities

The tribals are one social group that comes closer to the dalits in terms of exclusion and deprivation. The basis of tribal isolation and exclusion, however, is not caste or religion but ethnicity. They suffer from isolation, neglect and exclusion, which cause considerable deprivation and poverty among them (Thorat, 2006a). The Scheduled Tribe (ST) population spread over nine states with areas marked as 'scheduled areas' is governed under certain constitutional provisions defined in its Fifth Schedule. Since it has a higher percentage of their population, the northeast part of India has been given a status of 'tribal areas' in the Sixth Schedule (which enjoys a higher level of autonomy than those in the Fifth Schedule Areas) in the Constitution. The ST populations in both the scheduled areas and tribal areas are considered to be economically less developed and therefore need social support (Mundu, 2006).

As per the 2001 census, the tribal population in India is estimated to be 84.3 million, i.e., 8.2 per cent of the total population of India, classified under 461 different communities. One of the distinguishing features is that majority of the tribals live in scattered habitations located in interior, remote and inaccessible, hilly and forest areas of the country. Nearly 22 per cent of tribal habitations have less than 100 people and more than 40 per cent have 100 to less than 300 people, while others have less than 500 people (Sujatha, 2000). The tribals, being isolated and not being able to relate with others (as compared with dalits and Muslims), face exclusion in more general ways. This possibly explains as to why poverty is highest among the tribals in rural areas despite better access to agricultural land (Thorat, 2006b). According to Amartya Sen, it is 'active and passive exclusion' affected by development policies of the states and other agents causing land alienation and displacement. Tribals also suffer from what Sen would call 'constitutive relevance'. This type of exclusion is a result of the inability of a group to relate to others and to take part in the life of the community.

Constitutional Safeguards for Scheduled Tribe Communities

Recognizing the special needs of tribal communities, the Constitution of India has made certain special safeguards to protect these communities from all the possible exploitation and thus ensure social justice. While Article 14 confers equal rights and opportunities to all, Article 15 prohibits discrimination against any citizen on the grounds of sex, religion, race, caste, etc.; Article 15(4) enjoins upon the State to make special provisions for the advancement of any socially and educationally backward classes; Article 16(4) empowers the state to make provisions for reservation in appointments or posts in favour of any backward class of citizens, which in the opinion of the state is not adequately represented in the services under the state; Article 46 enjoins upon the state to promote with special care the educational and economic interests of the weaker sections of the people and, in particular, the STs, and promises to protect them from social injustice and all forms of exploitation. Recognizing that the tribal communities are the most deprived and marginalized sections of Indian society, a host of welfare and developmental measures have been initiated for their social and economic development. In this regard, particular reference has to be made to the tribal sub-plan approach that came into existence as the main strategy from the Fifth Five-Year Plan. Along with core economic sectors, elementary education has been accorded priority in the tribal sub-plan approach. Table 11.1 illustrates the trends in literacy amongst the Scheduled Tribes and others.

Table 11.1

Literacy Rate of the Scheduled Tribes and Total Population

Year	*Total Population*			*STs*		
	Male	*Female*	*Total*	*Male*	*Female*	*Total*
1961	40.40	15.35	28.30	13.83	3.16	8.53
1971	45.96	21.97	34.45	17.63	4.85	11.30
1981	56.38	29.76	43.57	24.52	8.04	16.35
1991	64.13	39.29	52.21	40.65	18.19	29.60
2001	75.26	53.67	64.84	59.17	34.76	47.10

Source: Selected Educational Statistics 2002–03, Ministry of Human Resource Development.

Although there has been a substantial increase in the literacy rates of the STs during the last four developmental decades, the gap between the literacy rates of the STs and those of the general population persists. Although the female literacy rate, which is an important indicator in the field of education, amongst the STs has increased substantially from 4.85 per cent in 1971 to 18.19 per cent in 1991 – but the gap between the Scheduled Tribe females and those of general population has also been widening during the same period, though with a slight decrease after 1981. The literacy rate of STs was 8.53 in 1961 census, and has steadily increased to reach 47.1 in the 2001 census, yet it is still far below the overall national literacy rate of 64.8 as per the 2001 census.

Problems of Tribal Education

Sujatha (2000) in her *India Education Report* has analysed the problems of tribal education in detail. She has categorized the reasons into external, internal, socio-economic and psychological.

External Constraints

The perspective adopted for educational development among tribal communities fails to adequately address the specific disadvantages characterizing tribal population. In formulating policies and programmes for tribal education it is essential to understand the complex realities of tribal life and the expectation of tribals from the system, and this has never been done either by the tribal welfare department or by the education department. One of the major constraints of tribal education at planning level is the adoption of a dual system of administration. The tribal welfare department deals with tribal life and culture and administers development work at the local level, including education, but it lacks expertise in educational planning and administration in general and academic supervision and monitoring in particular. On the other hand, the education department formulates implementation guidelines and instructions regarding curriculum, textbooks, teacher recruitment, transfer policies, and so on, which are uniform for the entire state. The school calendar is a case in point, where vacations and holidays cater to the needs of the formal school set-up in a non-tribal context, with little consideration for local context and tribals festivals. This lack of sensitivity to their problems and failure in understanding tribal social reality, coupled with faulty selection and appointment of teachers in tribal areas, have resulted in poor performance and teacher absenteeism in tribal schools.

Internal Constraints

The internal problems of tribal education refer to the quality of school provision, suitable teachers, relevance of content and curriculum, medium of instruction, pedagogy, and special supervision. A majority of schools in tribal areas are without basic infrastructure facilities. Normally, school buildings in tribal areas have thatched roofs, dilapidated walls, and non-plastered floors. Research evidence shows that a large number of tribal schools do not have teaching-learning materials, or even blackboards. In tribal areas the opening of a school is equated with the posting of a teacher and same is the case with 'ashram' schools. It is found that in most of ashram schools which are residential in nature, there is no space for the children to sleep. Consequently, the classroom turns into the dormitory and vice versa. Due to lack of minimum sanitary provisions, it is not uncommon to find that many children studying in ashram schools are afflicted with contagious diseases like scabies and diarrhea, leading to high dropout rates. Schools in tribal areas just function with bare minimum facilities.

Content and Curriculum

The uniform structure and transaction of curriculum has put tribal children at a disadvantage. In respect of pedagogy, it has been found that the rigid systems of formal schooling, which emphasize discipline, routine norms, teacher-centred instruction, etc., have made the children wary of school. This goes against the culture of free interaction and absence of force as embedded in tribal ethos and culture prevalent at home. This has led to sharp division between home and school leading to lack of interest among the children towards school, and research findings have shown this as a major factor behind non enrolment. Another area is the inherent fear of tribal children towards the teacher, and their inability to establish a communication link with the teacher and this is reflected in low attendance and high dropout rates. The Constitution of India allows the use of tribal dialect (mother tongue) as the medium of instruction in case the population of the said tribe is more than one lakh. But this has not been adopted on the grounds of feasibility and viability of introducing and sustaining such a change.

Socio-economic and Cultural Constraints

In a broad sense, these socio-economic and cultural factors can be outlined as poverty and poor economic conditions, social customs, cultural ethos, lack of awareness and understanding of the value of formal education, conflict and gap between the home and school, etc. Studies on educational deprivation of tribals have inevitably linked it to their poor economic condition and poverty. The main occupation of tribals is agriculture, practiced either through shifting cultivation or terrace cultivation where productivity remains very low. Consequently, children play an important role, contributing directly or indirectly to family income by participating in the family occupation and household works like cattle grazing and fuel and fodder collection, etc. Even though elementary education is deemed free and additional incentives are given to children, in practice, it is not free due to several reasons. First, the incentive schemes do not have full coverage, and thus, have limited value at community level. Second, many of the benefits do not reach the beneficiaries. Third, even though incentives like slates and uniforms are given, they are of poor quality and do not reach in time, thus nullifying the entire purpose. It should be noted that the impoverished economic status of tribals makes even the small amount of private expenditure involved in procuring writing material, clothing, etc., a serious burden on the family. Under these circumstances, it is not surprising if education is not given priority. In an economy dominated by struggle for survival, options are limited. Since education does not provide any visible and immediate benefit and tribals do not see beyond their present state, the participation of tribal children in education also becomes limited. Another reason for low participation is the opportunity cost involved, as the majority of non-enrolled children are required to work in households or family occupations. Even if the economic contribution of children is indirect, they certainly facilitate the participation of parents in economic activity. Poor health is another major hindrance in the promotion and participation of tribal children in education. Contagious diseases like scabies, eye infection, malaria, and diarrhea are common in tribal areas, and also affect children's attendance at school. Further, some tribal communities are seasonal migrants and this leads to absenteeism among their children and makes it difficult for them to effectively benefit from schooling.

Conclusion and Recommendations

It is necessary to critically analyse the government's obligations and commitments to promote tribal education. Though the education is inclusive for tribals, the content, approach and methodology of the education has to be different from the educational content and methodology for mainstream population. More specifically there is need to make tribal education effective and sustainable by promoting collaborative relationship between government and civil society organizations to facilitate and monitor universalized enrolment and retention at the primary level and ensure education relevant to tribal context both at the primary and secondary levels. It is essential to promote 'holistic purposeful education' for tribal communities that focuses on human rights education, especially in the current context where there is an increasing threat to indigenous communities' access and control of natural resources.

Recommended Inclusive Measures

- *Tribal context:* The school schedule must be prepared as per the local requirements (e.g., festivals and seasons).
- *Language:* To enable comprehension of lessons taught, tribal children will be taught in their mother tongue at least in the classes I to III. While teaching in the local/tribal dialect, Hindi/English as language of social and economic opportunity cannot be ignored.
- *Curriculum:* The curriculum must be relevant to daily life, local history and culture of the tribal areas.
- *Textbooks:* Textbooks will be prepared in tribal languages and will acknowledge the role of tribal leaders and tribes people in the struggle for Indian independence and their contribution in other areas.
- *Teachers:* There is a need for teachers, as much as possible, to be drawn from the tribal communities and who are motivated and sensitized towards working in tribal areas.
- *Infrastructure:* A normative network of primary, secondary and high schools equipped with proper school buildings, hostels and other requisite infrastructure facilities will be worked out for all tribal areas.
- *Teacher absenteeism:* To prevent teacher absenteeism in tribal areas, local and tribal teachers from local panchayats will be given preference in employment, and the teaching and non-teaching staff of primary schools will be placed under the control of the village management committee (VEC) appointed by the gram sabha or gram panchayat.
- *Gender equity and quality education:* The prime focus should be on gender equity and provision of quality education that makes tribal communities economically effective and independent.
- *Anganwadis/crèches*: Anganwadis to be linked with schools so that girls are not required to do baby-sitting of their younger siblings, which in turn affects their education.
- *Relevant knowledge and skill development:* Strengthening traditional knowledge and skills through syllabus, skills of articulation and negotiation to safeguard sources of livelihood to be included in the curriculum.

References

Beall, Jo and Carine Clert. 2000. *Social Exclusion and Globalization: Implications for Social Policy and Urban Governance*, Department of Social Policy, London School of Economics, Monograph Prepared for the African Technical Families, Macroeconomics 2, The World Bank, London.

Buvinic, Mayra. 2005. 'Social Inclusion in Latin America', in Mayra Buvinic and Jacqueline Mazza (eds.), *Social Exclusion and Economic Development*, Johns Hopkins University Press, Baltimore.

Duffy, K. 1995. *Social Exclusion and Human Dignity in Europe*, Council of Europe, Strasbourg.

Kabeer, Naila. 2000. 'Social Exclusion, Poverty and Discrimination: Towards an Analytical Framework', *IDS Bulletin*, 31(4): 83–97.

——. 2006. 'Social Exclusion and the MDGs: The Challenge of 'Durable Inequalities' in the Asian Context', paper presented in ASIA 2015 Conference, held in March, Institute of Development Studies, University of Sussex, Brighton.

Kleinman, M. 1998. 'Include Me Out? The New Politics of Place and Poverty', CASE Monograph 11, Centre for Analysis of Social Exclusion, London School of Economics, London.

Mander, Harsh and M. Kumaran. 2008. *Social Exclusion in ICDS: A Sociological Whodunit? A Research Study*, www.google.com, accessed in June 2008.

Mundu, Bineet J. 2006. On the Future of Indigenous Traditions: The Case of Adivasis of Jharkhand, India (Masters thesis) University of Tromsϕ Tromsϕ.

Room, Graham. 1995. *Beyond the Threshold: The Measurement and Analysis of Social Exclusion*, Polity Press, Bristol.

Sen, Amartya. 1992. *Poverty Reexamined*, Harvard University Press, Cambridge.

——. 1999. *Development as Freedom*, Knopf, New York.

Sujatha, K. 2000. *Education among Scheduled Tribes*, India Education Report, CED.

Thorat, Sukhadeo. 2006a. 'Paying the Social Debt', *Economic and Political Weekly*, June 17.

——. 2006b. 'Exclusion and Poverty: Need for Socially Exclusive Politics and Development Approach', *People's Democracy*, Vol. XXX, No. 5, January 29.

12

Assertion of Rights and Ensuing Reprisals

Atrocities on Dalits in Andhra Pradesh

V. Sreemannarayana Murthy

The exclusion of Dalits from the mainstream society stems from the Hindu religious texts. The Hindu social structure as said to be ordained by divinity does not accord a place for the Dalits within its framework. Dalits (Marathi term meaning oppressed) are the ex-untouchables of the Indian society and are not a part of the varna system which consisted of Brahmins, Kshatriyas, Vaisyas and Shudras. The phenomenon of untouchability as such does not figure in the Vedas though there did exist ideas and beliefs that had the potential to develop into an iniquitous and divisive institution. The Chandala one of the groups whom the Vedic Aryans detested, were watchmen at cremation grounds. The Vedas mention other non-Aryan groups besides the Chandala, namely, *Ayogava Paulkasha* and *Nishada*. The four varnas and the Nishadas were collectively referred to in the later Vedas as the Panchajanah. The precise manner in which untouchability developed from the four Vedic Varnas is not clear, though there is no doubt that such a development was linked with the elaboration of the notions of ritual purity and impurity. Thus, certain duties were considered ritually defiling. Untouchability and casteism became more pronounced in the later Vedic period when Dharmashastras gained prominence (Srinivasulu, 2002). In the later Vedic period, those who were dealing with menial and servile tasks that seemed to be defiling in nature were treated as untouchables.

The stratified society of India on caste lines allowed no room for mobility with each stratum making a watertight compartment. The transition from Vedic to post-Vedic era reinforced the caste ties and closed doors on mobility. Thus, those who performed servile and mean tasks continued with them generation after generation. The top castes in the Varna system, especially the Brahmins, secured their position through the religious texts, which convinced the untouchables that their faith is preordained (Ghurye, 1969). Religion, more than rationality, ruled the roost in India, which is a land of mystical aura.

Ironically, the rigid caste system had certain openings in its strata which allowed the lower caste people to move over to the upper stratum through sanskritization, a process according to M.N. Srinivas where the people of the lower castes imitate the lifestyles of the upper castes, frequently twice-born castes, in order to improve their status in the society. Sanskritization is a process of cultural and social mobility during these periods of relative closure of the Hindu social system.

It is an endogenous source of social change. From a social psychological standpoint, sanskritization is a culturally specific case of the universal motivation towards 'anticipatory socialization' to the culture of a higher group in the hope of reaching its status in future. The specific sense of sanskritization lies in the historicity of its meaning based on the Hindu tradition. There are two levels of meanings that are implicit in sanskritization which interchangeably have been used by Srinivas; they are 'historical-specific' and 'contextual-specific' connotations of sanskritization.

In historical-specific sense, sanskritization refers to those processes in Indian history which led to changes in the status of various caste groups and their cultural pattern. In contextual-specific sense, sanskritization denotes contemporaneous processes of cultural imitation of upper castes by the lower castes or subcastes in various parts of India (Singh, 1986). It was observed by Srinivas (1971) that on several occasions in Indian history many warring tribes laid claim to Kshatriya status by virtue of their physical prowess and control of territory and could achieve it by tracing their origin to mythical characters. As a contemporaneous process, sanskritization helped only the intermediary castes, while the untouchable castes, especially those in the rural areas, still remain an excluded group.

Missionaries, Constitution and the Dalits

The untouchables for several generations continued with their ignominious tasks. Since there appeared to be no way out to escape the scourge of untouchability, they found an opportunity to depart from their slavish jobs when conversions in the name of Islamization gave them some scope to escape the bondage of Hindu caste system. The inroads of Muslims into the Indian subcontinent and their attempts to consolidate their occupied territories by forcing conversions on vulnerable populace paved the way for the depressed classes to embrace Islam, which accorded them special privileges in Islamic governance. Another channel that enabled them to escape the draconian treatment of the caste Hindus was to embrace Christianity. The missionaries from the West who came on a devoted task to spread the holy message found in Dalits potential followers who would yield to conversion if their well-being was looked after. The Dalits found in them the saviours who could pull them out of the thralldom of the Hindu social structure. Humanitarianism was one of the important motives of missionaries in fighting caste oppression. Conversions were believed to be definite means of escaping from social disabilities and hierarchically structured caste society. They helped in delegitimizing the traditional notions of purity and pollution (Satyanarayana, 2005).

Conversions to Christianity became rife with the advent of Portuguese rule. They received a fillip during the British rule. The converts gained a new social identity from Christianity, which symbolized advancement in civilization by treating Hinduism as obscurantist. Today majority of the Dalits are converts to Christianity though they claim to be following Hinduism in order to retain the Scheduled Caste (SC) status to which alone accrues the affirmative action in a full-fledged manner.

Though the Dalits were ranked low in the social order, the signs of social change were conspicuously experienced for the first time ever since the introduction of Western education. It is assumed that the introduction of Western education and the concomitant flow of Western ideas not only inculcated a new spirit among the Indian people but also acted as a catalyst of 'social change' in modern India. While the privileged tried to reassert their hegemony over the entire society, the underprivileged developed an urge to use education to acquire self-respect, equality and social prestige. The principal architect of the Indian Constitution being a Dalit provided necessary safe-guards to the Dalits. But the basis for the exclusion of these groups is deeply entrenched in the obscurantist mindset of the Hindus. As the hierarchy has a religious basis and given the fact that certain callings have been attached to the caste groups, the upper castes would not accept the prosperity of the Dalits. It is not only the upper castes in the Hindu hierarchy that practice social distance, but the intermediary castes are more vocal and emphatic in practising untouchability. The assertion of constitutional rights by the Dalits was resisted by the non-Dalits who are not necessarily the upper castes but the dominant castes of the region in question. According to Srinivas, "a caste may be said to be 'dominant' when it preponderates numerically over the other castes, and when it also wields preponderant economic and political power" (Srinivasulu, 2002).

The concept of reservation introduced by the erudite constitution makers is to bring in the excluded groups to the mainstream of the society. The intermediary groups are a part and parcel of the Jajmani system of village India and hence do not constitute an excluded group. Their educational needs must be promoted because each caste is attached to an occupation and hence despite the wide-ranging opportunities available in education they prefer to continue with their occupation.

The Upper/Intermediary and Backward Castes vis-à-vis Dalits

The Other Backward Castes (OBCs) never faced Dalit exclusion and humiliation and hence cannot claim Dalit policies of reservation. The Dalit and OBC or Shudra movements have distinct ideological underpinnings. The Dalit movements while fighting the system seek reforms in it. They seek annihilation of the caste order and are often inclined towards modernity and democracy. Contrarily, the OBC movements fight the system but do not see the need for reforms from within. They aim to dismantle the hegemony of the Brahmins. Their ideology is anti-Brahmin and not anti-caste. Shudras and Dalits become one social block under the banner of lower castes. They are represented as repressed and stigmatized equally. This distorted proposition hurts the Dalits most as the lower castes that never face Dalit-like discrimination claim Dalit-like public policy. The plight of Dalits cannot be compared with any other doctrine of discrimination. Untouchability condemns Dalits into unsociability, which denies Dalits any space unless the state intervenes (Prasad, 2008).

Numerous incidents of atrocities go unreported, yet some incidents came to light when the Dalit leaders converged on the places where atrocities were committed and launched agitations to bring the culprits to book. In 1985, in a village called Karamchedu in Prakasam district, seven Dalits were killed by the people of Kamma caste when a petty argument snowballed into a major controversy. The upper caste

Kammas could not tolerate a sign of assertion by the Dalits and they were chased out of the village enmasse. In 1987, in the village of Neerukonda in Guntur district, the political assertion of Dalits against the Kammas was seen as a case of lower caste disloyalty and the Dalits had to face the brunt of the Kamma onslaught. In 1983, armed hooligans led by upper caste gentry attacked the Dalit hamlet in the village Padirikuppam, Chittoor district, and killed four persons, burnt 86 houses and destroyed property worth about 6 lakhs (Desai, 1986).

The backward castes who like to be benefited out of the affirmative action on par with Dalits also maintain social distance from Dalits, and their repugnance for Dalits is demonstrated in several incidents of violence which are akin to the Belchi massacre in Patna district of Bihar in 1977, where eleven Dalits (agricultural labourers) were burnt alive by the Backward Caste Kurmi landowners, as the former demanded better wages. The committee constituted by the Bihar Assembly under the chairmanship of Vijay Kumar Misra considered the atrocity to be the outcome of the clash between the oppressor and the oppressed (Nedumpara, 2004). In 1986, in the village of Gudiada in Vizianagaram district, one Dalit was killed and eighteen others were injured when people belonging to the Backward Caste Koppula Velama attacked them for cultivating on the government land with the permission of the District Magistrate. In 2005, in a village called Vempeta in Kurnool district, five Dalits were killed by the people of Gandla caste, which is a backward caste, as a group of Dalits were suspected to be sympathizers of extremists. The backward castes, by virtue of their dominant caste status, always tried to suppress the Dalits.

Conclusion

Constitutional safeguards and progressive legislation did little to rid the social order of the widespread evil of caste discrimination. Taboos imposed by tradition and belief still exert their stranglehold across most of India and impose social disabilities and economic deprivation on the Dalits.

There are two main acts to check the violation of the rights of the Dalits. They are the Protection of Civil Rights Act 1955 and the Scheduled Castes and Scheduled Tribes (SC and ST) (Prevention of Atrocities) Act, 1989. Most of the Dalits in rural areas are hardly aware of the fact that they are protected by such stringent legislations. Even if they are aware, they are not in a position to invoke these acts against the culprits. In most of the cases, the police are not responsive to the appeals of Dalits against the atrocities unleashed on them. As per the SC and ST Act 1989, any case registered under this act must be investigated by a police official not less than the rank of Deputy Superintendent. But this norm is not always adhered to. Some incidents end up with out-of-court settlements. In the era of globalization, though Dalits in cities and urban areas to certain extent escape the scourge of untouchability, their brethren in the rural areas are still under the shadow of age-old traditions and the hierarchical social order. Hence the government while enacting laws must take into consideration the rural milieu and introduce a monitoring mechanism to provide immediate relief to the victims. Vote bank politics and expedient political calculations drive political parties to treat the OBCs on par with SCs. This kind of policy must be reviewed and more should be done in the direction of changing the mindset of the non-Dalits.

References

Desai, Akshayakumar Ramanlal. 1986. *Violation of Democratic Rights in India*, Popular Prakashan, Mumbai.

Ghurye, G.S. 1969. *Caste and Race in India*, Popular Prakashan, Mumbai.

Nedumpara, Jose J. 2004. *Political Economy and Class Contradictions*, Anmol Publications, New Delhi.

Satyanarayana, A. 2005. *Dalits and Upper Castes*, Kanishka Publishers, New Delhi.

Singh, Yogendra. 1986. *Modernization of Indian Tradition*, Rawat Publications, Jaipur.

Srinivas, M.N. 2002. *Collected Essays*, Oxford University Press, New Delhi.

Srinivasulu, K. 2002. Caste, Class and Social Articulation in Andhra Pradesh: Mapping Differential Regional Trajectories, Working Paper 179, ODI, London.

13

A Study of Child Labour in the Hotel Industry in Kakinada

P. Subba Rao and T.V. Ramana

Caste and income inequalities are the predominant features of the Indian society. The inherited property rights and abundant opportunities to earn good income have created a distinct affluent class belonging to all upper castes. Simultaneously, due to lack of opportunities and disempowerment many of the lower castes have remained poor. Thus, the inequalities – both social and economic – persist. A direct consequence of such inequalities is child labour. Owing to poverty, the poorer sections engage their children in income-generating activities as a result of which they are denied access to education and the attendant benefits. Child labour therefore has become a ubiquitous phenomenon and a conspicuous feature of urban 'blight'.

In this paper, an attempt is made to delineate the extent, causes and problems of child labour. Further, the paper shall find out to which strata of the society most of them belong. In other words, the paper would test the hypothesis that a majority of them belong to the socially disadvantaged groups. It aims to evaluate the performance of the institutional mechanism which prevents and controls child labour. At the end, we provide suggestions for the eradication of child labour.

In consonance with the above objectives a study of child labour in the hotel industry in the city of Kakinada of East Godavari district was conducted. There are approximately 200 hotels in the town of Kakinada and nearly 150 children are working in them. Due to non-availability of some of the children and the unwillingness of some to give information, the investigators could interview only 70 of them. The secondary data were obtained from concerned departments, newspapers, census reports, websites, NGOs and the Labour Department. Cross-table analysis has been adopted for data analysis.

In this study, an attempt is made to analyse the demographic features, nature, composition and extent of child labour. The caste-wise classification of child labour, indicating the concentration of child labour, is presented.

Demographic Particulars

As per the 2001 Census, there are 1,348 inhabitant villages, 56 uninhabited villages and 22 towns in the district. The population of the district is 49.01 lakhs and area 10,818 km^2. The city of Kakinada has a population of 5,04,920. Males constitute 50 per cent of the population and females 50 per cent. Scheduled Castes (SCs) constitute 19.80 per cent of the population while it is 0.88 per cent in case of the Scheduled Tribes (STs). (It is 17.99 and 3.91 respectively in case of the district as a whole.) Main workers constitute 28.19 per cent of the working population, 1.32 per cent are cultivators and 8.76 per cent are agricultural labourers. Kakinada has an average literacy rate of 66 per cent, higher than the national average of 59.5 per cent; male literacy is 71 per cent, and female literacy is 61 per cent. In Kakinada, 11 per cent of the population is under 6 years of age.

Nature and Composition of the Child Labour Force

Child labour means the employment of children, either male or female (5–14 years of age), in gainful occupations, which are deleterious to their physical, mental, moral and social development. Since poor families have meagre incomes, the children of their families are compelled to join the labour force to supplement the family income. Hence, they are withdrawn from their schools or never sent there. Ultimately, the intellectual growth, health and socialization process of such children are hampered. Child labour is mainly concentrated in urban areas.

Industrial revolution and green revolution had resulted in urbanization. India has reaped the benefits of all these revolutions, which led to greater urbanization and consequently migration to cities from villages due to push and pull factors. Technological progress led to adoption of capital-intensive methods in production, which hastened the process of industrialization. However, low levels of labour absorption capacity of the urban modern sectors led to mass urban unemployment and underemployment. Further, it led to extreme poverty in these areas. Meanwhile, the pressure of labour supply was manifest in the proliferation of certain occupations characterized by low skill, low productivity and meagre incomes. Most of these occupations are found in the informal sector. Due to the lower incomes of the urban poor a large number of their children are employed in agriculture, manufacturing sector, services, retail trade, etc.

Extent of Child Labour

Child labour is a global phenomenon. Globally, out of an estimated 210 million children in the age group of 5–14 years who are engaged in some form of economic activity, 186.3 million qualify to be defined as child labour. Around 111.01 million children are engaged in hazardous occupations. In other words, more than two-thirds of the child labour is still engaged in hazardous forms of child labour. The Asian Pacific region harbours the largest number of child labourers in this age group, i.e., 127 million, constituting 19 per cent of the total child population.

In India, according to the 1991 Census the number of working children in the country was 11.28 million, constituting 3.59 per cent of the total working force. According to the 2001 Census figures, there are 1.25 crore working children in the age group of 5–14 years as compared to the total child population of 25.2 crore, of which 1.07 crore working children are in the age group of 10–14 years.

Andhra Pradesh has the dubious distinction of being home to 14.5 per cent of the child labour (the highest) in the country. It is interesting to note that a backward state like Bihar registered only 8.3 per cent of the country's child labour (Table 13.1). A majority of the child labourers work in the informal sector.

Table 13.1

Child Labour in Major States in India

State	*Percentage*	*State*	*Percentage*
Andhra Pradesh	14.5	Rajasthan	6.9
Uttar Pradesh	12.5	West Bengal	6.3
Madhya Pradesh	12	Tamil Nadu	5.1
Maharashtra	9.5	Gujarat	4.6
Karnataka	8.7	Orissa	4.0
Bihar	8.3		

Hotel Industry and the Extent of Child Labour

According to different surveys conducted by the Government of Andhra Pradesh, NGOs and other organizations, there are around 800 children presently working in different establishments, which include domestic help. Child employment exists in several scheduled employments like automobiles, general engineering, brick-kilns, shops, establishments, agriculture, etc. Child employment in domestic houses, which is called domestic help, could not be checked completely as the implementation of laws and enforcement of the provisions is not an easy task. It is very difficult for the government officials to go into individual houses and catch hold of the children working there and prosecute the erring people.

According to recent surveys there are around 200 hotels, restaurants, lodges, fast food centres, messes and *dhabas* along National Highway 214 and the road laid with the help of the Asian Development Bank. According to the surveys conducted by the state government and information available with the Labour Department, Education Department, Sarva Siksha Abhiyan, the National Child Labour Project (NCLP) and different NGOs, there are around 170 children working in the above establishments including bars and restaurants.

Majority of Child Labourers Belong to the Downtrodden Communities

Certain cultural factors and practices of some families force their children to enter into the labour market. Some deep-rooted social practices are associated with the caste-ridden society. The social fabric is developed in such a way that certain kinds of employment that are caste-specific are inherited in India. For instance, in Andhra Pradesh, a Brahmin family, though poor, may not wish to send its children to work. Some families belonging to Backward Classes, though not in need of any financial assistance from their children, send their children to work. Therefore, it indicates (Table 13.2) that employment of children is closely associated with the caste group and the experience reveals that most of the child labourers are from Scheduled Castes (57.14%) followed by Backward Classes (38.57%) and Scheduled Tribes (4.29%). Of the total number of poor people, nearly 60 per cent belongs to the downtrodden communities (Scheduled Castes and Scheduled Tribes).

Table 13.2

Caste-wise Child Labour in Hotel Industry

Caste	*No. of Child Labourers*	*Percentage*	*Percentage of Population in Total*
Scheduled Caste	40	57.14	17.99
Scheduled Tribe	3	4.27	3.91
Backward Caste	27	38.57	78.1*
Total	70	100.0	100.0

* including other communities.

Other Factors Influencing Child Labour

Child labour is a complex phenomenon, deeply rooted in the economic and cultural milieu of the society. Though poverty is believed to be the main reason for child labour, it cannot, however, be said that poverty necessarily causes child labour. The main reasons for child labour in the study area are improper utilization of the earnings of incomes members due to the consumption of liquor by (20.0%) the fathers of the children. Nearly 30 per cent of the children enter the informal labour market as child labourers due to the weak financial conditions of the family. Injury or illness to an adult earning member in the family and the abandonment of the family following divorce are other factors that are often at the root of child labour. If the parents are educated, even though they are poor, they wish to send their children to school so that the child can lead a better life. The reverse is true in case of illiterate parents. Irrespective of economic status or income levels, many illiterate parents prefer to send their children to work in accordance with the customs and practices prevailing in their respective castes and communities. Such families constitute 10 per cent of the families in the study area. Migration of families from rural areas to the city to take up odd jobs was mentioned as the cause for 13.5 per cent of the sample. They spend money to meet their family needs (Table 13.3). Insecurity of food in time also propels them to work in fast food centres and hotels. They opined that they can get food in addition to their salaries or wages. Non-availability of schools within reasonable distance and ineffective implementation of birth control measures by the state and central governments are among the reasons for child labour. The employers engage children in their business establishments as the wages to be paid are very meagre.

Table 13.3

Factors Influencing Child Labour

Causes	*No. of Child Labourers*	*Percentage of Child Labour*	*Rank*
Due to financial problems	21	30.0	1
Due to orphanage	7	10.0	4
Due to migration of the family	10	14.5	3
Due to illiteracy of the family	7	10.0	4
Due to big family	4	5.5	5
Due to lake of awareness	7	10.0	4
Due to addiction of liquor	14	20.0	2
Total children interviewed	70	100.0	—

The distinction based on gender is highly prevalent in the Indian society. The status of the girl child is very low in certain families and the parents feel that no useful purpose would be served if the girl child is educated. Therefore they prefer to send boys to school and spare girls to attend to a variety of household chores. The girls slowly land up in vocations generally pursued by women of that area, depending mainly on the availability of employment opportunity.

The population explosion at the macro level is therefore responsible for child labour. It is also the size of the family that compels the child to participate in work. The illiterate and ignorant parents who are trapped in the vicious cycle of poverty have less capacity to rear. Therefore, they try to convert every child into an earning member and prefer to put the child to work as soon as he/she starts to walk freely.

Tribulations of Child Labourers

Generally, the employers try to maximize their profits through cheap labour cost. In India, as labour supply exceeds the demand, wages are lowered. Moreover, the owners of the industry give priority to children because of their inability to demand higher wages. Child labourers get Rs. 10–20 while it is Rs. 80–100 for an adult. This discrepancy leads to high exploitation. The working conditions are also very unsatisfactory. Sometimes they are the last ones to take food in the hotels. The management does not provide medical treatment at the time of illness. Further, it is found that they work amidst unhygienic conditions and are not entitled to holidays and additional remuneration for extra work. In course of time their skills get blunt and turn out to be unproductive. It ultimately leads to economic and social disparities at a higher level and consequently it may result in unrest in the society.

Mechanism to Exterminate Child Labour in the Study Area

The following measures should be taken into consideration to eradicate child labour which is the by-product of the stratified society.

The government has to make provision for medical examination and certification of the age of children and adolescents before they get into some kind of employment. The children should be entitled to leave provision with wages after 12 months of continuous service at the rate of one day for every 15 days of work, subject to a minimum of 14 days. However, all these legislative measures have not given relief because the provisions are generally evaded in most of the cases. It was found in the study that some of the child labourers were not willing to continue with the same work and were interested to join schools.

To eradicate child labour, many prohibition and regulation acts were enacted. Some of them are Children's (Pledging of Labour) Act, 1933, Employment of Children Act 1938, the Factories Act, 1948, Plantation Labour Act, 1951, Mines Act, 1952, Motor Transport Workers Act, 1961, Beedi and Cigars Workers Act, 1986 and Andhra Pradesh Shops and Establishment Act, 1988. In addition to these acts some of the legislative frameworks are also adopted by the states in this regard. The Government of Andhra Pradesh launched many programmes to eradicate child labour under NCLP. This project covered thirteen districts in Andhra Pradesh including the East Godavari district.

During the period 1998–99, there were around 2,000 children working in the hotel industry at Kakinada, resulting in massive exploitation of child labourers. In the month of September 1998, the state labour department in collaboration with NGOs, NCLP and other departments under the chairmanship of the District Collector, East Godavari, conducted a seminar which declared that most of the children were, working in the hotel industry at Kakinada. It was decided to prosecute the erring employers and file cases against them by imposing penalties up to ten times of the actual difference in wage payment. The NCLP has taken up the task of identifying those children who are out of schools and enrol them by convincing their parents (Table 13.4).

A project titled Sarva Siksha Abhiyan was introduced by the Government of India in coordination with the Government of Andhra

Pradesh with the aim of identifying the problems of child labour. The project is intended to create awareness among the people about the importance of education for children and the fact that school and not the workplace is the right place for the child. With the coordination of the school education committee, villagers, DWRCA groups and mother committees, the programme has been trying to eliminate child labour. NGOs are involved in the identification of children engaged in work and in enrolling them in the bridge schools of NCLP, government hostels, residential hostels, social welfare and Backward Classes welfare hostels and regular schools.

Table 13.4

Particulars of Children Enrolled in Regular Schools from NCLP Bridge Schools

Year	*Boys*	*Girls*	*Total*
1999–2000	210	150	360
2000–2001	340	180	520
2001–2002	190	210	400
2002–2003	225	140	365
2003–2004	135	165	300
20004–2005	120	100	220
Grand total	1,220	945	2,165

The state labour department has also started inspection of different hotels, restaurants, eating houses, fast food centres, canteens, bars, restaurants and liquor shops. Open courts were conducted and a great deal of awareness was created among the public. This has yielded a tangible result and child employment was reduced drastically. In this way, during 1999–2003, 282 prosecutions were filed, about 344 children were identified and 272 children were rehabilitated.

M.V. Foundation is one of the identified NGOs which runs eight schools with a strength of 20 children each. Viswa Geetika (V.G.) Foundation also enrolled 200 children. Padamavathi Education Society, Yetimoga is also working on the same lines.

Some Policy Implications

After observing the situation in the hotel industry at Kakinada, the following suggestions are offered for examination:

In most of the cases it is observed that insufficient income of the parents is not sufficient to meet the ends of the family. But it is not true in the case of most families. If the parents, especially the father, bring the whole amount to home, there is no need to send the child to work. Hence, stringent measures have to be adopted to curb drinking habits among the males.

People should be convinced of the birth control measures. More educational institutions like residential and bridge schools for the masses are to be established to meet the increasing demand. Stringent measures like punishment up to 10 years imprisonment and payment of huge compensation (ten times the prescribed wages) will act as effective deterrents for the employers of child labourers.

Dropouts should be identified on war footing and sent to bridge schools. Street corner meetings and door-to-door campaigns will have to be organized to let people know the impact of illiteracy on their children. Methods like displaying slides in the cinema theatres, erecting hoardings at crossroads, pasting posters on walls and, performing skits and rallies will be effective in spreading the message.

Select References

Dubey, M.K. 2000. *Rural and Urban Development in India*, Commonwealth Publishers, New Delhi.

Dutt, R. and K.P.M. Sundaram. 2008. *Indian Economy*, S. Chand & Co., Delhi.

Hirway, Indira. 2001. 'Review on Informal Sector in India', *EPW*, 22 Sept.

Mishra, S.K. and V.K. Puri. 2006. *Indian Economy*, Himalaya Publications, Delhi.

Ramana, T.V. 2005. Work Force Participation of Child Labour in SKL, (seminar volume).

Record of Chief Planning Officer, KKD. Records of NCLP, KKD and RSSA.

Reports of State Labour Department, KKD.

Satyanarayana, D.S.V. 2003. *Project Work on Child Labour*, Andhra University Campus, Kakinada.

14

The Concomitant Effects of Geographical and Cultural Isolation on Chenchu Leading to Social Exclusion

Jesurathnam Devarapalli

Almost every nation-state in this modern world is faced with the problem of addressing to exotic cultural groups which are still found lying at the early rungs of human civilization. Though the level of development of such autochthonic groups varies from country to country, the basic reasons for such a scenario are geographical and cultural isolation, ethnocentric attitudes and apathy of general public or establishment towards such peoples. In the recent decades, though the governments at various levels and the international bodies have been paying considerable attention to ameliorate the conditions of such populations called aborigines, first nations, native populations, indigenous groups, autochthons, tribals and so on, the success achieved and the progress made in that direction are miniscule. Many times approaches were adopted, but the results obtained were inappropriate and negative. The open apology tendered by Kevin Rudd, the Prime Minister of Australia, to the aborigines for injustices committed on them for over two centuries by laws and assimilative policies of successive parliaments (*The Hindu,* 13 and 14 February 2008) speaks about one of the numerous historical tragedies that took place throughout the history of human civilization but have not come to light.

The tribal situation in India is very complex and has many problems that overshadow triumphs during the long history of pre and post-independence eras of the country. The existence of the tribes in the subcontinent dates back to prehistoric times. The varna system, which is based on skin colour, hints about the origin of colour discrimination, which started with the encounter of the fair complexioned Aryans with the local inhabitants who were dark-skinned and called 'dasas' (Kuppuswamy, 1977). It is generally opined, as pointed out by Mathur (2004), that the Aryans pushed the original inhabitants of the land into the interiors of the dense forests and on to the hill tops and hill plains. These populations began living in seclusion in the areas that were not at all easily accessible and developed their own means of living and social organization (Chauhan, 1965). Thus, the tribal communities in India live in a world of physical isolation and distinct cultural identities, strongly adhering to tradition and very slow to accept modernity. However, we may still find a few of the communities living in close association with the non-tribals which is due to the organized encroachment and infiltration. The ancient Hindu rulers and their chiefs encouraged the Brahmins to penetrate into these exclusive tribal belts by giving them lands (Kosambi, 1965). In order to support agriculture, artisan castes also entered into the tribal areas. In course of time with an intention to exploit the resources of the forest areas, a host of outsiders including traders and money lenders infiltrated into these areas.

Thus, in addition to the sufferings resulting from poverty, ill-health and strong traditionalism, the tribes suffered more due to the exploitation by non-tribal intruders. The unbridled exploitation by outsiders excluded the tribes from reaching the fruits of development. With this premise it is intended to substantiate the misery of the Chenchu who were stuck in thick forests for generations together without seeing the light of progress. The core issue of this paper revolves around insularity and the concomitant problems of the tribe.

The Chenchu

They are one of the few living examples of foraging people of India displaying the cultural features of the Palaeolithic period. Bhowmick (1989: 13) expressed the view that Chenchu share early traditions of human society. They are found inhabiting the Nallamalai Hills, which are the southernmost part of the Eastern Ghats. Though a degree of suspicion prevails in the ascertaining of the origin of the word 'Chenchu' and its meaning, it is often believed that as they dwell under trees, they are called Chenchu, because in Telugu a tree is called *chettu*. There is also another notion that they had the habit of eating mice, which is locally called *chunchu* and hence the name. But in their known ethno-history there is no report of mouse eating. The Chenchu are typically dark in complexion with shiny skin, piercing eyes and bewildered looks. They are generally slender and of medium stature with scanty growth of facial hair. They have wavy or curly and invariably black head hair. They are found distributed in the forest areas of six districts of Andhra Pradesh, namely Kurnool, Prakasam, Mahaboobnagar, Guntur, Rangareddy and Nalgonda.

Life of Isolation

The Nallamalai forest, the natural abode of Chenchu since times immemorial, is extended over a length of 430 km having an average width of 30 km, with an elevation ranging from 275 to 915 m above mean sea level (MSL). Its topography is generally of undulating hilly terrain with free surface rocks and boulders and a few patches of soil on the plateaus. The river Krishna passes through the forest dissecting the area into deep winding gorges. The ridge of the Nallamalai Hills runs in a general north-south direction with many plateaus and valleys. The plateaus of Amrabad, Pecheruvu and Guttalachenu rise to an average elevation of 700–800 m above MSL. Durgamkonda has the highest elevation, which rises up to 915 m above MSL, while the Nagarjuna Sagar Dam has the lowest, which is less than 100 m above MSL. The Nallamalai forest is considered to be one of the world major centres of plant diversity. Nallamalai contains good samples of nearly all the vegetation types known from the Eastern Ghats, namely, dry deciduous, moist deciduous, dry evergreen, riverine and scrub forest.

Due to its lush green belt and great biodiversity the wildlife is also plentiful in this forest which is home to a variety of carnivores including tigers and leopards apart from different kinds of birds and smaller mammals. Due to these reasons the Nallamalai forest has two wildlife sanctuaries, namely Nagarjunasagar-Srisailam Tiger Reserve and Gundla Brahmeswaram Metta wildlife sanctuary.

The rich biomass of the Chenchu habitat is an indicator of great resourcefulness of the area. It forms a formidable barrier to interaction with the outer world in addition to the non-negotiable terrain infested with wild animals. Due to the presence of surface boulders and shallow surface soil this area could not attract farming communities except the Lambada (a farming tribe) into its core area.

However, the fringe areas abutting the rural side are monopolized by caste populations and some Chenchu serve them as farm guards.

Under these physical and physiographic conditions of the habitat, the Chenchu have developed a lifestyle of their own with certain characteristic features that reflect in their economy, food habits, behaviour and worldview.

Economy

The economic activities of the Chenchu are based on the forest ecosystem. They are traditional forgers, a practice still in vogue among the forest-dwelling Chenchu. They get the major portion of their food from gathering and hunting. They collect honey and a variety of tubers, roots and berries from the forest. Normally women are involved in this activity, while men help them in uprooting the tubers. The honey is collected exclusively by men. They also go for hunting animals like deer, antelope, wild sheep, Nilgai, rabbit and wild boar. This mode of economic activity does not allow them to save food for tomorrow as they gather food on the basis of daily requirements, and if there is big game the meat is distributed among all the members of the hamlet. The foraging activities are not sufficient to sustain the Chenchu due to outsiders' interaction and they have to search for alternate economic activities, which are again based on the forest.

Food Habits

Along with the changes in economic activities their food habits have also undergone changes. They collect a variety of tubers varying from a small onion size to a very large size of tapioca. Of all these tubers *chenchu gadda* is their staple food as it is the largest sweet edible wild tuber without any cognizable ill effects. Due to extensive deforestation these tubers have also become scarce, forcing the people to purchase agricultural products. In spite of these changes, wild leaves, berries, nuts, tubers, honey and game meat still form an important part of their food. Consumption of homemade as well as purchased liquor is a common habit among men and women. Men have the habit of smoking beedies and most of the men and women chew tobacco

Behaviour and Worldview

The Chenchu are highly tradition-bound. It is observed that the children are given much liberty during their childhood. This, however, does not mean that parental care is lacking. The child is fed with breast milk till the next child is born. The growing child is allowed to join the peer group and learn to kill small animals and gather berries and nuts. Despite strong and secure family ties, a high degree of individualism is displayed by men and women. Both men and women are free to choose their mates and break the marital bonds at will. Though pre-marital sex is not taken seriously, extra-marital relations often lead to breakups in marriage. Bonhomie prevails in the community while sharing food, extending a helping hand in the time of need and helping in avoiding competition for resources. The Chenchu are pleasure lovers. They drink and dance, and liquor forms the basic payment in solemnizing marriages. They have unshattered faith in the forest environment and all ill effects and mishaps are attributed to the discontent of the supernatural. They take pride in claiming to be the kings of the forest but do not have a clear political set-up at least of a traditional type commonly seen among many tribes. Though they can be alone day and night in the thick forest amidst wild animals, the Chenchu are very timid. They hesitate to speak to the visiting officials and avoid outsiders. Due to their shyness and timidity they fail to question the exploitation by the non-tribals. They suffer from inferiority complex and hence hesitate to interact with the people from the plains.

Their cultural traits help them cope with the exigencies of the nature and train them to minimize their material needs. The indicators of growth and development reveal that the situation of the Chenchu is very discouraging.

Housing

The Chenchu live in very simple huts in the forest. They experienced a shift from nomadic to semi-nomadic life as a result of which settled life housing assumed significance in their lives. Their traditional houses are made of locally available materials (Devarapalli, 2008). These houses suit their lifestyle as well as the forest environment. However, these houses provide the least protection and safety during heavy rains with strong gales. In recent decades some of them relocated to the fringe or rural areas to stay either in thatched houses or in small masonry structures of inferior quality which never satisfied them. Many of them went back into the deep forest as they found their food there.

Drinking Water

The Chenchu have failed to develop a proper water management system as they are foragers and not cultivators. As they solely depend on the hill streams for drinking and domestic use they make their settlements and hunting campsites close to a natural water body. These water bodies are not protected from contamination and carry with them vegetative parts and develop into breeding grounds for many harmful micro- and macro-organisms. When the water bodies dry up, the Chenchu move out in search of water. Though the government has installed hand pumps in a few large settlements, they were rendered useless and the Chenchu had to depend on the traditional sources. The hunters during their expeditions have to quench their thirst with the dripping water from the cuts of a creeper. The stream water is loaded with harmful creatures that cause a number of health problems such as dysentery, diarrhoea, vomiting, skin diseases and so on.

Electricity

Though the Srisailam Hydroelectric Project is located in the heart of the Chenchu land, their hamlets are still groping in darkness. They still have to wait for kerosene supplies from the fair price shops which are located in distant places. Most of the Chenchu houses in the core area have no light in the house and they at the most have to depend on the red coals (which are common in winter) meant for providing warmth in the house. As the majority of Chenchu habitats are situated in the core of the forest, they cannot be provided with power supply because that may be harmful to the wildlife. But incidentally the high power lines pass through the core area to provide power to the well-developed urban centres.

Nutrition

Food contents of the Chenchu are drawn from both forest and the outside market. Because of the non-tribals' interference the natural ecosystem is disturbed and many food sources of the Chenchu are becoming scarce, while some of them have already disappeared. As such they are unable to get their traditional staple food *chenchu gadda* and other tubers. The forest laws infringe upon their hunting rights and collection of forest produce for sales. On the other hand, the agricultural food stuffs are not available at nearby places and are also very expensive. As a result, the Chenchu have inadequate food with low nutritive value. This in turn has led to malnourishment among children, pregnant women, nursing mothers and the aged.

Health

Health is another important indicator to gauge the miserable hardships faced by the Chenchu in their homeland. It is the most neglected aspect by the Chenchu themselves as they have a different yardstick of health and disease. As modern health care facilities are not available for them in the vicinity they leave the subject to fate when all their ethno-medical practices fail to yield any result. Though big claims are made by the public health care providers, practically the Chenchu hamlets are not provided with any assured medical facilities. The facilities available are of inferior type concentrated outside the fringe area while the majority of the Chenchu dwell in the core area.

Education

The concept of formal education is something alien to Chenchu parents and therefore they are least bothered in inculcating interest in the child to attend schools. Though a few schools are seen in the core area the teachers are rarely available at the schools. The only person available at the school is the *kamati* (cook). The school begins and ends with consumption of food. The Chenchu children after collecting their food go back to play. Only a few Chenchu children are found at the upper primary level. The Chenchu boys and girls who get till tenth class (they mostly live outside the forest) are given jobs as teachers or other menial staff as an incentive, irrespective of whether they pass or not. The overall educational levels, educational facilities and educational infrastructure are at a dismal state.

Communication

Communication is the lifeline for all developmental processes in any society. The Chenchu community is denied of the minimum communication facilities like road and transport means. Once again the rugged nature of the terrain and inhibiting forest laws are the major causes for this state. Due to the lack of communication facilities the developmental personnel and the infrastructural facilities could not reach the community in full swing and hence the people have remained insulated. The Chenchu love to listen to radios for only music and songs but not for news and other items of awareness or educational importance.

Deprivation of Resources

The tribal areas are the last pockets to be brought under the British rule. Ever since, there is increasing interference of the union and state government in the tribal habitats. A number of laws were clamped on the tribal areas with regard to forest protection and resources utilization. This practically has curtailed the Chenchu's movement in the forest and they were suspected and constantly troubled by forest personnel. They no more had the freedom to get their food through hunting, and restrictions were imposed on their collection of timber and firewood. Rather, most of the forest resources like medicinal herbs, timber, non-wood produces and wildlife were cleverly taken away by non-tribal contractors and traders. Mishra (2002: 21) pointed out that the laws disinherited the tribals from their ownership of the resources of their region and resources became national property without obtaining their consent. Thus they became intruders in their own areas and were treated as criminals when they exercised their traditional rights. The Scheduled Tribes and other Traditional Forest Dwellers (Recognition of Forest Rights) Act, 2006 is yet to be implemented in its full form.

Conclusion

A close examination of Chenchu life reveals those basic problems that have already been overcome to a large extent by the population who are considered to be advanced. The major cause for continuation of these problems is their physical isolation within the inaccessible forest area which is shielded with many Forest Acts that virtually hinder the implementation of developmental strategies. It is needless to say that their ethnocentric attitude and worldview offer formidable resistance to the developmental interventions. Under these circumstances the Chenchu are practically excluded from the purview of national growth and progress and are thus deprived of the minimum required amenities in day-to-day life. Considering their stagnant population growth, pre-agriculture economy and high illiteracy, they are declared as one of the 75 primitive tribes of India. Touching the outsiders' intrusion Sharma (1995: 21) says that the state, industrialists, contractors, middlemen and the non-descript crowd of outsiders have descended on the tribal areas in search of new opportunities. Thus, non-tribal intrusion into Nallamalai not only exploited the forest but also the Chenchu and ultimately reduced the quality of environment so that it no longer remained the sole source for their sustenance. Such a situation has led to widening of the socio-cultural gap between tribals and nontribals. All these developments pushed the Chenchu into poverty, hunger, illiteracy, ill-health, ill-communication and insecurity barred from the neighbouring caste population with distinct boundary. Furer-Haimendorf (1977: 533) underlined the frustration, inferiority complex and timidity that had enveloped the tribals in the Deccan and hinted for special consideration to preserve the confidence and pride of the people.

References

Bhowmick, P.K. 1989. *The Chenchus of the Forests and Plateaux: A Hunting-Gathering Tribe in Transition*, Institute of Social Research and Applied Anthropology, Calcutta.

Chauhan, B.R. 1965. 'Tribalisation' *Tribe*, Vol. 1, p. 65.

Devarapalli. J., 2008. 'Hidden Wisdom under the Primitive Huts', in V. Subramanyam (ed.), *Indigenous Science and Technology for Sustainable Development*, Rawat Publications, New Delhi.

Furer-Haimendorf, C.V. 1977. 'The Position of Tribal Population in India', in H.M. Mathur and C.V. Furer-Haimendorf (eds.), *Anthropology in the Development Process*, Vikas Publications, New Delhi.

Kosambi, D.D. 1965. *The Culture and Civilization of Ancient India in Historical Outline*, Routledge & Kegan Paul, London.

Kuppuswamy, B. 1977. *Dharma and Society: A Study in Social Values*, Macmillan, Delhi.

Mathur, L.P. 2004. *Tribal Revolts in India under British Raj*, Aavishkar Publications, Jaipur.

Mishra, P.K. 2002. 'Issues in Sustainable Development Debate: Development of Tribes and Ecological Considerations', in K. Viswanatha Reddy (ed.), *Cultural Ecology of Indian Tribes*, Raj Publications, Delhi.

Sharma, B.D. 1995. *Globalisation: The Tribal Encounter*, Har-Anand Publications, New Delhi.

15

Population, Literacy and Educational Status of Scheduled Tribes in India

D. Pulla Rao

The Scheduled Tribes (STs) are the most segregated and isolated communities and are concentrated in the states of Orissa, Bihar, Madhya Pradesh, Andhra Pradesh, Maharashtra, Gujarat and Rajasthan. In these states they constitute about 80 per cent of the total ST population of India. The STs constitute 8.20 per cent of the country's population as per 2001 Census and live mainly in forest and hilly regions. They are sons of soil and live in isolation from other communities. Most of the tribes constitute separate socio-cultural groups having distinct customs, traditions, marriage, kinship and property inheritance system and they live largely in agricultural and pre-agricultural level of technology. Among these tribes, there are food gatherers, hunters, forest land cultivators, shifting cultivators and minor forest produce collectors. The essential characteristics of these communities are primitive traits, geographical isolation, distinctive culture and inhibition in communicating with outsiders. There are 635 STs living in different parts of the country, having their own languages different from the ones that are mostly spoken in the state where they live. There are more than 270 such languages in India. Educational and economic backwardness is also a common feature. They are isolated from the rest of the society due to poor transportation and communication facilities and have remained as educationally, culturally, economically and socially disadvantage sections. Being mostly illiterate, they are subjected to all kinds of exploitation – social, economic and political.

Definitions of Tribe

A tribe is a collection of families bearing a common name, speaking a common dialect, occupying or professing to occupy a common territory and is not usually endogamous, though originally it might have been so.

—Imperial Gazetteer of India

A tribe is a group of people in a primitive or barbarous stage of development acknowledging the authority of a chief and usually regarding themselves as having a common on sector.

—Oxford Dictionary

In its simplest form the tribe is a group of bands occupying a contiguous territory or territories and having a feeling of unity deriving form numerous similarities in culture frequent contacts, and a certain community of interest.

—Ralpla Linton

A tribe is an independent political division of a population with a common culture.

—Lucy Mair

A tribe is a group united by a common name in which the members take pride by a common language, by a common territory, and by a feeling that all who do not share this name are outsiders, 'enemies' in fact.

—G.W.B. Humtingford

Constitutional Safeguards

After independence, the framers of Indian Constitution included certain special safety and security measures for the tribals. These measures provide some protective discrimination to the tribals against the non-tribals. Table 15.1 shows what various articles and schedules meant for the tribes provide for. They constitute the base for development approach in tribal areas. As a part of two-pronged strategy of development and protection, the Department of Tribal Welfare has geared up the enforcement machinery for the effective implementation of the protective regulations which are promulgated by the Governor in exercise of powers conferred under para 5 (2) of Fifth Schedule to the Constitution to provide the much-needed protection of tribals.

Table 15.1
Constitution for Scheduled Tribes

Article and Schedule	*Information*
342	Definition of tribal.
46	Educational and economic interests of Scheduled Castes and Tribals.
244	Empower the tribal people in tribal areas
339	Welfare Schemes for the STs.
275	Funds for tribes to the State Government.
330 332 334	Provide for reservation of seats for STs in the house of the people and the state legislatures.
335	Reservation in the various services.
15 16 19	Tribes are also equality of citizens.
338	The machinery for implementing the safeguard of the STs and the programmes for their development.
5	Powers and lays certain duties on the Governor of every state.
6	The way of living.

Demographic Profile of the Scheduled Tribes in India

The Census experience indicates that the population of STs increases faster than the overall population of the country. Table 15.2 shows that the overall population of the country (Census, 1951) was 36.1 crore, of which the ST population was 1.9 crore. The decadal growth rate of ST population was high (52.6) in 1961 and the proportion of ST population to overall population was 6.6 per cent. The sex ratio of STs was in a better position at 987 as against the overall sex ratio, which was 941 in 1961. As per the 2001 Census, the overall population increased to 102.8 crores of which the population of the STs was 8.4 crore. The decadal growth rate of ST population was high (23.5) as against the overall population (21.5). The proportion of ST population to overall population was 8.2 per cent. The sex ratio of STs was 978, which was higher than the sex ratio of overall population (933) in 2001.

Table 15.2

Overall and Scheduled Tribe Population (in Crore) and Sex Ratios in India

Year	Overall Population	Decadal Growth Rate of Overall Population	Scheduled Tribes		% of ST Population to Overall Population	Sex Ratio	
			Population	Decadal Growth Rate		Overall	ST
1951	36.1	—	1.9	—	5.2	946	988
1961	43.9	21.6	2.9	52.6	6.6	941	987
1971	54.8	24.8	3.8	31.0	6.9	930	985
1981	68.3	24.6	5.2	36.8	7.6	935	983
1991	84.6	23.9	6.8	30.8	8.0	927	972
2001	102.8	21.5	8.4	23.5	8.2	933	978

Source: Selected Educational Statistics, MHRD, GoI, New Delhi, 2002–03.

According to the 2001 Census, STs inhabit the entire country except Haryana, Punjab, Chandigarh, Delhi and Pondicherry. While the highest concentration of the ST population is found in the North Eastern states of Mizoram (94.46%), Nagaland (89.15%), Meghalaya (85.94%) and Arunachal Pradesh (64.22%) and in the union territories of Lakshadweep (94.51%), and Dadra and Nagar Haveli (62.24%), there are heavy concentrations in the states of Manipur (34.20%), Chhattisgarh (31.76%), Tripura (31.05%), Jharkhand (26.30%), Orissa (22.13%), Sikkim (20.60%) and Madhya Pradesh (20.27%). The lowest concentration of ST population is found in Uttar Pradesh (0.06%), Bihar (0.91%), Tamil Nadu (1.04%), Kerala (1.14%) and Andaman and Nicobar Islands (1.27%) (Table 15.3).

Table 15.3

Total Population and Percentage of Scheduled Tribe Population, 2001 Census

India/State/Union Territory	Total Population ('000)	Scheduled Tribe Population ('000)	Percentage of ST Population to Total Population
INDIA	1,028,610	84,326	8.20
Jammu & Kashmir	10,144	1,106	10.90
Himachal Pradesh	6,078	245	4.02

Cont'd

Cont'd

Punjab	24,359	0	0.00
Chandigarh	901	0	0.00
Uttaranchal	8,489	256	3.02
Haryana	21,145	0	0.00
Delhi	13,851	0	0.00
Rajasthan	56,507	7,098	12.56
Uttar Pradesh	166,198	108	0.06
Bihar	82,999	758	0.91
Sikkim	541	111	20.60
Arunachal Pradesh	1,098	705	64.22
Nagaland	1,990	1,774	89.15
Manipur	2,167	741	34.20
Mizoram	889	839	94.46
Tripura	3,199	993	31.05
Meghalaya	2,319	1,993	85.94
Assam	26,656	3,309	12.41
West Bengal	80,176	4,407	5.50
Jharkhand	26,946	7,087	26.30
Orissa	26,805	8,145	22.13
Chhattisgarh	20,834	6,617	31.76
Madhya Pradesh	60,348	12,233	20.27
Gujarat	50,671	7,481	14.76
Daman and Diu	158	14	8.85
Dadra and Nagar Haveli	220	137	62.24
Maharashtra	96,879	8,577	8.85
Andhra Pradesh	76,210	5,024	6.59
Karnataka	52,851	3,464	6.55
Goa	1,348	1	0.04
Lakshadweep	61	57	94.51
Kerala	31,841	364	1.14
Tamil Nadu	62,406	651	1.04
Pondicherry	974	0	0.00
Andaman and Nicobar Islands	356	29	1.27

Note: 1. India and Manipur figures exclude those of the three sub-divisions, viz., Mao Maram, Paomata and Purul of Senapati district of Manipur as population census 2001 in these three subdivisions were cancelled due to technical and administrative reasons although a population census was carried out in these subdivision also as per schedule.

Source: Census of India, 2001.

Literacy Profile of STs in India

Literacy and level of education are two basic indicators of the level of development achieved by a group or a society. High levels of literacy result in a greater degree of awareness besides contributing to the overall improvement of health, hygiene and other social conditions. As per the figures based on the 2001 Census, in the field of literacy, the disparities between males and females are still large. Table 15.4 shows the gap between the literacy rates of the overall population and ST population, overall males and ST males and overall females and ST females. It shows how the difference has been persisting since 1961. In 1961 the total ST literacy rate was 8.53 per cent as against 23.30 per cent among overall population. The difference in 1961 was 14.77 per cent. In the same year, the literacy rate of ST males was 13.83 per cent as against 4.40 per cent among overall males and the difference between ST males and overall males was 26.57 per cent. In the case of female literacy rate, it was only 3.16 per cent for ST females as against 15.35 per cent among overall females and the difference was 12.19 per cent.

According to the 2001 Census, the literacy rate of the STs increased to 47.10 per cent as against 65.38 per cent of the overall population. The difference between the literacy rate of total STs and overall population was 18.28 per cent. The literacy rate of ST males increased to 59.17 per cent as against 75.85 per cent among overall males and the difference was 16.68 per cent. In case of female literacy rate, it was 34.76 per cent among ST females as against 54.16 per cent of overall females and the difference was 19.40 per cent. Understandably, female literacy rates at all points of time are lower than those of males. The disparity in literacy rates between overall population and ST population is higher among females than among males.

Table 15.4

Genderwise Literacy Rates of Overall Population and ST Population in India

Year	*Overall literacy*	*Total ST literacy*	*Differ-ence*	*Overall Male literacy*	*ST Male literacy*	*Differ-ence*	*Overall Female Literacy*	*ST Female Literacy*	*Differ-ence*
1961	23.30	8.53	14.77	40.40	13.83	26.57	15.35	3.16	12.19
1971	34.45	11.30	23.15	45.96	17.63	28.33	21.97	4.85	17.12
1981	43.57	16.35	27.22	56.38	24.52	31.86	29.76	8.04	21.72
1991	52.21	29.60	22.61	64.13	40.65	23.48	39.29	18.19	21.10
2001	65.38	47.10	18.28	75.85	59.17	16.68	54.16	34.76	19.40

Source: Census of India, relevant issues.

The literacy rate of STs and the overall population of the major states of India is shown in Table 15.5. As per the 2001 Census, more than half of the tribal population in the country is illiterate. The position in this regard is further worsened in the states of Bihar, Andhra Pradesh, Orissa and Madhya Pradesh, which account for more than 30 per cent of total ST population in the country. In all points of time, the literacy rates of overall population are much higher than that of the STs. The growth in literacy of the STs is very slow compared to overall population during the period of 1961–1991. But the growth in literacy of STs is higher than that of the total population from 1991 to 2001.

Table 15.5

Literacy Rates (%) of Overall Population and STs in Major States of India

State	*Overall Population*					*Scheduled Tribes*				
	1961	1971	1981	1991	2001	1961	1971	1981	1991	2001
Andhra Pradesh	21.19	24.57	29.94	44.09	61.11	4.41	5.34	7.82	17.16	37.04
Bihar	18.40	19.94	26.20	38.48	47.53	9.16	11.64	16.99	26.78	28.17
Gujarat	30.45	35.79	43.70	61.29	69.97	11.69	14.12	21.14	36.45	47.74
Karnataka	25.03	31.52	38.46	56.04	67.04	8.15	14.85	20.14	36.01	48.27
Madhya Pradesh	17.13	22.14	27.87	44.20	64.11	5.10	7.62	10.68	21.54	41.16
Maharashtra	29.82	39.18	47.18	64.87	77.27	7.12	11.74	22.29	36.79	55.21
Orissa	21.66	26.18	34.23	49.09	63.61	7.36	9.46	13.96	22.31	37.37
Rajasthan	15.21	19.07	24.38	38.55	61.03	3.97	6.47	10.27	19.44	44.66
West Bengal	29.28	33.20	40.94	57.70	69.22	6.55	8.92	13.21	27.28	43.40
India	23.30	34.45	43.57	52.21	65.38	8.53	11.30	16.35	29.60	47.10

Source: Census of India, relevant issues.

Recognized Schools and Enrolment of ST Students by Sex in Primary and Upper Primary Education in India

The educational problems of STs are more serious than that of any other section of the society because of their special geographical and environmental constraints. The enrolment status of ST children in primary and upper primary stages is presented in Table 15.6.

The enrolment of ST children at primary and upper primary stages corresponds to the proportion of their number in the overall population. Table 15.6 shows that during 1990s, the enrolment of ST children including girls at the primary stage has been about 7–9 per cent, which approximates the percentage of their population (8.20%) in the overall population of India in 2001. But at upper primary level their enrolment has not been satisfactory. It may be seen that the enrolment of ST children at the upper primary stage varies between 5 and 6 per cent. This data indicate that the progress of education of ST children at upper primary stage is not satisfactory and sustained efforts have to be made to raise their educational status during the years to come. The government should provide attractive financial incentives to enhance the enrolment of ST children, especially at upper primary stage in view of their specific problems emerging out of their geographical and environmental location. The total number of primary schools in India increased from 4.94 lakh in 1980–81 to 6.39 lakh in 2000–01, and the total number of upper primary schools has increased from 1.18 lakh in 1980–81 to 2.06 lakh in 2000–01.

Government should set up more schools in the vicinity of ST habitations. Attempts may be made to utilize the services of voluntary agencies by way of helping them in opening non-formal education centres and pre-primary schools.

Table 15.6

Number of Recognized Schools and Enrolment of ST Children by Sex in Primary and Upper Primary Education in India

Year	*Primary (Classes I–V)*			*Upper Primary (Classes VI–VIII)*		
	No. of Schools	*Total enrolment*	*Girls enrolment*	*No. of Schools*	*Total enrolment*	*Girls enrolment*
1978–79	NA	3398 (7.0)	1124 (4.3)	NA	1279 (4.8)	401 (6.8)
1980–81	4.94	4660 (6.3)	1527 (5.4)	1.18	742 (3.6)	205 (3.0)
1985–86	5.29	6580 (7.5)	2406 (6.8)	1.35	1283 (4.7)	390 (4.1)
1990–91	5.61	7869 (8.1)	2911 (7.2)	1.51	1707 (5.0)	576 (4.6)
1995–96	5.9	8794 (8.0)	3608 (7.6)	1.71	2545 (6.2)	938 (5.9)
2000–01	6.39	10995 (9.4)	4665 (9.4)	2.06	3084 (7.2)	1205 (6.9)

Note: The figures within the parentheses indicate the ST enrolment as per cent of the total enrolment at the corresponding stages.

Sources: 1. Government of India, Education of Scheduled Castes and Scheduled Tribes 1988–89, MHRD, Department of Education, New Delhi, 1993.
2. Government of India, Selected Educational Statistics 2002–03, Department of Education, MHRD, New Delhi.

Gross Enrolment Ratios of STs in Primary and Upper Primary Education in Major States of India

The gross enrolment ratio for ST girls and boys for grades I to V and VI to VIII are shown in Table 15.7. As can be seen from this table that from grades I to V, the gross enrolment ratio of ST girls and boys in Andhra Pradesh is higher than the gross enrolment ratios of ST girls and boys in Kerala and Tamil Nadu. But at the upper primary stage, the gross enrolment ratio of ST girls in Andhra Pradesh declined sharply to 38.5 per cent and is substantially lower than the gross enrolment ratios of ST girls of Kerala (80.8%) and Tamil Nadu (99.2%). It is interesting to note that both in primary and upper primary stages, the gross enrolment ratios of ST boys and girls in Uttar Pradesh is higher than the other states in India. Bihar recorded the lowest gross enrolment ratios for both boys and girls than the other states in the country.

Table 15.7

Gross Enrolment Ratio of Scheduled Tribe Students by Sex in Primary and Upper Primary Stages in Major States of India, 2002–03

State	*Primary Classes I–V (6–11 Years)*		*Upper Primary Classes VI–VIII (11–14 Years)*	
	Boys	*Girls*	*Boys*	*Girls*
		North East		
Meghalaya	90.2	93.0	41.6	51.3
Mizoram	119.3	122.7	78.3	78.0
Nagaland	72.9	70.9	38.0	38.3
		East		
Bihar	59.6	32.5	18.6	8.5
Orissa	103.4	87.3	38.4	26.6
West Bengal	108.1	94.6	60.5	29.8
		Central		
Madhya Pradesh	91.9	71.8	41.6	24.6
		West		
Gujarat	111.6	107.9	67.8	58.2
Rajasthan	118.7	106.4	64.8	31.8
Maharashtra	116.6	106.4	72.9	63.8

Cont'd

Cont'd

		North		
Uttar Pradesh	130.4	124.6	108.6	99.3
Himachal Pradesh	126.5	122.1	100.6	75.9
		South		
Andhra Pradesh	118.1	113.6	54.3	38.5
Kerala	112.9	107.7	84.6	80.8
Tamil Nadu	105.7	113.2	85.6	99.2
INDIA	104.8	92.3	55.0	40.8

Source: Selected Educational Statistics, GoI, Ministry of Human Resource Development, 2002–03.

Dropout Rates of ST Students in Primary and Upper Primary Education in Major States of India

Dropout rate is another important factor that hinders the progress of literacy among the STs. The dropout rates of STs in major states is shown in Table 15.8. The table shows that the dropout rate of ST girls in Andhra Pradesh is 68.7 per cent at the primary level, Which it is much higher than the dropout rate of girls in other states in India. The dropout rate of ST boys in Bihar is 66.6 per cent at the primary stage, which is much higher than the dropout rate of boys in other sates in the country. At upper primary stage of education, the dropout rate of both girls and boys is increasing. The dropout rate among ST girls in Andhra Pradesh is next only to that of Bihar (85.6%), which is also higher than the national average (71.2%). The highest dropout rate of ST boys was 82.4 per cent at upper primary stage in Bihar. It is evident that apart from gender disparities in the gross enrolment ratios and dropout rates, the gross enrolment ratios are declining and the dropout rates are increasing among the ST students at upper primary level of education, particularly in case of ST girls in Andhra Pradesh. This may be due to the relatively higher poverty levels and lower human development levels in Andhra Pradesh compared to other southern states of Kerala, Karnataka and Tamil Nadu. Most of the ashram schools are not being maintained properly and are suffering from lack of basic facilities. The location of the schools is not convenient for the students as well as the teachers, thus leading to absenteeism on both sides. The quality of teaching, the attitude of the teachers towards the cultural background of the tribal students, the meagre number of teachers and the meagre funds allocated for tribal literacy improvement are all responsible for the discouraging situation.

Table 15.8

Statewise Dropout Rates of Scheduled Tribe Students by Sex in Primary and Upper Primary Stages in Major States of India, 2002–03

State	*Primary Classes I–V*		*Upper Primary Classes I–VIII*	
	Boys	*Girls*	*Boys*	*Girls*
		North East		
Meghalaya	61.4	59.3	81.1	80.3
Mizoram	55.9	54.9	59.9	56.3
Nagaland	37.4	37.0	42.8	44.2
		East		
Bihar	66.6	65.4	82.4	85.6
Orissa	58.0	53.5	77.5	79.1
West Bengal	53.7	59.3	60.7	42.4
		Central		
Madhya Pradesh	51.9	50.5	65.6	70.2
		West		
Gujarat	36.1	43.1	58.3	67.0
Maharashtra	28.8	40.2	61.0	66.4
Rajasthan	50.6	59.9	52.6	73.2
		North		
Uttar Pradesh	31.2	30.0	37.0	36.5
Himachal Pradesh	16.2	21.7	26.8	37.4
		South		
Andhra Pradesh	63.3	68.7	78.6	84.3
Kerala	2.2	6.0	33.6	40.0
Tamil Nadu	27.2	21.0	57.0	54.4
INDIA	50.8	52.1	66.9	71.2

Source: Selected Educational Statistics, GoI, Ministry of Human Resource Development, 2002–03.

Conclusion and Suggestions

STs are considered as the most backward population and still live relatively in isolation. They were denied all educational opportunities in the past. They are living mainly in forest and hilly regions. Being mostly illiterate, they are subject to all kinds of exploitation – social, economic, political and educational. After independence, the Government of India provided some constitutional safeguards for their upliftment – social, economic, political and educational. Yet, the desired result has not been achieved.

The government therefore needs to undertake some more special measures to encourage this population send their children, especially girl children, to schools compulsorily and regularly. The government should provide attractive financial incentives to enhance the enrolment of ST children even in the school stage and should set up more schools in the vicinity of ST habitations. Attempts may be made to utilize the services of voluntary agencies by way of helping the students in opening non-formal education centres and pre-primary schools in the tribal habitations. It is more appropriate to implement some strategies of schooling in tribal areas, such as mobile schools, alternate intake schools, non-graded schools, mosque schools, learning post schools, etc. Attempts must be made to involve the parents actively in the educational process such that parents will know in advance the end results of education and the need to send their children to the schools regularly and punctually.

Select References

Ahmed, A. 1984. *Education of Scheduled Tribes: Some Aspects of Inequality*, National Institute of Educational Planning and Administration, New Delhi.

Ambasht, N.K. 1970. *A Critical Study of Tribal Education*, S. Chand and Co., New Delhi.

Chalam, K.S. 1988. *Education and Weaker Sections*, Inter-India Publication, New Delhi.

Das Gupta, N.K. 1963. *Problems of Tribal Education and the Santals*, Bharatiya Adimjati Sevak Sangh, New Delhi.

Dube, S.C. 1968. 'Approaches to Tribal Problems in India', in L.P. Vidyarth (ed.), *Applied Anthropology in India*, Kitab Mahal, Allahabad.

Government of India. 1986. *National Policy on Education: Programme of Action*, Government of India, New Delhi.

Mishra, B.C. 1996. *Education of Tribal Children*, Discovery Publishing House, New Delhi.

Naik, J.P. 1975. *Elementary Education in India: A Promise to Keep*, Allied Publishers, Bombay.

Nair Gopinathan, P.R. 1981. *Primary Education, Population Growth and Socio-Economic Change*, Allied Publishers, New Delhi.

Patel, M.L. 1984. *Planning Strategy for Tribal Development*, Inter-India Publications, New Delhi.

Rajaiah, B. 1987. *Economics of Education*, Mittal Publication, New Delhi.

Rath, R. 1976. 'Problems of Equalization of Educational Opportunities for the Tribal Children', *Indian Educational Review*, IX (2).

Shah, G. 1984. *Economic Differentiations and Tribal Identity*, Ajanta Publications, Delhi.

Srivastava, L.R.N. (ed.) 1967. 'Tribal Education in India', in *Report of the National Seminar on Tribal Education in India*, NCERT, New Delhi.

16

Exclusion of Dalits in India

A Violation of Human Rights

N.A.D. Pal and D. Raja Kumar

On January 26th we are going to enter into a new life of contradictions. In politics we will have equality and in social and economic life we will have inequality ... We must remove this contradictions at the earliest possible moment or else those who suffer from inequality will blow up the structure of political democracy which has been so laboriously built up.

—Bharat Ratna Dr B.R. Ambedkar

The establishment of an egalitarian society is one of the cherished goals of our nation. This was clearly articulated by the national movement and enshrined in the Constitution of India. This entails equality and justice for all sections of the society without any discrimination on the basis of religion, caste, colour, race, gender, age, language and place of birth, etc. The Indian social structure itself is based on inequality because of the caste system. Due to this social exclusion, discrimination are being observed on the basis of ethnicity, gender, religion in general and caste in particular. Consequently, in India, certain communities like Dalits, tribes, backward castes and religious minorities experience a systematic exclusion from the mainstream of development and are denied equal rights and opportunities on par with others.

Concept

Dalits: A Scheduled Caste

The rigid caste system for centuries had divided the Indian society vertically. The institution of caste entails a hierarchical relationship on the basis of purity-pollution. Social hierarchy on the basis of caste system exhibits social discrimination and inequality. The Dalits are branded as out caste and accorded the lowest social status as they were placed at the bottom of the social hierarchy.

The term 'Dalit' is not a new concept. Etymologically, Dalit means oppressed or broken. Apparently the term Dalit was used in 1930s as a Hindi and Marathi translation of depressed classes by the Britishers. The word was also used by Ambedkar in his Marathi speeches ... with the same meaning. The Dalits are oppressed and depressed classes or broken people and they are now called as Scheduled Castes (SCs). In the past the SCs were also known as Atishudra, Avarnas, Panchamas, Chandalas or untouchables, etc., and were placed outside the Chatuvarna Vyavasta.

The concept of Scheduled Castes has been used in the Indian Constitution. The constitution does not give any specific definition for the term 'Scheduled Caste'. According to Article 341 of the Indian Constitution, the President of India is empowered to declare any group as Scheduled Caste and accordingly such groups is entitled for protection under various provisions of the Constitution.

Social Exclusion

The term 'exclusion' as a social phenomenon has found expression in different forms throughout the world. Social exclusion and discrimination are observed on the basis of ethnicity, gender and religion. In Indian society, basically, the caste and patriarchical systems are the sources of social exclusion. Social hierarchy of traditional social system in India exhibits inequality between the highest and lowest castes. As a result, the lowest and downtrodden communities are excluded from interaction and denied access to resources through iniquitous social arrangements.

The concept of social exclusion has been defined differently by social scientists. According to Buvinic (2005), social exclusion means "the inability of an individual to participate in the basic political, economic and social functioning of society and it involves the denial of equal access to opportunities imposed by certain group in society upon others". Narayan (1999) stated that social exclusion refers to the norms and process that prevent certain groups from equal and effective participation in the social, economic, cultural and political life of societies.

Noble laureate Amartya Sen observed that social exclusion leads to various kinds of deprivation (Sen, 1997). He mentioned that it leads to the impoverishment of human life through their casual consequences. The consequences of macro-economic policies such as poverty, unemployment and involuntary migration exclude the victims from economic, cultural and political activities. Institutional inequality and discrimination has been a pervasive feature of our society. In simple words, social exclusion can be termed as a process through which, certain groups are wholly or partially restricted from full participation in the development activities – social, economic, cultural and political life of societies.

Social Exclusion: Violation of Human Rights

The traditional Hindu social system is a unique system of inequality sustained by religious and ritual concepts of purity and pollution. The hierarchy built upon the caste system determines an individual's status and total life. In this kind of social organization, inequality is accepted as a fundamental value, which is against the very spirit of human rights. The caste system, the root cause and the very source of social exclusion, has given rise to the idea of high and low and untouchability.

The untouchables were placed at the bottom of the Indian society. Untouchability denied vast multitude of the population access to the very basic human life and evolved into the highest form of social exclusion in India. It is not simply a form of social discrimination but a systematic method of excluding the SCs from participation in the developmental process. The Dalits are still, being assigned menial jobs – scavenging and agricultural labour – and are being exploited by the upper castes. They are kept in physical and social isolation, which is against the principles of human rights. They are prevented from appearing before the caste Hindus and are subjected to various forms of humiliations. Their very presence, touch or contact is supposed to bring impurity.

This led to several inhuman practices such as segregation of Dalits in villages, denying them access to sources of drinking water, prohibiting them from entering temples, preventing them from praying Gods they revere and studying religious scriptures, denying them entry to educational institutions and hotels, etc.

Further, the SCs were being subjected to heaviest physical punishments, exorbitant taxes, highest fines and inhuman practices. Centuries of subjugation of Dalit people to all sorts of humiliation and indignities excluded them from mainstream of social life by denying basic human rights. The social system prohibited Dalits from skills, opportunities and means of production. It legitimized the violation of human dignity. The Indian social system, which was based on the principle of purity and pollution, was a system of inequality. This system denied equality before law, equal opportunities and equal protection of the law. Thus it was a source of social exclusion and thereby a source of violence and violation of human rights.

Every human being by virtue of being human is entitled to certain human rights for overall development. In simple sense, human rights means right to be human. But, in traditional India society, Dalits were denied minimum basic human rights such as right to life, right to equality, right to food, right to shelter, right to clothing, right to education, right to name, right to family, right to work, right to leisure, right to fair wages, right to decent working conditions, right to physical and mental health, right to property, right to access to natural resources, right to religion, etc. Thus, due to social exclusion, Dalits have been denied, in different forms, social, economic, cultural and political rights due to social exclusion.

Constitutional Concern: An Inclusive Strategy

The very Preamble of the Constitution of India itself is a clear strategy of inclusive policy. The framers of the Constitution under the leadership of Dr B.R. Ambedkar, the chief architect of the constitution, had visualized the evil consequences of caste system and its repercussions in the development of SCs, STs and other weaker sections of the Indian society. Therefore, they carefully drafted the Fundamental Rights and Directive Principles of State Policy for the protection and betterment of socially excluded sections.

Part III of the Constitution of India, which deals with Fundamental Rights, provides a number of safeguards and protections for the realization of equality and other basic human rights.

Article 14 guarantees to all citizens equality before law and equal protection of law. Article 15 prohibits social discrimination on the basis of religion, race, caste, colour, sex, place of birth, age or any of them. This Article prohibits both citizens as well as the state from making such discrimination with regard to access to shops, hotels, public resort, wells, tanks, roads and all places of public entertainment. It is a well-known fact that untouchability and other practices of discrimination are practised by a sizable section of upper castes. Article 15 is an inclusive strategy giving power to the state to prohibit the practise of untouchability and to provide the SCs access to all places and things. *Article 16 guarantees the right* to equal opportunity and access to public employment. Article 17 abolished untouchability in any form and declared it an offence and punishable legally.

Further, the Directive Principles of the State Policy under Part IV of the Constitution are the directives for inclusive strategy. Article 46 of the constitution directs that the state shall promote with special care the educational and economic interests of the weaker sections of the people and SCs and STs in particular. The state should protect them from social injustices and all forms of discrimination and exploitation.

Under the doctrine of protective discrimination, the Constitution of India provides reservations to the SCs and STs mainly in three fields as an inclusive strategy.

1. Under Article 15 (4): Reservations are provided to in educational institutions.
2. Under Article 16(4): Reservations are provided to SCs and STs in the appointments under the state.
3. Under Articles 330 and 332: Reservations are provided in legislative bodies (central, state and local bodies).

This inclusive strategy certainly enables the SCs and STs and so far other socially excluded sections to have a meaningful life with dignity by realizing all basic human rights.

Conclusion

Social divisions on caste basis have been a ubiquitous feature of the Indian society. The caste system is the very source of social exclusion and due to this certain communities in general and SCs in particular have been excluded from equal and effective participation in developmental process.

As a result of several constitutional guarantees, safeguards and legislative action and influence of modern values, the extent of social exclusion and discrimination has only lessened. But still the social exclusion and oppression of Dalits continues in several parts of the country in different forms and different proportions, particularly in rural areas where they are more in number.

To liberate Dalits from the iron clutches of social exclusion, their human rights have been protected and promoted through special policies framed for their upliftment. This provides Dalits with opportunities to participate in the mainstream development process. Dalits should be absorbed into this development exercise both as participants and beneficiaries and only then the establishment of a more egalitarian society committed to the principles of social justice and economic equality is possible. Accordingly, a sound inclusive policy with an effective implementation mechanism is the need of the hour.

Select References

Basu, Durga Das. 2008. *Introduction to the Constitution of India*, Wadhwa and Company, Nagpur.

Buvinic, Mayra. 2005. 'Social Inclusion in Latin America', in M. Buvinic and J. Mazza (eds.), *Social Exclusion and Economic Development*, Johns Hopkins University Press, Baltimore.

Singh, Dhian B. and Priyanka D. Singh. 1996. 'Socio-Economic Disparities and Violation of Human Rights: An Analysis', in B.P. Singh Sehgal (ed.), *Human Rights in India: Problems and Perspectives*, Deep & Deep Publications, New Delhi.

Narayan, Deepa. 1999. Bonds and Bridges: Social Capital and Poverty, Policy Research Working Paper 2167, Policy Research Department, Washington DC, World Bank.

Pandey, J.N. 2007. *Constitutional Law of India*, Central Law Agency, Allahabad.

Sen, Amartya K. 1997. *On Economic Inequality*, 2nd edition, Clarendon Press, Oxford.

Thorat, S. and Katherine S. Newman. 2007. 'Caste and Economic Discrimination: Causes, Consequences and Remedies', *Economic and Political Weekly* (special issue), Oct. 13, Mumbai, pp. 4121–24.

Webster, John C.B. 1999. 'Who is a Dalit', in S.M. Michel (ed.), *Dalits in Modern India: Vision and Issues*, Vistaar Publications, New Delhi.

17

Social Exclusion and the Disabled

S. Haranath, N. Indira Rani and P. Arjun

Social exclusion can encompass life and livelihood as a whole and can severely restrict participation in social services, welfare, security networks, consumer culture, political choice, bases of popular solidarity and also in the understanding of the circumstances surrounding the people at large. According to Kabeer (2000), social exclusion revolves around social identities of people or groups and reflects the cultural devaluation of people based on their identities. Caste, ethnicity, religion and gender are examples of such group identities. Thus, social exclusion is more than an economic phenomenon. It refers to the alienation of or 'leaving out' certain people within a society, which has consequences of social and cultural dimensions. It is argued that social exclusion based on identities is a process independent of income characteristics or the merit of individuals. The excluded are resorting to such strategies as low aspiration, despair, apathy, fatalism, pledging labour, migration, etc. Social exclusion is synonymous with the concept of marginalization and is related to poverty, unemployment, deprivation, withdrawal, underclass, alienation and disabled.

Disability not only creates but also increases poverty by increasing isolation and economic strain not just for the disabled person but for the entire family. This is the reason why people with disability tend to be the poorest of the poor in developing countries. Disability is also a development issue because it dehumanizes. It dehumanizes because, on the practical level, disabled people are left out of development planning and their voice is not heard in decision-making circles. On the philosophical level we know instinctively that if we deny the humanity of another, we ourselves are dehumanized (Coleridge, 1993). Crippling attitudes towards disabled people, compounded with institutional and environmental barriers, result in the blatant discrimination and exclusion of this most marginalized section. The aim of this paper is to discuss the issues of persons with disabilities (PWDs) as an excluded group and suggests strategies for their inclusion into the mainstream society.

According to a conservative estimate, there are about 600 million disabled people across the world, of these, 420 million (70%) live in developing countries. Eighty per cent of the disabled population in developing countries lives below the poverty line, which is a staggering 335 million disabled people. The hard facts collected by various agencies clearly indicate that one out of five of the poorest of the poor is a PWD. This means that 20 per cent of the poorest of the poor and most marginalized are PWDs.

These facts are also true of India. The following is an extract from a report prepared by the World Bank in 2007:

While official estimates of disability are low (around 2%), alternative estimates using better methods and more inclusive definitions suggest a higher incidence of disability (4–8%). The 2001 census found 21.91 million PWD (2.13% of the population), while the 2002 NSS round's disability estimate is 1.8 per cent of the population. The share of *households* estimated by NSS to have a disabled member was 8.4 and 6.1 per cent in rural and urban areas respectively (though this share seems high given the number of disabled individuals and survey results on their household size). Alternative estimates from a variety of sources suggest that the actual prevalence of disability in India could be easily around 40 million people, and as high as 80–90 million if more inclusive definitions of mental illness and mental retardation in particular were used. Just as importantly, the bulk of disabled people in India have mild to moderate disabilities. Out of this 80 per cent live in rural areas, and 49 million disabled people in India live below the poverty line.

According to a study conducted by McKinsey and Company, it is costing the nation as much as Rs. 72,000 crore per annum to care for its disabled citizens. Mostly it is the parents, siblings, friends or welfare organizations which bear the 'burden' (InfoChange, 2003). Despite the challenges, various UN and other agencies have collected a wide range of data over the years. Although presenting precise figures are not possible, the rough estimates have been backed by experience and are useful for planning. The following is a summary of key points from this data. General estimates provide that 10 per cent of the world's population is disabled persons including about 100 million people thought to be disabled as a result of malnutrition. Further research from different sources provides more specific data although it is subject to how disability is defined. In poorer countries, people with mild impairments may be severely disabled because of lack of opportunity for appropriate equipment or rehabilitation that can easily be provided for richer countries (e.g., providing spectacles, cleft palate operations). Hence, mild impairments are more visible and common. Conditions such as HIV/AIDs, mental health problems, tuberculosis and chronic malaria, female genital mutilation, psychological trauma in conflict and refugee situations can all give rise to permanent impairments that result in exclusion and discrimination. If these people are included, then the prevalence rates will be much higher.

The World Bank report (2007) gives the socio-economic profile of PWDs as follows:

The medical causes of impairments are rapidly changing in India – from communicable disease to non-communicable disease and accidents. Between 1990 and 2020, there is predicted to be a halving of disability due to communicable diseases, a doubling of disability due to injuries/accidents, and a more than 40 per cent increase in the share of disability due to non-communicable diseases. This reflects long term trends in fertility reduction and aging, increased road congestion, poor workplace safety practices, stubbornly poor nutritional outcomes, and progress in reduction of communicable diseases.

For some impairments (e.g., speech and hearing), illness and disease remain major causes, while for others such as visual disability age is a major driver. For mobility disabilities, the causes are shifting from a dominance of polio to a more mixed set of causes. For several disabilities, in particular mental illness and mental retardation, the causes of disability are often unknown, indicating the major knowledge gaps in current disability research.

Physical and mental impairments are compounded by poor education outcomes, and children with disabilities (CWD) have very high out of school rates compared to other children. Disabled people have much lower educational attainment rates, with 52 per cent illiteracy against a 35 per cent average for the general population. Illiteracy is high across all categories of disability, and extremely so for children with visual, multiple and mental disabilities. Equally, the share of disabled children who are out of school is around five and a half times the general rate and around four times even that of the ST population.

Disabled people also have significantly lower employment rates than average, and this gap has been increasing over the past 15 years. The large majority of PWD in India are capable of productive work. Despite this fact, the employment rate of disabled population is lower (about 60 per cent on average) than the general population, with the gap widening in the 1990s. People with certain types of disabilities, e.g., hearing, speech and locomotor disabilities, and those with disability since birth also have better chances of getting a job. Mental illness and particularly mental retardation have a strong negative impact on the probability of being employed, even in cases where such disabilities are not severe.

A recent adverse development is the decline in the employment rate of working age disabled people, from 42.7 per cent in 1991 to 37.6 per cent in 2002. The gap between the disabled and general population employment rates also widened for all education levels during the 1990s, and disabled people with lowest educational attainment have fared the worst.

The attitudes of communities and families in which disabled people live, as well as of PWD themselves, contribute to converting impairments into disabilities. Qualitative research into attitudes to PWD in India finds that households generally believe that disability is due to the "sins" of disabled people or their parents and hence deserved in large measure. Equally, communities have poor assessments of the capacities of disabled people to participate in key aspects of life, with negative opinions on the capacity of disabled children to participate in regular school and for disabled adults to be effective members of the workforce still dominant. Negative attitudes towards some disabilities are much more pronounced than others, with those with mental illness and mental retardation the most marginalized. Most worrisome, both families of disabled people and people with disabilities themselves often share the low opinions of their communities of the capacities of disabled people to be independent and productive members of society. This internalization of negative attitudes reinforces social marginalization.

Low educational attainment, poor employment prospects and stigma mean that PWD and their households are notably worse off than average. The households with disabled members are poorer and more vulnerable than the general population.

Different Groups of PWD and Vulnerable Situations

Disabled Women

Women with disabilities are at a particular disadvantage. In most countries women are discriminated against in terms of basic rights, livelihood, education, health care and employment. Therefore, while the disabled form a minority in any population, women with disability form a minority within a minority. They face multiple discrimination because they are women and disabled and triply so if they are from the developing world.

Poverty and limited opportunities define the status of women with disability. They are constantly confronting problems of access to housing and transportation. Society considers women with disability asexual. They are often denied their sexuality and control over reproduction. These barriers, coupled with unique challenges exclusive to women with disability – negative attitudes, lack of role models, lack of education and many forms of violence – prevent them from taking their rightful place in society.

People with Severe and or Multiple Disabilities

People with severe disabilities are those who require ongoing, extensive support in more than one major life activity in order to participate in integrated community settings and enjoy the quality of life available to people with fewer or no disabilities. They frequently have additional disabilities, including movement difficulties, sensory losses and behaviour problems.

People with Mental Illness

Although tremendous advances have been made in the understanding and treatment of mental illnesses, the stigma surrounding them persists. For example, people with mental illness may be blamed for their illness or viewed as lazy or irresponsible. Mental illness may be seen as less real or legitimate than physical illness, leading to reluctance on the part of policy makers and insurance companies to pay for treatment. Parents may be blamed for causing mental illness in their children. The public may shun people with mental illness and avoid living near them working with them, and socializing with them.

Disabled People in Disaster Situations

In any crisis be it man-made or natural disaster, PWDs are likely to feel the negative impact of the crisis more keenly than other citizens. Very often, their ability to cope and survive is completely dependent upon others, and the capacity of any family and community to support its disabled members is keenly tested in any disaster situation. Anecdotal evidence from acute emergencies suggests that disabled people suffer particularly high rates of mortality and morbidity. Frequently, the breakdown of support structures within a disaster-affected population further endangers the position of disabled people; they may lose their ability to function independently and with their dignity. Disabled people tend to be invisible to emergency registration systems. They are frequently left unregistered, which means they fail to receive their basic entitlements to food, water and clothing and their specific needs are not met either. This was painfully true of the post-tsunami scenario as well.

Disabled People in Institutions

Disabled people in institutions are usually the most 'invisible' of all disabled people. The nature of being institutionalized is such that the disabled people have very little control over their lives. It is well known that institutional environments do not do justice to the needs of PWDs nor do they offer sufficient protection against abuse, neglect and exploitation. Institutions invariably tend to be charity based and its residents are powerless and passive recipients of 'rehabilitation'. The involvement of family and the community in the life of disabled people in institutions is non-existent.

Inclusive Approach

Inclusion in its widest and real sense means change, acceptance, participation, decision-making, involvement, access, freedom, independence, empowerment, holistic development, contribution of PWDs in the development process and enjoying a life of dignity. Inclusion does not merely mean including PWDs in processes as passive recipients and providing them rehabilitation services. Inclusion is not just only about PWDs but also about all of us. While working with PWDs we need to adopt some models, and of the entire models, social model is very prominent.

Social Model

Social model sees disability as the social consequence of having impairment. The inequities faced by disabled people can only be overcome if society becomes inclusive. The social model of disability recognizes that some people have impairments that affect how they function physically or mentally. But these people are disabled by the barriers that exist in a society that does not take account of their needs. These barriers may be in the physical, organizational or personal aspects of society, for instance, stairs without ramps or lifts, information not available in large print/Braille or people's negative attitudes. The social model sees disabled people as having the same wants, needs and aspirations as non-disabled people. Disabled people should enjoy the same freedom and choices as enjoyed by non-disabled and be allowed equal responsibility in determining their life choices. Disability should not be seen as something invoking pity or in need of a cure. Indeed it may be viewed as a positive asset. Equality for disabled people is seen in the same light as equality for other under-represented groups. According to the social model of disability, it is not the individual medical condition but society which disables people with impairments. It is the way in which others react to disabled people that determines whether impairment will result in the exclusion of disabled people from mainstream activities. Coleridge (1993) argues that if able-bodied people did not react with horror, fear, anxiety, distaste, hostility or patronising behaviour towards disabled people, then there would be no problem. It is discrimination and prejudice that create the sense of being disabled. In this sense social interaction is the most important aspect of disability.

Recommendations

The following are recommendations to include PWDs in the mainstream society:

- Strengthen leadership of people with disabilities with special emphasis on disabled women. Facilitate women with disability in joining other women's movements.
- Conceptualize and create capacity building programmes that aim to fight exclusion and discrimination.
- Facilitate critical analysis of the structural causes of disability. The vicious cycle of poverty and disability can be prevented by using gender-sensitive participatory methodology.

- Campaign to create new laws and amend existing laws in India is the need of the hour, so as to be in keeping with the United Nations Convention on Disability. Ensure participation of disabled people in all discussions related to laws and policies that concern them.
- Influence policies, laws and the planning commission on appropriate allocation and optimal utilization of budgets on disability. Track budgets (both central and state) to understand allocation. This will consequently feed into and support our campaigns.
- Assess the implications for women and girls with disabilities of any planned action concerning disability including legislation, policies or programmes, as well as the implementation, monitoring and evaluation, in all areas and at all levels as a strategy so that women and men with disabilities benefit equally.
- Identify and address specific rehabilitation needs of PWD in extreme circumstances. Create community preparedness to cope with disasters and conflict situations. Campaign for appropriate protections mechanisms in disaster-related situations.
- Creating state- and national-level networks of Civil Society Organizations to create a common resource pool for disability work. This will give all disability organizations a common platform and greater credibility. This way of funding the disability work will avoid duplication of work and create greater impact.
- Build and support network/alliances of disabled peoples', organizations to claim their rights at district, state and national level. Promote the concept of inclusive development with other international development agencies.

References

Coleridge, P. 1993. *Disability, Liberation and Development*, Oxfam Publications, Oxford, produced in association with Action on Disability and Development.

InfoChange. 2003. News and Features, www.infochangeindia, accessed in July 2008

Kabeer, Naila. 2000. 'Social Exclusion, Poverty and Discrimination: Towards an Analytical Framework', *IDS Bulletin*, 31(4): 83–97.

The World Bank. 2007. *People with Disabilities in India: From Commitments to Outcomes*, Human Development Unit, South Asia Region.

18

Hindu Code Bill

A *Coup De Grace* to Systemic Gender Exclusion in India

C. Pradgna

Although gender is the only stratification found in any society, it has led to virulent forms of discrimination in combination with other forms of inequalities like race, class and ethnicity in different societies. In India, caste and gender together resulted in highly noxious and systemic inequality. Several approaches analysing gender inequality being available, this paper finds the perspective of exclusion offering useful insights for diagnostics of the interface between caste and gender and the remedial inclusive policy. The attempt is to show how Ambedkar's Hindu Code Bill displays the relational features of gender exclusion in India and the socio-legal programme incorporated in the bill envisages inclusion of women, who constitute nearly half of the population of the country.

In Indian society, sexuality, reproduction and social production are regulated by patriarchal values expressed through specific cultural metaphors. Overt rules existing in the society prohibit women from specific activities and deny equal rights to them. The sexist ideology expressed through various symbolic ways give messages of inferiority of women through legends highlighting the self-sacrificing, self-effacing pure image of women through the ritual practices that day in day out emphasize the role of woman as a faithful wife and devout mother. Brahmanical world view is grounded on the understanding that inequality is a natural phenomenon. The woman who is considered naturally inferior is bound to suffer exclusion from social, political, economic and religious realms. This totalitarian exclusion relegated women to a subhuman existence. The caste system ideologically provides justification for subordination of women. The relation between caste and gender is such that the emergence of caste system is through endogamy, which is nothing but the regulation of women's sexuality. And it is the caste system again that reinforces and rationalizes gender exclusion.

Ambedkar was the first to link caste with gender inequities. Even during his early student days in the Columbia University (1916), he analysed these connections between the genesis and perpetuation of caste system and oppression of women. The morbid fear of miscegenation can be observed in the strict rules of caste endogamy, control and regulation of women's sexuality and life choices in order to maintain the purity of castes. The Brahmanical system imposes stringent restrictions on women because purity of women is central to Indian patriarchy, as purity of castes is contingent upon it (Nanda, 2006: 21). Controlling women's sexuality, especially of those belonging to the upper castes, was the easiest way of making them not accessible to men of lower orders, which resulted in harsh rules and inhuman traditions like child marriages, withdrawal from productive work outside the home, forceful widowhood and even sati. The women belonging to the lower castes were turned into drudges and subhuman beings who suffer from triple oppression – as women, as belonging to the lower castes and poverty associated with inferior castes. We can understand that the entire ideology of *Pativrata* (worshipping the husband like god) is the mechanism of the Brahmanical ideology to ensure endogamy and purity of castes. Thus gender ideology legitimizes not only the structure of patriarchy but also the very organization of caste (Liddle and Joshi, 1986). Ambedkar's analysis displays that the system of caste determines the division of labour, sexual division of labour and division of sexual labour (Rege, 1995). Ambedkar was fully aware of the sufferings and marginalization of women along with men. In order to mitigate their sufferings, he consciously involved women in his prolonged struggle. Initially, mobilizing women for nominal recognition for their just cause, he ultimately come up with the Hindu Code Bill towards annihilating the root cause.

Hindu Code Bill

Realizing that the constitutional provision of caste equity in the public sphere would be meaningless without social provisions for women's equality in the private sphere, Ambedkar embarked upon the task of reconstituting the society. The Hindu Code Bill, which was introduced in the Constituent Assembly in 1947, encompasses total liberation to women. Although in the past there were some attempts to reform the conditions of women like Vittal Bhai Patel's bill of 1919, Dr Gour's modifications of Hindu Law in 1923, several committees in 1937 and the Rao committee in 1941, Dr Ambedkar in this legislation sought to bring about a revolutionary change in the society through liberation of women. This bill was referred to the select committee in April 1948 and the debate continued for more than four years, before it got killed. Among other things, the Hindu Code Bill mainly focused on four aspects:

- The abolition of castes as a necessary requirement for a valid marriage.
- The prescription of monogamy
- Right to divorce
- Right to property to women

By abolishing caste as a requirement for a valid marriage, Ambedkar wanted to show that castes are the artificial barriers for penetration and endosmosis of human relations; caste is not divine in origin. He maintained that caste is a device, designed to divide. In the words of Mahaveer Tyagi, "Marriages are the 'root cause' and elections are the 'fruit cause' for all these differences, because it is primarily at the time of the marriage that one enquires into the caste of the other. The next occasion when the caste of a person is enquired into, when one stands for election". Therefore, Ambedkar sought to destroy the existing Brahmanical social order through this clause, attacking endogamy and social exclusion of women.

Another important aspect of the Hindu Code Bill is the prescription of monogamy. The clause of monogamy is a direct attack on the male chauvinism, patriarchy and gender exclusion. The right to divorce removes the Brahmanical religious notions of sanctity around marriage and makes it a civil contract between man and woman. Finally, Ambedkar wanted to debunk the Brahmanical code that woman is man's property by giving woman the right to property. Thus by making daughter equal to son, he sought to tackle the economic exclusion. Through Hindu Code Bill, Ambedkar strived to provide the rights of women in regard to inheritance, in regard to marriage, in regard to property, in regard to divorce and in regard to personal freedom. The principles of the Bill are in harmony with the Constitutional philosophy of equality of sexes. It dealt with multiple deprivations – civil, economic, political and religious – that women suffered as a result of exclusionist ideology.

By pitching the conscience and reason against orthodoxy, Ambedkar was shaking the very structure, the very foundations of the caste society. In the Hindu Code Bill, we can clearly observe that he is continuing the legacy of Buddha and Phule in ennobling and elevating women, opening for them the way to liberty, to acquire dignity and to be human. Ambedkar says "To leave inequality between class and class, between sex and sex which is the soul of Hindu society untouched and to go on passing legislation relating to economic problems is to make a farce of our Constitution and to build a palace on a dung heap" ... Many great leaders, including women, opposed this Hindu Code Bill and though they pretended working for the emancipation of women, in reality, they were all against the complete liberation of women.

Representations as Inclusive Policy

The Constitution of India, in order to reconstitute the society on the democratic foundations of equality, liberty, fraternity and justice, incorporated legislations for equality between the sexes, enfranchisement and equal opportunity in all spheres of life. Road map is laid for a democratic and inclusive society through reservations as representations. Participation in political sphere, it was envisaged, would lead to equal participation in social as well as economic spheres. Ambedkar advocated for true and adequate representations. As a part of the democratic process, women are entitled to political representations based on their prorata (as the most agreeable criterion) of their population. Even after sixty three years of independence, the Indian government is grappling with the issue of providing 33 per cent reservation for women in Parliament and legislative assemblies. The Bill despite odds has been passed and presented to Rajya Sabha. "The demand for the number – 33 per cent (called critical mass) is partly based on research in seventies conducted in the United States on women's participation in business"(Gokhale, 2008). It has been shown that 30 per cent representation by minorities could significantly influence the majority verdict within a decision-making body. By this logic, women are treated as a minority though they account for nearly 48 per cent of the total population. Even this concessional percentage of representation is being opposed by the same Brahmanical obstructionist forces that siphoned away the juice out of the Hindu Code Bill. This exclusionist view still prevails in treating the rights provided in the Constitution to women as mere concessions. Several arguments inside and outside the Parliament reveal the attitude of treating women as a national liability.

The ongoing debate over Women's Reservation Bill essentially highlights the fact that women are being marginalized by the concept of public 'majority' morality, traditional patriarchal family structures and the oppressive elements of Brahmanical ideology, which pretends to allow certain concessions to women only to reinforce its dominance over their lives. We should not overlook the fact that when the question of reservations to socially and educationally backward classes is being discussed in the constitutional debates, the Brahmanical forces, including women leaders, rejected reservations to women. They stated that what they wanted was equality and not special privileges! A modicum of reservation was retained by a directive that there must be one or two women representatives on different bodies, as a result of persuasion by Ambedkar. Now this appears like a liberal gesture, those who opposed any change in the traditional position of women are supporting 33 per cent political reservation to women. Some even tossed up a tricky proposal (which now became a procedure in implementing reservations to OBCs in higher education institutions) to raise the seats in the parliament and state legislatures by 33 per cent, and offer them to women, keeping the present number intact for men. However, there is vehement opposition to the policy of representing all women, i.e., quota within quota in the state legislatures and parliament, even though such provision already exists in the Panchayats and local bodies. Barring a few (for their obvious reasons), all political parties and all women's organizations – Right, Left or Centre – are opposed to the provision of quota within quota. Apart from the apparent explanations for such a stand, there lies a complex interface between caste and gender that operates through structuring several hierarchies and overlaps.

Multiple Patriarchies and Layers of Gender

In Indian society, women are not a homogenous group but have multiple and layered identities derived from social relations within unequal, patriarchal, sexist and exclusionist caste system. Gender, caste, class and sexuality intersect each other, resulting in processes that position women as both collective and oppositional subjects. The existence of multiple patriarchies and many of their overlaps are integral to the Brahmanical social order: "... through history, there has been a Brahminical refusal to universalize a single patriarchal mode. Thus, the existence of multiple patriarchies is a result of both, a Brahmanical conspiracy and of the relation of the caste group to the means for production" (Rege, 2005). There are, therefore, discrete (specific to caste) as well as overlapping patriarchal arrangements (Sangari, 1995). These Brahmanical hierarchies prompt different experiences, perceptions and behaviours of women belonging to different castes and classes towards their common oppressions.

An analysis of practices of violence against women by caste shows that incidences of dowry deaths and violent controls and regulations on mobility and sexuality by the family are frequent among the dominant upper caste women, whereas Dalit women are more likely to face the collective and public threat of rape, sexual assault and physical violence at workplace and in public (Rege, 1994). In operation, inter-caste relations at local level often get mediated through a redefinition of gendered spaces. It can be seen that women belonging to upper castes react differently to different situations – sexuality and caste become hidden issues when they protest as 'citizens' during anti-Mandal, anti-reservation agitations declaring that they were against all kinds of reservation (including those for women), abetting their men during atrocities on Dalit men and women (Pimpri, Khairlangi in Maharashtra) as 'protecting' their honour as upper castes (Tharu and Niranjana, 1994). It is but obvious that Dalit women talk differently when their life experiences and assertions are different, and especially when their voice of difference gets inaudible (Guru, 1995; Rege, 2005).

Brahmanism an exclusivist ideology is left unchallenged in the women's movements led by the Left as caste is collapsed into class and in the case of the autonomous women's groups, caste is collapsed into sisterhood, built as a counterforce to patriarchal power. On the other hand, movements led by the Bahujan women (SCs, STs, OBCs and minorities) oppose all social inequalities that patriarchies are related to, embedded in and structured by Brahmanism. They need to talk differently to express their dissent against their exclusion from both the political and cultural arena (Guru, 1995). In order to address all these specificities of women's oppression, which cut across various castes, classes and religious communities, quota within quota becomes necessary. All women need to take part in the process of participation in the democratic agenda. And those who oppose, either intend to shoot from the shoulders of their women, as no political party is sure of getting an absolute majority in the era of coalition politics, or incapable of grasping the Brahmanical cultural politics. On the other hand, those political parties demanding for quota within quota also should be made accountable for the political space that they allow for women within their parties otherwise the bogey raised by them only indicates the unwillingness of male leaders to part with any part of political power.

In the discourse of representations, though numbers are important, it is ultimately how effectively these representations strengthen the movement for women's political empowerment and thereby lead to inclusion of women in the society that matters most. Despite many social movements against the caste system, untouchability and gender bias, social isolation and exclusion at various civil, political, economic and religious realms still continue. We have to keep track of the dynamics of exclusion in the changing society where one form of exclusion gets expressed overtly in certain situations blinding the other. As long as the customs and traditions that we follow are on the side of inequality that results in gender exclusion in combination with several forms of exclusion, the laws that are on the side of equality are meaningless. Hence, it is the responsibility of the civil society, especially the educated sections, to create social and moral consciousness and build a humane society.

References

Akerkar, S. 1995. 'Theory and Practice of Women's Movement in India', *Economic and Political Weekly*, 30(17): 2–24.

Ambedkar, B.R. 1917. 'Castes in India', in *Dr Babasaheb Ambedkar, Writings and Speeches*, Vol. I, Government of Maharashtra, Bombay.

——. 1947. 'The Hindu Code Bill', in *Dr Babasaheb Ambedkar, Writings and Speeches*, Vol. 14, Parts I and II, Government of Maharashtra, Bombay.

Gokhale, Sandhya. 2008. 'The Women Reservation Bill, Quota within Quota?' *Combat Law*, 4(6).

Guru, Gopal (ed.). 2005. *Dalit Intellectual's Collective: Atrophy in Dalit Politics*, Intervention I, Vikas Adhyayan Kendra, Mumbai.

——. 1995. 'Dalit Women Talk Differently', *Economic and Political Weekly*, Oct. 14–21, pp. 2548–49.

Liddle, J. and R. Joshi. 1986. *Daughters of Independence: Gender, Caste and Class in India*, Kali for Women, New Delhi.

Nanda, Meera. 2006. 'A Prophet Facing Forward', *Critical Quest*, New Delhi.

Rege, Sharmila. 1995. 'Caste and Gender: The Violence Against Women in India', in P.G. Jogdand (ed.), *Dalit Women*, Gyan, New Delhi.

——. 2005. 'Dalit Women Talk Differently: A Critique of 'Difference and towards a Dalit Feminist Standpoint Position', in Gopal Guru (ed.), *Dalit Intellectual's Collective: Atrophy in Dalit Politics*, Intervention I, Vikas Adhyayan Kendra, Mumbai.

Sangari, Kumkum. 1995. 'Politics of Diversity: Religious Communities and Multiple Patriarchies', *Economic and Political Weekly*, Dec. 23.

Sangari, K. and S. Vaid (eds.), 1989. *Recasting Women*, Kali for Women, New Delhi.

Tharu, S. and T. Niranjana. 1994. 'Problems for a Contemporary Theory of Gender in India', *Social Scientist*, Vol. 22, March–April.

19

Ambedkar and Women's Rights

B. Ratna Kumari

Weighed down by the oppressive hierarchies of caste, class and gender, rural Dalit women experience discrimination and untouchability in multiple spheres and these elements shape their lives. Like Dalit men, they bear the brunt of poverty and political subordination as well as the social stigma of caste. At the same time, they have to contend with the patriarchal power that makes them vulnerable not only to domination by upper castes but also by Dalit men. Two aspects of Dalit women's lives are of special concern: (1) the gendered division of labour that exposes women to specific forms of untouchability, and (2) sexualized forms of oppression.

Dalit women constitute less than 17 per cent of the total female population in India. According to the 2001 Census, 81 per cent of the Scheduled Caste (SC) women live in rural areas. The male/female ratio among SCs is 1000:922 (NIPCCD, 2005) because of this predominant caste polarization and globalization processes. In the case of SCs and STs women and men, the participation rates of female labourers are higher than for others as a whole. This is also evidenced in the higher work participation rates of SCs and STs people in all the census from 1961 to 2001 and this is due their being available for work at the lower level of skills, wages and literacy.

The Dalit women are thrice at disadvantage because they are enmeshed in problems typical of the backward areas such as poverty and have secondary status because of gender as well as being a member belonging to the depressed group. The government has introduced affirmative action policies with special budgetary allocations to help the underprivileged women in the past three decades. Even after the declaration of International Women's Decade (1975-85), the status of Dalit women was unable to create enabling conditions for the upward social mobility. Moreover, Dalits or untouchables in general and marginal women in particular remain at the bottom of most human development indicators due to gender, racial and caste discrimination and violence.

The main aim of this article is to discuss Ambedkar's views on women's human rights and emancipation. In this paper an attempt is made to

1. highlight Ambedkar's pro-woman stand and struggle against oppressive Brahmanical ideology and his alternative vision of conversion;
2. discuss Ambedkar and human rights of women and also constitutional rights guaranteed to women;
3. focus on the welfare and social security for women and Ambedkar's contribution in this field; and
4. deal with Ambedkar's struggle for Hindu Code Bill and women's rights in the family.

... *Na stree swatantramarhati* – meaning a woman is never fit for freedom in *Sanskrit* – is one of the many retrogressive statements made by the Manusmriti, the erstwhile political constitution of Brahmanical Hinduism. Hinduism imposed sanctions on women's liberty, which thus resulted in the most infamous girl (child) marriage, enforced widowhood, *Sati*, *Devadasi* (temple prostitutes) and dowry systems. Brahmanical Hinduism curtailed freedom of women in every aspect of life (Geetha and Rajadurai, 1998). Ambedkar observed this 'freedom curtail' as Brahmanical counter-revolution of Hinduism against women. He says, "The triumphant Brahminism began an onslaught on both the shudras and the women in the pursuit of the old idea, namely, servility, and Brahminism did succeed in making the shudras and women the servile classes: Shudras the serfs to three higher classes and the women to their husbands. Of the black deeds committed by Brahminism after its triumph over Buddhism this one is the blackest. There is no parallel in history for so foul deeds of degradation committed by a class of usurpers in the name of class domination" (Moon, 1989).

Manu was hardly tender to women than he was to Shudras. Women were not supposed to be free under any circumstances. In

Manu's opinion, their nature was to seduce men. A woman was never supposed to be fit to be independent. Study of Vedas and the performance of sacrificial rites were forbidden to them. Manu said that the ideal life of a woman was to be loyal to her husband, worshipping him as a god. Explaining reasons for this inhuman discrimination and hatred against women, Ambedkar rightly says, "Manu was the greatest opponent of the Buddhist religion. This is the secret of many inequalities, which he heaped upon women as he knew that the home must be put under restrain. And he did it. All responsibility for the decline and fall of women in India must be fastened upon Manu and not upon the Buddha" (ibid.).

Manu's laws were cruel towards women. He denied social justice to women and made 'injustice' a state law. Manu says, "Anger, lie, betrayal were created for women (Manusmriti Ch. 9–5–59). An infidel, immoral bad character husband indulging in adultery must be worshipped like God by his wife (Manusmriti Ch. 5–5–148). Woman must remain under the servitude of father in infancy, of husband in youth and of son in widowhood (Manusmriti Ch. 11–5–65). Killing woman or a Shudra is no sin".

For this reason, Ambedkar burnt 'Manusmriti' publicly on 25 December 1927 and gave a clarion call for women liberation. 'Emancipation of women' was the central theme of his speeches. "I measure the progress of a community by the degree of progress which women have achieved" (Moon, 1989).

'Ambedkarism' is today a living force in India, much as Marxism. It defines the ideology of the Dalit movement, to a large extent, as a broader anti-caste movement. Yet, just as 'Marxism' as a trend in the working class movement has to be distinguished from the actual theorizing of Karl Marx, so the urge to abolish the social and economic exploitation involved in caste and capitalism (which is the main significance of 'Ambedkarism' as a general movement ideology) must be distinguished from the complex grappling of an individual activist-theoretician with the interpretation of Indian reality.

Ambedkar's thoughts were not always consistent and did not (and the same of course can be said for Marx) fully resolve the problems he grappled with. But some themes stand out:

First, an uncompromising dedication to the needs of his people, the Dalits (as he said once in response to a Legislative Council claim that he should think as 'part of a whole' – 'I am not a part of a whole; I am a part apart'), which required the total annihilation of the caste system and the Brahmanic superiority it embodied.

Second, an almost equally strong dedication to the reality of India – but an India whose historical – cultural interpretation he sought to wrest from the imposition of a 'Hindu' identity to understand it in its massive popular reality.

Third, a conviction that the eradication of caste required a repudiation of 'Hinduism' as a religion, and adoption of an alternative religion, which he found in Buddhism, a choice which he saw as not only necessary for the masses of Dalits who followed him but for the masses in India generally.

Fourth, a broad economic radicalism interpreted as 'socialism' ('state socialism' in some versions; 'democratic socialism' in others) mixed with and growing out of his democratic liberalism and liberal dedication to individual rights.

Fifth, a fierce rationalism which burned through his attacks on Hindu superstitions to interpret even the Buddhism he came to in rationalistic, 'liberation theology' forms.

And finally, a political orientation that linked a firmly autonomous Dalit movement with a constantly attempted alliance of the socially and economically exploited (Dalit women and Shudras, 'workers' and peasants' in class terms) projected as an alternative political front to the Congress party he saw as the unique platform of 'Brahmanism' and 'capitalism'. However, Ambedkar, like Marx, did not spend the major part of his active life in research and writing, with political activism as a sideline; rather, the demands of leadership absorbed the major part of his time.

It would be worthwhile to repeat what Ambedkar said at the Depressed Classes Women's Federation at Nagpur on 20 July 1942: "Learn to be clean. Keep free from all vices. Give education to your children. Instill ambition in them. Inculcate in their minds that they are destined to be great. Remove from them all inferiority complexes. Don't be in a hurry to marry, marriage is a liability. You should not impose it upon your children. Unless financially sound they cannot meet the liabilities arising from marriage. Those who will marry must bear in mind that having too many children is a crime. The parental duty lies in giving each child a better start than parents has had. Above all teach each girl who marries stand upto her husband, claim to be her husband's friend and equal and refuse to be his slave."

Ambedkar thought Hinduism cherished wrong ideals and propagated wrong social life. He believed that inequality is the official doctrine of Brahmanism and so he inclined towards Buddhism claiming that Buddhism means casteless society based on equal rights, which encourages equality between women and men. That is why, he made his famous statement in Yeola Conference on 13 October 1935 that he was born a Hindu but he would not die a Hindu. To fulfil his dream, he had to wait for 20 years and on 14 October 1956, he publicly embraced Buddhism in Nagpur. By doing so he showed a path of liberation to women and Dalits. According to Ambedkar, conversion is an act of liberation against Brahmanical Hinduism. The reasons why Ambedkar embraced Buddhism can be summarized as follows:

1. Buddha was nearer to untouchables and women. He preached equality and social justice.
2. Ambedkar tried to prove that untouchables were Buddhists. In his thesis on the origin of untouchability, he made it clear that today's Untouchables were once Buddhists.
3. The religion of Buddha is morality and its founding pillars are liberty, equality and fraternity.

By advocating conversion, Ambedkar challenged the spiritual fascism of Hinduism and propagated social democracy for women and untouchables (Dalits).

Ambedkar and Women's Rights

Ambedkar was the pioneer in championing the cause of rights of Indian women and their social security. Rights of women are incorporated in the Indian Constitution. In the Constitution of India, the assurance of equality is explicit in the Preamble in the Fundamental Rights and the Directive Principles of State Policy sections. The Preamble assures of equality of status and opportunity and of social, economic and political justice. The constitution provides equal rights for its citizens under Articles 14, 15 and 16. This was a departure from the Vedic and Puranic ages in which the position of the women was equal with cattle. Article 14 guarantees equality before the law and equal protection of the laws. Article 15 forbids discrimination on the grounds of sex. Ambedkar being the chief architect of the constitution recognized the unequal position of women by empowering the state under Article 15(3) to make special provision for women. This Article provides for affirmative action and for protective discrimination to the women by the state. Article 16 provides for equality of opportunity relating to appointment to any office and prohibits discrimination on grounds only of sex. Article 23 prohibits traffic among human beings. Article 39 enjoins the state to direct its policy towards securing adequate means of livelihood for both men and women equally (in clause a), equal pay for equal work for men and women (in clause d). Article 42 directs the state to make provisions for securing just and humane conditions of work and for maternity relief. Never before in the history of India, had the "Hindu State" sanctioned these rights to women. The Brahmanical state treated them as second-class citizens. Ambedkar made women 'equal' citizens in India by including rights for them in constitution.

Ambedkar opined that man makes laws for mankind and law has not created man but man has created law for his own happiness. But he also cautioned, "Rights are protected not only by law but by the social and moral conscience of the society. If social contract is such that it is prepared to recognize the rights which law chooses to enact rights will be safe and secure. But if fundamental rights are opposed by the community, no law, no Parliament, no Judiciary can guarantee them in the real sense of the word (1936)". He warned that the effects of Brahmanism were not confined only to social rights, but also civil rights. The Golden Jubilee Republic message of the then President of India K.R. Narayanan reminds us this warning of Ambedkar. K.R. Narayanan said, "Fifty years after the adoption of our constitution, the plain truth is that the female half of the Indian population continues to be regarded as it was in the 18th, 19th centuries. In parts of rural India forms of Sadism seem to be earmarked for Dalit women". He reiterates Ambedkar's warning: "If things go wrong under the new constitution, the reason will not be that we had a bad constitution. What we will have to say that man is vile". To say in one word, it is a fact that whether they are implemented properly or not certain women-specific legislations have been passed to protect women from exploitation. Important among them are the Equal Remuneration Act, 1976, and the Maternity Benefit Act, 1961. Maternity benefit is also provided to women workers under the Employees State Insurance Act, 1948. There are certain family laws ensuring at least some 'equality' to women, that too mostly for Hindu women. Apart from personal laws, women can obtain maintenance from their husbands under Section 125 of Cr.P.C.

Ambedkar and His Contribution to Women Labour Welfare and Social Security

Ambedkar was the pioneer in the field of welfare of women and their social security. The "Labour Charter" propounded by him in the Viceroy Executive Council on 2 September 1945 later on became the basis and guiding principle of the labour welfare schemes in India. Dr Ambedkar became the labour member for the Viceroy Executive

Council on 20 July 1942 and resigned in June 1946. In November 1946 he was elected to the Constituent Assembly from Bengal. In August 1947, he was appointed by the Constituent Assembly on the drafting committee, which elected him as its chairman. Ambedkar was chosen as Minister for Law in independent India's first cabinet on 15 August 1947. On 11 November 1951, he resigned from the Nehru Cabinet accusing the government of apathy towards women, SCs and BCs. During the four years as a labour member and four years as a Minister of Law, he strived for the welfare and social security of women labour.

It was during his service as labour member (1942–46) that the Factories Act was amended to ensure holiday with pay and shorter hours of work and the Indian Mines Maternity Benefit Act was amended to provide larger benefits and better facilities to woman workers. It was during the same period that an important piece of legislation was passed to reduce to writing the terms and conditions of employment. It was also the period of constituting statutory welfare funds in the field of social insurance.

Tripartite approach, which today, is playing an important role in the evolution of labour policy and formulation of schemes, took institutional shape when Ambedkar was in office. The Coal Mines Labour Welfare Fund ordinance was promulgated on 31 January 1994 and the lean on underground employment of women was enacted on 1 February 1946 at the insistence of Ambedkar.

A bill to establish a fund to finance welfare activities of the labour in mica mines industry was introduced by Ambedkar in the Central Legislative Assembly on 8 April 1946. Similarly, the Indian Mines Act, 1923, was amended twice to construct and maintain crèches for the use of children where their mothers were employed and to provide separate bathing places for women labour.

During his tenure social security benefits for women were raised. Factories Act, 1934, was a mended thrice to ensure holiday with pay and reduced working hours. The measure enacted on 4 April 1946 provided for 48 hours a week and nine hours a day in lieu of then existing 54 hours weekly and 10 hours daily for perennial factories and 50 hours in place of 60 hours a week and 10 hours a day in place of 11 hours a day for seasonal factories. The work in excess of that was to be treated as overtime and payment made at double the normal rate (Remember those were the World War II days!).

A bill was suggested for a unified (social security) scheme comprising workmen's compensation, maternal benefit and sickness insurance on 6 November 1946 and it was passed on 19 April 1948. Ambedkar in the Central Assembly introduced the Industrial Employment (Standing Orders) Bill on 8 April 1946. A bill to constitute wage-fixing machinery for fixing and upwardly revising minimum wages in certain industries where labour was unorganized was moved by Ambedkar on 11 April 1946. (The bill was enacted into law on 9 February 1948 as Minimum Wages Act, 1948.) All these legislations have much benefited women labour. He always reminded labour that Brahmanism and capitalism are two enemies of the working classes in the country.

Ambedkar and his Struggle for Hindu Code Bill

The effects of liberalization and globalization on income distribution and poverty within and across different social groups and countries have been the subject of intense debate and critique (Cornia et al., 1987; Sen and Grown, 1987; Commonwealth Secretariat, 1989). Just as they did across countries, the effects of globalization have also differed across groups within countries differentiated by gender (alongside class, race and ethnicity). This is because, as pointed out, a discrepancy exists in almost all economies between women and men's access to resources, knowledge, ownership and control over assets, patterns of paid and unpaid work, the ability to generate income, educational patterns and political and economic power. In the case of Dalit women, Black women and marginal women, the impact of globalization on their pattern of culture, work, education, health and livelihoods (in terms of economic social and political status) made a great difference.

Feminist researchers and activists have repeatedly pointed to a variety of gender biases of structural adjustment and macro-economic stabilization policies since the mid-1980s. In fact, these critiques have to some degree found their place in policy making and international mandates such as the Beijing Platform for Action.

Ambedkar gave more of his time to working for the upliftment of the status and lives of the women in India. This was especially in the case of providing Hindu women equal rights along with men. A select committee of Ambedkar and 16 others prepared a report to amend and codify certain branches of Hindu law. For this purpose Hindu Code Bill was suggested. Ambedkar strived for this bill to enact as legislation in his tenure as Law Minister. The aim of the Hindu Code Bill was to codify "the rules of Hindu law scattered in numerous decisions of the High Court and of the Privy Council, which form a bewildering mostly to the common man and give right to constant litigation". The select committee reports on Hindu Code Bill contained nine parts: Preliminary, Marriage and Divorce, Adoption, Minority and Guardianship, Joint Family Property, Succession, Maintenance and Miscellaneous. This was presented to the Constituent Assembly of India on 12 August 1948.

Prior to the Hindu Code Bill another bill prepared by Hindu Law Committee was introduced in the Legislative Assembly on 11 April 1947. This bill more or less resembled the report prepared by Dr Ambedkar's Committee. The house on 17 Nov 1947 had also adopted a motion for the continuance of the bill. Dr Ambedkar remarked, "I am orthodox, but the right to divorce must be given to women (1946)". He knew how the Hindu women suffered under the laws of Manu, Brahmins and upper caste men. However, SC/ST women did not come under this bill. Yet, Ambedkar was the only one to propose such bill in the Parliament, even though he was an untouchable. He even remarked later that none of prominent Hindu (women) leaders were really interested in the social progress of their women. Brahmanical politicians opposed the Hindu Code Bill. It hung in the air due to divided convictions.

The results of Ambedkar's endeavours ended in a terrible failure. It was a failure, not for Ambedkar's commitment and his attitude towards women, but for the suffering Hindu/non-Dalit and upper caste women. Ambedkar's intention to reform Hindu religion was defeated. The bill was dropped (rejected). This movement could have been a moment of sadness for Ambedkar, but actually it helped him to free himself to serve his people in a better way by resigning from Nehru's cabinet.

Sticking to his ideals Ambedkar made his greatest sacrifice by stating, "For a long time I have been thinking of resigning my seat from the Cabinet. The only thing that held me back from giving effect to my intention was the hope that it would be possible to give effect to the Hindu Code Bill before the life of the present Parliament comes to an end. I have agreed to break up the bill and restricted it to marriage and divorce in the fond hope that at least this much of our labour may bear fruit. But even that part of the bill has been killed. I see no purpose in my continuing to be a member of your cabinet" (statement in parliament when he resigned from Nehru's cabinet on 11 October 1951).

This resignation took place because of the liberal Brahmanical approach of the then Prime Minister Pandit Jawaharlal Nehru. The reason for Babasaheb's behaviour was the result of his versatility and humaneness. Babasaheb had in mind at all times the thought of the liberation of Hindu women. After resigning he wrote a great article titled 'The Rise and Fall of Hindu Women'. In this article, he established the fact that Buddhism strived for the women's liberation and to counter Buddhism, Manu made his Brahmanical law as 'Law of the State' to suppress women.

Conclusion

Ambedkar led women and Dalit protest movements on a number of occasions in his lifetime. He addressed many women conferences. His message to them was clear: "you must abolish your slavery yourselves. Do not depend for its abolition upon God or a superman. Your salvation lies in political power and not in making pilgrimages and observance of fasts. Devotion to scriptures would not free you from your bondage, want and poverty. Your forefathers have been doing it for generations, but there has been no respite or even a slight difference in your miserable life in any way. Like your forefathers, you wear rags. Like them you subsist on thrown-out crumbs; like them, you perish in utter slums and hovels; and like them you fall easy victims to diseases with a death rate that rages among poultry. Your religious fasts, austerities and penances have not saved you from starvation (1947)".

He set the goal very clearly to Indian women by saying, "unless the Indian people secure political power and this power does not concentrate in the hands of the socially suppressed section of the Indian society, it is not possible to wipe out all social, legal and cultural disabilities from which this section suffers" (1947). Ultimately, these initiatives brought by Ambedkar led to women's emancipation and development in our country.

References

Ambedkar, B.R. 1946. *Who Were the Shudras? How They Came to be the Fourth Varna in the Indo-Aryan Society*, Thacker and Co., Bombay.

——. 1936. 'Annihilation of Caste', in Vasant Moon (ed.), *Dr Babasaheb Ambedkar: Writings and Speeches*, Vol. 1, Education Department, Government of Maharashtra, Bombay.

——. 1936. 'Slavery (in the Civilized British Government under the cloak of Brahmanism)', reprinted as Jotirao Govindrao Phule (ed.), *Dr Babasaheb Ambedkar: Writings and Speeches*, Vol. 3, Education Department, Government of Maharashtra, Bombay.

——. 'Annihilation of Caste', in Vasant Moon (ed.), *Dr Babasaheb Ambedkar: Writings and Speeches,* Vol. 1, Education Department, Government of Maharashtra, Bombay. p. 49.

——. Ambedkar, 'The Evolution of Provincial Finance', p.75.

——. 1947. 'States and Minorities: What Are Their Rights and How to Secure Them in the Constitution of Free India', (first published in 1947) in *Writings and Speeches,* Vol. I, p. 408.

——. 1987. *Dr Babasaheb Ambedkar: Writings and Speeches*, Vol. III, Government of Maharashtra Education Department, Bombay, p. 444.

Geetha, V. and S.V. Rajadurai. 1998. *Toward a Non-Brahmin Millenium: From Iyothee Thass to Periyar,* Samya, Calcutta.

Jadhav, Narendra. 1993. *Dr Ambedkar: Economic Thought and Philosophy*, Sugawa Prakashan, Pune.

Joshi, Shashi. 1989. 'The Untouchables: Children of India's Ghetto', in *Writings and Speeches,* Vol. V, Government of Maharashtra, Bombay, pp. 115–16.

Moon Vasant. 1989. 'The Communal Deadlock', in *Dr Babasaheb Ambedkar: Writings and Speeches,* Vol. I, Government of Maharashtra, Education Department, Bombay, pp. 355–80.

20

Women Employment in Media

A Case Study of Andhra Pradesh

D.V.R. Murthy and G. Anita

Caste composition in the media has not been considered a serious issue for many years. However, with the exception of researchers like Robin Jeffrey who made an effort to document the absence of Dalits in the Indian language print media, there has been no attempt made to seriously examine or address this issue (Anand, 2005). However, Jeffrey (2000) did not probe the caste/communal composition of non-Dalit journalists – how many Brahmins, Jats, Yadavs, Muslims, Nadars are working in the media. Nevertheless, Uniyal (cited in Anand, 2005) in *The Pioneer*, who looked up the Accreditation Index (1996) of the Press Information Bureau (PIB) in New Delhi, observed that of the 686 accredited correspondents listed in it, as many as 454 bore their caste surnames, and of them as many as 240 turned out to be Brahmins, 70 Punjabi Khatris, 44 Kayasthas, 26 Muslims with as many Baniyas, 19 Christians, 12 Jains and 9 (Bengali) Baidyas. I checked out the case affiliation of 47 of the remaining 232 correspondents at random. None of them turned out to be a Dalit either.

The media institutions in the country, being privately owned and controlled, mostly by extended families, recruit people without giving much importance to the caste composition. Chandra Bhan Prasad, a Dalit journalist has been writing a weekly column on the Dalit issues in a mainstream English language newspaper for over four years. However, others who work in the media do not reveal their caste background for the reasons not known to us.

Media Scenario in India

With the growth of the new communication technologies such as cable television, computers, the Internet, satellites and telecommunications, information dissemination has been increasingly influencing the Indian society (Singhal and Rogers, 2001:19). Consequently, the mass communication channels in India have been expanding. With the availability of new technology, newspaper publication has increased manifold and India publishes more daily newspapers than any other country in Asia, covering a range of languages and cultural diversity that is unparalleled in the world (Singhal and Rogers, 2001:54).

By the turn of 2006, there were over 55,000 newspapers and periodicals published in ninety-three languages. In respect of radio broadcasting, there were only six stations of All India Radio (AIR) located in metropolitan cities in India at the time of independence (Kohli, 2006). The AIR has 110 primary channels, 30 Vividh Bharthi stations, 75 local radio stations and 4 FM channels (Kohli, 2006). The FM radio has grown in the country with over 40 stations. By 2006, broadcasts of AIR programmes were heard in 110 million households in 24 languages and 146 dialects. Further, television too has grown immensely. About 50 per cent of India's population regularly watches television networks like Zee TV, STAR TV, SONY, CNN, BBC and many other channels that broadcast various programmes. In particular, the federal state of Andhra Pradesh has witnessed a media boom. Newspapers with chain editions, FM radio stations and new television networks continuously supply news and entertainment programmes. For example, *Eenadu,* the largest circulated daily has 23 chain editions. While the television networks such as *ETV2, Gemini* and *TV9* telecast 24-hour news. Because of the proliferation of mass communication channels, the employment of women in various mass media channels is growing.

In this context, this chapter makes an attempt to ascertain the caste composition of women journalists working in the media organizations in Andhra Pradesh.

Study Sample

In view of the purpose of the study, we proposed to use a survey method while adopting a purposive sampling method to collect data pertaining to the study. Since the study focuses on working media women, we in a preliminary survey listed out the total number of media women working in three mass communication channels, i.e., newspapers, TV networks and radio network, that come under the study across state. It was found out that a total of 145 women were working in different organizations located in Hyderabad, Visakhapatnam and Vijayawada. Many newspaper publications such as *Eenadu, Andhra Bhoomi, Vaartha, Deccan Chronicle and The Hindu* as well as All India Radio AM and FM stations and the headquarters of TV networks are located in these three cities. Once the total number of women working in these three cities in different media organizations was available, we, keeping in view the objectives of the study, decided to administer a questionnaire. We approached the respondents with a request to fill the questionnaire. The process of data collection took three months, i.e., November, and December 2006 and January 2007. Since the authors worked as journalists, before they found it easy to approach the respondents with a questionnaire who in turn obliged by filling the questionnaire.

Results

A total of 127 respondents have come up for the final analysis. Out of these, 178.7 per cent respondents were from Hyderabad while 14.2 per cent were from Visakhapatnam and the remaining 7.1 per cent were from Vijayawada. Of these 127 respondents, 88 (69.3%) were from print media, while 39 (30.7%) were from electronic media such as radio and television networks.

Table 20.1

Distribution of Respondents by Their Organization

Media Organization	*f*	%
Newspaper		
Andhra Bhoomi	2	1.6
Andhra Jyothi	8	6.3
Deccan Chronicle	3	2.4
Economic Times	3	2.4
Eenadu	11	8.7
Indian Express	4	3.1
Prajasakhti	8	6.3
Times of India	8	6.3
The Hindu	15	14.8

Cont'd

Cont'd

Vaartha	8	6.3
Visakha Samcharam	1	0.8
Visalandhra	6	4.7
Television channel		
ETV	18	14.2
ETV2	7	5.5
TV9	14	11.0
Excel	1	0.8
Radio		
All India Radio	10	7.9
Total	127	100

However, the 69.3 per cent respondents who represent print media. belong to twelve newspapers, while 30.7 per cent journalists representing electronic media belong to four TV channels and one radio network, i.e., government-controlled AIR. Out of the eighty-eight print media journalists, majority (11.8%) of the respondents were from English daily, *The Hindu* followed by Telugu daily *Eenadu* (8.7%). Four other dailies, namely, *Andhra Jyothi, Prajasakhti, Times of India* and *Vaartha* were in the next place. In respect of television networks, ETV (14.1%) had more percentage of respondents followed by TV9 (11.0%), ETV2 (5.5%) and Excel media (0.8%). With regard to radio, all the respondents belonged to AIR (Table 20.1).

Age

The age distribution of the respondents shows that more than half of them (54.4%) were in the age group of 21–30 years, while 31.5 per cent were in the group of 31–40 years, 10.2 per cent were in the 41–50 years group and 3.9 per cent were in the 51–60 years group. The minimum and maximum ages of the respondents were 21 and 59 years, respectively. The mean age of the respondents was 31.29 years, while the median age of the respondent was 28 years. One interesting finding is that the respondents working in TV channels were below 40 years, with majority of them being in the age group of 21–30 years (Table 20.2).

Table 20.2

Distribution of Respondents by Age from Different Media Organizations

Media organization	21–30 (Years)		31–40 (Years)		41–50 (Years)		51–60 (Years)	
	f	%	*f*	%	*f*	%	*f*	%
Newspaper								
Andhra Bhoomi	—	—	2	5.0	—	—	—	—
Andhra Jyothi	—	—	4	10.0	3	23.0	1	20.0
Deccan Chronicle	2	2.9	—	—	1	7.7	—	—
Economic Times	3	4.3	—	—	—	—	—	—
Eenadu	5	7.3	4	10.0	2	15.4	—	—
New Indian Express	3	4.3	1	2.5	—	—	—	—
Prajasakhti	5	7.3	1	2.5	2	15.4	—	—
The Hindu	6	8.7	7	17.5	2	15.4	—	—
Times of India	8	11.6	—	—	—	—	—	—
Vaartha	—	—	6	15.0	2	15.4	—	—
Visakha Samcharam	—	—	—	—	—	—	1	20.0
Visalandhra	1	1.4	4	10.0	1	7.7	—	—
Television channel								
ETV	17	24.6	1	2.5	—	—	—	—
ETV2	6	8.7	1	2.5	—	—	—	—
Excel	—	—	1	2.5	—	—	—	—
TV9	11	16.0	3	7.5	—	—	—	—
Radio								
All India Radio	2	2.9	5	12.5	—	—	3	60.0
Total	69	100	40	100	13	100	5	100

N = 127

Designation

This study found that the respondents represented varied jobs in the mass media and yet broadly they belonged to reporting, editing, script writing, producing and anchoring of the programmes. Further, though the nature of the job apparently was the same, their designations varied depending upon the organization in which they worked. Therefore, the distribution of respondents by their designation shows that nearly 30 per cent of them worked as subeditors, 18.9 per cent as reporters in print media and 17.3 per cent as copy editors, working for various television channels. In the senior media women category, 6.2 per cent were senior sub-editors. Next place is occupied by radio jockeys (3.9%) of FM radio in AIR. Chief subeditors and reporter/subeditor are 3.1 per cent each and senior reporters and principle correspondents are 2.4 per cent. Proof readers and transmission executives are 1.6 per cent each. Remaining categories like bureau chief, news editor, programme associate, station director, script writer, photographer, senior announcer, senior feature writer, feature editor, copy editor/news reader, radio producer are 0.8 per cent each (Table 20.3).

Table 20.3

Distribution of Respondents by Their Designation

Designation	*OC*	*BC*	*SC*
Bureau chief	—	1	—
Chief subeditor	4	—	—
CGO operator	1	—	—
Copy editor	19	4	—
News reader	1	—	—
Photographer	1	—	—
Principle correspondent	3	—	—
Producer	1	—	—
Programme associate	—	1	—
Proof reader	1	1	—
Radio jockey	4	1	—
Rep/sub	3	1	—
Reporter	19	—	—
Senior reporter	3	—	—
Feature writer	1	—	—
Senior subeditor	8	—	—
Senior announcer	1	—	—
Station director	1	—	—
Subeditor	35	3	1
Transmission executive	3	1	—
Trainee reporter	2	—	—
Feature editor	1	—	—
News editor	1	—	—
Total	113	13	1

N=127

Caste

In Indian society, caste hierarchy plays a predominant role and all individuals belong to some caste or the other. These castes for the purpose of government records are divided into three: open category, backward category and scheduled category or caste. Open category represents the upper castes in social hierarchy. Table 20.4 shows the caste distribution of the total 127 respondents. of these, 89 per cent belonged to open category, 10.2 per cent to Backward Class (BC) category and only 0.8 per cent belonged to Scheduled Castes (SCs). Media women who belonged to BCs were found working in all types of media organizations. Two women each who belonged to BCs were working in ETV, *Eenadu* and AIR. One each were with ETV2, Excel, *New Indian Express, Times of India,* TV9, *Vaartha and Visaalandhra.* The lone SC woman was with *Visaalandhra.*

Table 20.4

Distribution of Respondents by Caste in Different Media Organizations

Organization	*OC*		*BC*		*SC*	
	f	%	*f*	%	*f*	%
Newspaper						
Andhra Bhoomi	2	1.8	—	—	—	—
Andhra Jyothi	8	7.1	—	—	—	—
Deccan Chronicle	3	2.7	—	—	—	—
Economic Times	3	2.7	—	—	—	—
Eenadu	10	8.8	1	7.7	—	—
Indian Express	3	2.7	1	7.7	—	—
Prajasakhti	8	7.1	—	—	—	—
Times of India	7	6.2	1	7.7	—	—
The Hindu	15	13.3	—	—	—	—
Vaartha	7	6.2	1	7.7	—	—
Visakha Samacharam	1	0.9	—	—	—	—
Visalandhra	4	3.5	1	7.7	1	100
Television channel						
ETV	15	13.2	3	23.0	—	—
ETV2	6	5.3	1	7.7	—	—
TV9	12	10.6	2	15.4	—	—
Excel	—	—	1	7.7	—	—
Radio						
All India Radio	9	7.9	1	7.7	—	—
Total	113	100	13	100	1	100

N=127

Duration of Service

Table 20.5 explains the duration of service of the respondents. Interestingly, three-fourths (74.8%) of the respondents had less than five years of experience, while 20.5 per cent had worked for 6–10 years. Moreover 4.7 per cent respondents had more than 11 years of experience (Table 20.5). Further, all the respondents from BC had less than 15 years of service and one respondent from SC community had less than 10 years of service (Table 20.6).

Table 20.5

Distribution of Respondents According to Duration of Service

Duration of Service	*f*	*%*
Below 5 years	95	74.8
6–10 years	26	20.5
11–15 years	4	3.2
Above 15 years	2	1.5
Total	127	100

Table 20.6

Distribution of Respondents by Duration of Service

Duration of Service	*OC*	*BC*	*SC*
Below 5 years	28	9	—
6–10 years	40	2	1
11–15 years	23	2	—
Above 15 years	22	—	—
Total	113	13	1

Discussion

Caste is often examined as one of the variables in sociological studies in India as it impacts the social life. Caste plays a crucial role in society and social interactions. It helps an individual to better her/his life and may also deprive her/him of an opportunity. Therefore, the present study has made an attempt to ascertain the respondents' background in the profession of journalism or media. The study found out that 89 per cent of the respondents belonged to open category (OC), while ten per cent of the respondents were from BCs. Obviously, majority of the respondents from the OC are increasingly opting for a job in private sector because of the increasing number of jobs that are available for those with education and motivation. In the 1990s, India witnessed a fundamental shift from Nehruvian socialist style to a free market policy in which the country opened its economy to foreign investment and foreign consumer products. Thus, in the process, the role of the government had shrunk in the economy and laissez-faire policies prevailed (Singhal and Rogers, 2001:45). Because of the opening of the Indian economy there was a proliferation of television networks in 1990s, and nearly 300 television channels have been launched in the country so far. Because of these reasons, more number of women seek jobs in the media organizations, which are in private hands. The nature of media ownership is also seen as a reason for employment of open category people. Normally, an open category candidate is considered to belong to the privileged section of society. Because of the market-driven forces, the recruitment policy aims at selling the media product. Vilanilam (2005: 36) observes recruitment of media workers is also not always above board. Even in old, established newspaper organizations, young men and women belonging to the privileged sections are recruited and given in-house training aim at making them seekers of a product rather those upholders of serious socio-economic principles. Business management principles are more in application in such situations because what counts in media organizations these days is profit.

For instance, corporate media organizations such as *Eenadu*, ETV, ETV2, *Deccan Chronicle, Andhra Bhoomi, Times of India, Economic Times* and *The Hindu* recruit people who are young, urbane and educated. Moreover it can also be seen in this study that 54.4 per cent of the respondents were in the age group of 21–30 years. These people who are young graduates work in the urban-centric and glamorous television channels. It can also be seen from the study data that nearly half of this age group of people were working in popular and lead television channels such as ETV2 and TV9, which are news channels catering to the information needs of the people in the state. ETV2 and *TV9*, which are 24×7 television channels, offer jobs to the young, educated and dynamic women to work in the channels as news reporters and anchors. Furthermore, a number of universities in the country are also offering journalism programmes. It can also be observed from this study that 64.6 per cent of the respondents have journalism degrees or certificates. Also, the TV networks and newspapers have in-house training schools for the young people. Furthermore, one of the reasons why Dalit issues may figure less in the media is because of under-representation of these people in media organizations. Further research into this aspect has to be taken up to ascertain the exact reason.

References

Anand, S. 2005. 'Covering Caste: Visible Dalit, Invisible Brahmin', in N. Rajan (ed.), *Practising Journalism: Values, Constraints, Implications*, Sage Publications, New Delhi, pp. 172–97.

Jeffrey, R. 2000. *India's Newspaper Revolution: Capitalism, Politics and the Indian-Language Press* 2nd edition, Oxford University Press, New Delhi.

Kohli, V. 2006. *Indian Media Business*, 2nd edition, Sage Publications, New Delhi.

Singhal, A. and E.M. Rogers. 2001. *India's Communication Revolution: From Bullock Carts to Cyber Marts*, Sage Publications, New Delhi.

Vilanilam, J.V. 2005. *Mass Communication in India: A Sociological Perspective*, Sage Publications, New Delhi.

21

Social Exclusion of Women in India under Colonialism

Implications to the Modern Society

U.V. Shakkeela

The imposition of inhuman practices and restrictions like widow burning, enforced widowhood, child marriage and absolute illiteracy has been the means by which social exclusion of women has been maintained for long. Colonial period happened to be tumbled on these issues and for that reason had to pioneer a process that attempted a redefinition of women's role in Indian society. It is manifested through a number of reform movements that sprang up during that period. A perusal of the debates and discussions on women-oriented issues conducted in the colonial period may throw some light on the motives in which the parameters of women's inclusion are rooted. This in turn will help to make out the processes and prospects of women's inclusion/exclusion of the present.

The campaign against *sati,* a custom of self-immolation of women in the funeral pyre of their husbands, was the first notable move towards their integration into the mainstream society. Raj Ram Mohan Roy's name is intimately associated with the crusade against sati. Through his writings, he tried to unveil the pseudo-sanctity and the cruelty involved in the custom. The crusading spirit that he showed in the public debate on *sati* installed him as the champion of women's rights and this may not encourage a person to probe more into his views regarding women's emancipation.

A close analysis of his writings about women's issues reveals that he wanted a change in their existing position without delineating much from the outdated concepts in the *sastric* texts. The discourse on *sati* was not a debate based on a new conception of individual rights of women, it was rather a contest to decide the legitimacy of *sati* expounded in different law books. Throughout the writings about *sati*, Ram Mohan Roy refuted the pro-*sati* arguments by quoting holy books, which gave women the option of widowhood. Although the arguments and counter arguments were about women, they were not treated as individuals having a self of their own; they were not even a party to the discourse. On the contrary, women became the centre on which tradition was debated and reformulated. In fact, as Lata Mani argued that it was not women who were at stake but tradition (Mani, 1998).

Debate on *Sati*

Ram Mohan's ambiguity towards the government's decision to put an end to the practice of *sati* made one doubtful about his crusading spirit against *sati*. Bentinck who banned *sati* found Ram Mohan's attitude to the question disappointing. The last minute ambiguity of Raja Ram Mohan Roy on the legislation of *sati* was a surprise to the British government who in fact decided in favour of legislation on a popular ritual like *sati* based on the arguments of Ram Mohan. He is said to have opined that while the English were contending for power, they deemed it politic necessary to allow universal toleration and to respect our religion. He is considered as a great supporter of women's rights as revealed through his pamphlets, which were full of passionate pleas for the end of inhuman treatment of women. Any serious reader of the pamphlets might get the impression that he would not allow the practice of *sati* to prolong it for a day. It is hard to believe that Ram Mohan who himself witnessed the predicament of woman who decided to commit *sati* and his own helplessness in convincing her and her relatives of the futility of the practice, turned his back when the time came for its immediate demise.

In a passionate appeal, he criticized the sufferings of women under polygamy and the plight of the penniless widows. Based on the rights of women as provided by the ancient law givers, Ram Mohan in his tract on "Modern Encroachments on the Ancient Rights of Females According to the Hindu Law of Inheritance", wrote: "All the ancient law givers unanimously award to a mother an equal share with her son on the property left by her deceased husband in order that she may spend her remaining days independently of her children" (Kontala, 1975). If that had been the case, what was the initiative taken by Ram Mohan in that direction? Except the rhetoric on women's issues, he did practically nothing in women-related issues. He appealed to the slow, official mind of the government, which was afraid to interfere with the religious convictions of the people (Joy, 1933).

Ram Mohan's perception of women's emancipation did not go beyond the existing notion of their position in the society. He acknowledged the views expounded in *sastras* in perceiving his conception of women's emancipation of nineteenth century. He pleaded with the menfolk to change their attitude towards women so that they can enjoy respect and dignity. Thus, Ram Mohan's idea of the new femininity grew out of his somewhat paternalistic view of society. In other words, women can aspire for their right to dignity and self-respect as far as men stood for it.

Widow Remarriage

If one takes into consideration the campaign for widow remarriage in a wider perspective, the inherent ambiguity of the reformers including Vidyasagar was visible both at the ideological and practical level. Considering the stance of other contemporary radical *Brahmos* of his time towards widow marriage, Vidyasagar was not that much enthusiastic in defying the social imposition on women. The first widow marriage organized on 7 December 1856 under Vidyasagar was celebrated with all the paraphernalia and ritual usually observed in a Hindu marriage. Indeed, one cannot criticize Vidyasagar's attempt to make the widow marriage as conventional as possible in view of the extreme hostility of the opponents of the widow remarriage and the deep-rooted patriarchal nature of the Indian society. Nevertheless, one should bear in mind the fact that Vidyasagar subverted a number of standard orthodox arguments for his own purpose (obviously for widow marriage) through his mastery over *sastras* and interpretative logic. He did not show any such gimmick in eliminating the drawbacks inherent in the Hindu marriages as a social institution. In other words, Vidyasagar did not declare war with social institutions, but with social aberrations (Tripathi, 1998).

The consent of brides was rarely sought in the marriages organized under the reformers. The elders or male relatives arranged it all and brides as usual were not consulted, in spite of the fact that in many of the widow remarriages, brides were mature young women who were capable to take decision themselves. It was reported in an autobiography entitled *Atmakatha* written by Gurucharan Mahalonobis (1833–1916) that Vidyasagar was quite pleased when he heard that the author married a widow who has known to him for some time before the marriage. Vidyasagar was reported to have commented that an intelligent person should never agree to marry someone she/he had never seen. Vidyasagar might have appreciated the idea but never put the idea into practice in his lifetime. In imposing the restrictions on his widowed daughter, Vidyasagar was no different from any typical orthodox father of his period. In fact, there is no report that Vidyasagar ever asked his daughter to defy the traditional rules, the emancipation which had been a major impulse behind his entire reform drive (Bipan Chandra, 1998).

All the nineteenth century reformers who spearheaded the campaign for women's emancipations shared the ambivalence showed by Vidyasagar towards social issues. They made a life and death struggle for the cause of women but the social injunctions evolved out of its prejudices based on caste and custom turned them into scapegoats. Their helplessness was clearly visible the way they reinterpreted the issues regarding women. The compromise they made with tradition, caste and customs in their struggle for women's emancipation seemed to be ridiculous. Emulating the example of Vidyasagar in Bengal, Vishnusastri Chiplunkar organized the first widow marriage in 1896 at Bombay. As in Bengal, the marriage was conducted with all the rites involved in a traditional Hindu marriage. He himself married a widow after the death of his first wife. Although a staunch supporter of widow marriage, he was not in favour of eliminating completely the prejudices, which crept into the social structure in the name of tradition. On the other hand, he was an ardent proponent of tradition. In the opinion of Uma Chakravarti, he was the best example of the new–western educated *Brahmna* proponent of tradition (Chakravarti, 1998). The same ambivalence was showed by Debendranath Tagore, the founder of *Tatwabodhini Sabha* and a very well-known social reformer from Calcutta. He supported the widow marriage in theory without being involved actively in the campaign for widow marriage. This passive attitude, according to Meredith Borthwick was partly due to Debendranath's ambivalent attitude towards such issues but also because he felt that such things were personal and so it was not his place to intervene (Borthwick, 1977).

Mahadev Govind Ranade amply demonstrated the differentiation between personal and public in the matter of social reform in his marriage with an 11-year-old girl in 1873. It was his second marriage at the age of thirty-one after the death of his first wife. Ranade was a well-known public figure and a strong supporter of widow marriage in Maharashtra. He could have inspired hundreds and thousands of young men to break voluntarily the ban on widow marriage had he married a widow in 1873. All his friends were under the impression that he would set an example by marrying a widow. Contrary to the expectation of the leading reformers, he succumbed to the pressure of his family. In fact, he promised to his father that he would not marry a widow. He consoled himself and convinced others by arguing that things had already gone too far and withdrawal at that stage would mar the girl's future, break his father and cause general unhappiness. One can agree fully with S. Natarajan who wondered whether to marvel more at the concessions, which Ranade could make, to prejudices, or at the ingenuity and perseverance with which he turns the concessions in his favour (Natarajan, 1962). Ranade was of the view that *sati*, infanticide, suicide, etc., in the name of religious tradition had to be abolished with a single stroke in the name of humanity. Widowhood was not mentioned among these issues as the one, which deserved to be abolished as an act of humanity. His stance of compromise with tradition was quite clear when he stressed the point that the victory for social reform would come not by mere modification of social institutions in a formal way under duress but by changing the hearts of individuals (Parvate, 1963).

The problem of sustaining a widow's virtue was considered as one of the chief motive forces for the attempt to legalize widow marriage. For that reason, the sexuality of widow remained the focal point of much of male discourse in the nineteenth century (Chakravarti, 1998). Reformers in general considered women as morally weak. Vidyasagar himself was more concerned with the austerities of widowhood, which might lead widows to prostitution and foeticide and thus bring disgrace upon the families of their fathers, mothers and husbands. Reformers were in general anxious about the disgrace that the young widows would bring to the family through licentious activities. Very few men tried to reveal the consequence of these activities on widows' lives. Abortions many times terminated in the death or murders of pregnant widows by relatives. These abortions, deaths, and murders seldom came to light. Pregnant widows were frequently taken away to distant places and then such crimes were committed. It is a fact that a number of widows were thrown out of their homes to the street. The parental and natal families considered a widow a responsibility after the death of her husband. If she were allowed to stay at home after the demise of the husband, she had to do all menial work at the home. In one instance, an 11-year-old Brahmin widow worked 18 hours a day on domestic jobs for the family and as a cook and general drudge at a hotel for Hindus run by her brother-in-law.

Domestic labour was considered as a means to restrain women from immoral pursuits or illicit sexual activity. The burden of the household drudgery was such that many widows ran away from home and took to prostitution or worked as domestic servants and as cooks. Since widows have been hailed as the epitome of upper caste norms, the reformers were more concerned with the consequences of unregulated sexuality that might turn the widows to a potential agent of 'dehinduization', prone to running away with low caste or Muslim men (Sangari, 1999).

Instead of causing disgrace and infamy to the families by keeping her as a widow, marriage was taken as the best option. Vidyasagar observed that as long as that salutary practice was deferred, so long would the crimes of prostitution, adultery, incest and foeticide flow on in an ever-increasing current – so long would family stains be multiplied (Vidyasagar, 1975). These words revealed his anxiety about the consequence of the repressed sexuality of the widows. This concern of Vidyasagar was well explained by Uma Chakravarti as she considered this anxiety was common among the male reformers. The undertone to the widow remarriage movement was the anxiety about the unchannelled sexuality of the widow and this went along with the humanitarian rhetoric of the need to alleviate the miseries of the child widow (Chakravarti, 1998).

Age of Consent and Child Marriage

Child marriage was one of the issues that came up for discussion. A perusal of the observations made by eminent men on infant marriage revealed that they did not want to make any major breakthrough in the existing system for the benefit of women. Ranade's stance towards raising the age of consent reveals his reluctance to disregard the existing law of the age of consent, which set the age of consent for girls as ten. He defended the stance thus: "even the limit of twelve years is too low; but as that age has been laid down generally in the code, I do not seek to raise the limit above that age. Of course, it is very desirable on medical grounds that every effort should be made to put off the connection at least till fourteen" (Ranade, 1901). By suggesting 14 years as the limit, Ranade was not trying to deviate from the prevailing norms on the marital age of girls. His suggestion in favour of keeping 14 years for girls as the limit for consent was very much in line with the practice followed among the respectable families during the period. He pointed out that the practice in all respectable families is superior to the age prescribed in the law and efforts should be taken to bring up the law to the limit of practice in respectable families. This prudent stance on a much-debated issue indeed helped to keep Ranade aloof from critics who believed firmly in the relevance of *sastric* laws in purging the society out of its existing evils. Ranade's observation about the practice among the respectable families and his call for the introduction of the said practice as a remedy to the early marriage of girls seemed ridiculous and less convincing as his own experience provided a picture contrary to his observation.

Although from a respectable family, 32-year-old Ranade had given in to the pressures of his adamant father who arranged an 11-year-old maiden for his son. As a matter of fact, his in-laws, who offered an 11-year-old girl to a 30-year-old widower, also belonged to these so-called 'respectable families'. If one can take his wife's account about the proposed marriage as testimony, Ranade was found to be very much particular about the respectability of his bride's family than about her age, when he decided to succumb to the pressures of his father for a second marriage. Ranade sent a message to his father thus: "you are going to force me to marry. But please do this much. Do not select a girl from this place. She should be from another place and she should belong to a family of good repute. It should also be ascertained that the other antecedents and connections of the family are decent … Our relationship is likely to be a little more happy if a good family is given preference over good looks" (Deshpande, 1963). Quite a number of reformers wanted to do away with the custom of early marriage as it affected the education of young men. Some of the men stood against the abolition of child marriage as it deprived young men of the pleasures of romance and the lack of it may induce them to go astray.

Though the bill was introduced to raise the age of consent of girls with the intension of rescuing women from the pernicious custom of early marriage, the entire debate in public was centred on men and the apprehension about the possible infringement of their privilege of being men once the law had come into effect. Many dailies and weeklies expressed their concern of the effect of this law on men. These periodicals stood for an amendment to the harsh provision of the act in favour of lighter one. *Andhraprakasika*, a Telugu weekly, commented in its 28th February, 1891 edition: "The law is proposed to punish a person who has sexual intercourse with his wife less than 12 years before she has attained puberty. This punishment should be simple imprisonment for a short period or a fine." *Swadesmitran's* opinion was also found in line with the *Andhraprakasika*. It remarked that if the government passes the bill with amendments necessary for lessening the punishment and constituting offence committed by a husband not a case of rape, but one of immature coition, all the present opposition will gradually disappear. Ranade also shared the general apprehensions of the public about the stringent provision in the proposed law against the guilty. In the fifth national social conference held at Nagpur in 1891, Ranade remarked, "All reasonable apprehension can easily be set at rest by enacting certain provision by which the offence can be made a non-cognizable one, and permitting bail in cases where the offence does not result in serious crimes" (Chintamani, 1901). While the European medical practitioners highlighted the effect of infant marriage and subsequent childbirths on the physique of girls, the social reformers in general glossed over this aspect of infant marriage and discussed the early marriage of girls from a broad social spectrum. As the president of the fourth social conference held at Calcutta in 1890, Dr Mahendra Lal Sircar strongly criticized the child marriage by emphasizing its detrimental effect on the Hindu race as a whole. He exhorted the audience "... the Hindu race consists at the present day, if you would pardon me for the very strong expression that I am bound to utter, by virtue of this very blessed custom, of abortions and premature births. Are we all born at the proper time? If the laws of physiology are true, and I believe they are eternal verities, then every man and woman born of parents of such tender years as ten or twelve years for a girl and fifteen or sixteen for a boy must be pronounced to be either an abortion or a premature birth" (Chintamani, 1901).

Reformers in general supported the abolition of child marriage. But the growing consciousness of nationalism in the late nineteenth century compelled the reformers to compromise with their liberal views on women's emancipation for the sake of nationalism. Vishnusastri Chiplunkar vehemently attacked the social reformers for espousing the cause of social reform when the country was being ruined by foreign rule. He held that inwardly there was nothing wrong with our society and that neither religion nor social customs like child marriage or caste had anything to do with India's decline as alleged by the social reformers (Sangari and Vaid, 1979). Bal Gangadhar Tilak also shared the same view of Chiplunkar. Tilak criticized social reformers like Ranade for espousing the cause of women. Commenting on the agitation against the ban on child marriage and especially about the controversy on Hari Mohan Maite vs Phulomani case, Tilak writes:

> Hari Mohan could not be held responsible for intercourse with his eleven year old wife, an intercourse which neither he nor almost the whole of India, nor even her legislators, had reason to think to be dangerous to life or likely to cause grievous hurt to life. His rashness and negligence then made him guilty, and these consisted in nothing else than his having omitted to think on the possibility of his wife having an unusually dangerous organ and his having omitted to speculate upon the comparative dimension and vigour of the sexual organs of both either before or at time of his marriage or intercourse ... but how may men do, or even can, think and speculate as above? (Wolpert, 1991).

This verbal abuse from a respected nationalist like Tilak showed the increasing aversion of social leaders towards woman-related issues.

Views of Women Reformers

Women social reformers like Parvati Athavali, Ramabai Ranade and Pandita Ramabai Saraswati involved actively in the process of eliminating the social exclusion of women during the colonial period. Although their perception about the nature of inclusion of women differed at times with that of men, it did not rupture radically from the traditional notion. Separate curriculum for girls as envisaged by Pandita Ramabai for the uplift of women served only to perpetuate the already existing subordination of women. The attempt to make a refined woman through education was but an effort to fill up the old wine in a new bottle. It did not intend to provide individuality to her, nor did it help to bestow on women a wider social role. As observed by Meredith Borthwick, it implied some changes in domestic arrangements, but not necessarily in social relationships. The primary duty of the woman towards her husband continued as per the accepted norm.

Since women are intimately connected with the domestic realm from time immemorial, the programme of education envisaged for them was arranged in such a manner as not to disrupt the domestic chores. The unpaid domestic labour of women was a common ideal of family life. In fact, it was elevated to the status of dharma or religious duty and neglect of which was treated as unfeminine. The belief was so deep rooted that women reformers like Pandita Ramabai reaffirmed the importance of domestic duties by providing a separate curriculum for women. While discussing the proper conduct for women in her *Stri Dharma Niti,* she reminds women of the importance of domestic duties. She notes that a woman does not attain the rank of a housewife merely by virtue of being born into the female sex or by becoming a wife. It requires careful training. According to her, a woman should help her husband in everything and the most essential of these tasks, which also carry the greatest responsibility, are the domestic duties (Kosambi, 2000). The importance that Ramabai provides for domestic duties in her *Stri Dharma Niti* shows that she intended moderate education, which would equip a woman to run the house successfully. The kind of education prescribed for women did not encourage them to seek avenues outside the domestic realm. The past time other than domestic work, in the opinion of Ramabai, is to read moral philosophy, stories containing spiritual knowledge, the *sastras* that are within one's comprehension, newspapers, etc.

A only limited spiritual knowledge is allowed for women as the idle mind of a woman may go astray and break the boundaries prescribed for women. If she neglects her domestic duties for her spiritual uplift, she would be branded as dangerous and deviant. Ignorant of the underplay of the patriarchal structure, the women reformers extolled the virtues of a devoted wife. Pandita Ramabai says, 'It is a woman's primary duty to assist her husband in every act, every time by following his inclinations. Only the women who act accordingly may properly be called their husband's better halves. Women who do not help their husbands in any way are not called saintly' (Kosambi, 2000). In a society where both men and women compete to provide justification for the subordination of women to patriarchal structure, there is no space for the development of individuality! The problem lies in the fact that change was being sought within the patriarchal system. So it is not surprising that these reforms in reality did not go beyond the traditional boundaries of definitions of women, a point of view accepted by women activists themselves (Pande and Kameshwari, 1987).

The life of those women reformers who fought for emancipation of their fellow women is according to the ideology prescribed for women in a patriarchal structure. In her widowed state, Pandita Ramabai's life was different from that of the millions of fellow country women as she resumed the occupation of a lecturer on the education of women within a few months of the death of her husband (Dyer, 1974). But she did not give up the lifestyle of an orthodox widow of her period. Padmini Sengupta who wrote the biography of Pandita Ramabai was of the view that Ramabai, immediately after her husband's death, must have had her hair shorn, though not shaved, and thus remained with short cropped hair, wearing the widows' white sari but no ornaments in her life. Ramabai Ranade's reminiscences provided the picture of a girl who was nurtured by her husband's blissful paternalism. Throughout the memoirs she presented herself as a devoted, obedient wife to her husband.

Conclusion

It is generally accepted that the colonial discourse on women relieved them from their pathetic state of existence. In fact the East and the West conversed for some time on women's inclusion based on their concept of women and assigned them a place which the men, both the British and the Indian, found befitting to a woman in the society. Nevertheless, the discourse on women in the colonial period improvised/improved her present state in the society. The importance of the ideology of women's inclusion during the discourse shifted very often from the western concept of women to the concept upheld by *sastric* texts. Ultimately, the *sastric* interpretation of women gained currency. All the prominent exponents of emancipation made hair-splitting efforts to place the arguments in *sastric* texts to repudiate the irrelevance of spurious customs in practice against women. Obviously, the new woman evolved out of the discourse based on *sastras* did not deviate much from the old concept of woman. In fact, the objectives of women's inclusion during the colonial period were determined within the four walls of the patriarchal society. The views of a handful of women reformers fell on the margin and were rather reduced to a cry in the wilderness.

The debate on women's inclusion/exclusion initiated under colonialism continues in the post-independence period with new dimensions adding to it. The scope of women's empowerment has widened with more issues coming up for discussion to define their space in the public and private. The question of women's control over natural resources, involvement in decision-making process and economic independence are some of the key factors driving the women's empowerment movement. She enjoys more freedom than what she had 50 years ago. She is able to enter into almost all walks of life, which were considered previously as male domains. Both government and non-governmental organizations are contributing a lot to eradicate the social exclusion of women. This is evident from the measures taken to ensure her participation in politics by reserving a certain number of seats for her from the village level to the apex body of law making. Poverty eradication programmes, imparting legal awareness and introducing new laws and amending existing laws to ensure gender equality are some of the ongoing measures to bring women into the mainstream. Viewing from this backdrop, the programme for the social inclusion of women has travelled a long way from the nineteenth century.

The inherent ideology that guided the male/female reformers in the process of the social inclusion of women in the colonial period to some extent influences the ongoing scheme of women's empowerment. Patriarchy, female sexuality, caste and customs are still very much relevant in establishing gender equality. It is true that social anomalies like sati, widowhood, infant marriage and female illiteracy are no longer posing as strong impediments towards women's inclusion into the mainstream society, but it is still not time to pen off these issues from the agenda of women's empowerment. In spite of its barbaric nature, sati occurs sporadically.

The experience of a woman who actively participated in the movement against child marriage indicates the strong rooted belief of people in it. She was gang raped with the support of prominent men in the village. The court left them scot-free under the pretext that high caste men never rape a low caste woman! It not only makes us realize the strangle hold of outdated customs on modern Indian society but also the misogynic attitude of men who interpret the law. It is very true that one of the chief means by which the colonial society strove hard to terminate the exclusion of women is legislation. Quite surprisingly, modern India is still not able to rectify this malady in favour of women's inclusion. An interview conducted among 106 judges to know their opinion about atrocities on women reiterates the above mentioned observation. Their opinions are given below:

(a) 48 per cent supported wife beating under special circumstances.
(b) 74 per cent upheld that women are responsible for family integrity.

(c) 68 per cent argued that dress code causes sexual atrocities on women.
(d) 34 per cent emphasized the cultural aspect of dowry.

Judiciary is not the only field where women's rights as human beings are subordinated. Women have to appeal the sense justice of men to be treated equal in the economic sector. Tremendous achievement has made in eradicating female illiteracy and 72.1 per cent of girls between the age group of 6–17 years are school going. When they approach the job market, gender discrimination raises its head in the form of low remuneration. The case is pathetic in the case of women who work in the unorganized sectors. Their work incurs not even half the amount that men usually get for the same work. This is, to a great extent, due to the reluctance of patriarchal/patrilineal society to give away the privileges that it bestowed on men.

In fact, the processes towards social inclusion of women begin by curtailing step by step the privileges hitherto enjoyed by men. The Indian society began the work a century before and the greatest achievement is that the process did not encounter an abrupt end under any circumstances. This indicates the determination of Indian society's aspiration for progress. At the same time, the discrimination still in operation shows that the underlying principles that perpetuate women's exclusion are not dealt properly enough to give space for women.

References

Andhraprakasika. 1891. Telugu Daily, February 28.

Borthwick, Meredith. 1977. *Keshub Chundra Sen: A Search for Cultural Synthesis*, Minerva Associates, Calcutta.

Chakravarti, Uma. 1998. *Rewriting History: Life and Times of Pandita Ramabai*, Oxford University Press, New Delhi.

Chandra, Bipan. 1998. *Writing Social History*, Oxford University Press, New Delhi.

Chintamani, C. Yajnesvara (ed.), 1901. *Indian Social Reform*, Vol. 2, Thompson and Company, Madras.

Deshpande, Kusumavati. 1963. *Ranade: His Wife's Reminiscences*, Publications Division 1, New Delhi.

Dyer, Helen S. 1974. *Pandita Ramabai: The Story of Her Life*, Morgan and Scott, London.

Joy, Charles R. (ed.), 1933. *The Father of Modern India*, The Unity, Chicago.

Kosambi, Meera (ed.), 2000. *Pandita Ramabai: Through Her Own Words, Selected Works*, Oxford University Press, New Delhi.

Kotnala, M.C. 1975. *Raja Ram Mohan Roy and Indian Awakening*, Gitanjali, New Delhi.

Mani, Lata. 1998. *Contentions Traditions: The Debate on Sati in Colonial India*, Oxford University Press, New Delhi.

Natarajan, S. 1962. *A Century of Social Reform in India*, Asia Publishing House, New Delhi.

Parvate, T.V. 1963. *Mahadev Govind Ranade: A Biography*, Asia Publishing House, New Delhi.

Pande, Rekha and J. Kameshwari. 1987. "What is Women's History" Proceedings of A.P. History Congress, Nagaram, pp. 173-175.

Sangari, Kumkum and Sudesh Vaid. 1979. 'Recasting Women Essays in Colonial History', in S.P. Sen (ed.), *Social and Religious Reform Movements in the Nineteenth and Twentieth Centuries*, Institute of Historical Studies, Calcutta.

Sangari, Kumkum. 1999. *Politics of the Possible: Essays on Gender, History, Narratives and Colonial English*, Tulika, New Delhi.

Tripathi, Amales. 1998. *Vidyasagar: The Traditional Modernizer*, Bikalpa, Calcutta.

Vidyasagar, Eshwar Chandra. 1975. 'The Practice of Widow Marriage among Hindus', *Nineteenth Century Studies* (Quarterly), Bibliographical Research Centre, Calcutta.

Wolpert, Stanley A. 1991. *Tilak and Gokhale: Revolutions and Reform in the Making of Modern India*, Oxford University Press, New Delhi.

22

Rammanohar Lohia's Social Philosophy and Inclusive Politics

An Assessment

K. Sekhar and N. Babavali

Rammanohar Lohia (1910–1967) was one of the founders of the Indian Socialist Movement and was acknowledged as the most lively and thoughtful among its leaders (Krishna, 1968). As a Socialist ideologue, persistent rebel, sensitive individual and sagacious thinker, he keenly observed the social phenomena and developed a distinct thought that was holistic and people-oriented. Apart from Ambedkar and Periyar he was the only politician who in no uncertain terms described the caste system as a discriminatory mechanism that enslaved and disempowered a vast mass of population. He was the first socialist thinker who refused to have his mental horizon limited or dominated by the ideas drawn from the west or the Soviet Union (Limaye, 1978). His writings reflected his ardent wish to bring about social transformation through political action, and because of his comprehension of the dynamics of caste and its inextricable link with politics, he always wanted the fight against caste to be grounded in the ideology of the socialists. The first general elections witnessed an intense political rivalry between the three major political parties: (1) the Congress who carried the baggage of freedom struggle, (2) the Communists who drew inspiration from the Bolshevik revolution and fired the imagination of the nascent Republic with their armed struggle in Telangana, and (3) the Socialists a breakaway group of the

Congress comprising some committed and able leaders whose agenda displayed concern for the public.

Although the Socialists stood second in terms of the percentage of votes secured, the seat tally of the Communists was next to that of the Congress. The unimpressive electoral performance of the Socialists could be attributed to lack of strategy, disunity among the leaders and poor election management. Since then there have been numerous splits in the Socialist movement. The splits became a usual feature of the Socialist camp and no wonder the Indian Socialist movement, which always held promise for the progressive and left of the centre forces, earned the dubious distinction of experiencing more number of splits than the seats won.

After a series of splits and mergers, which were a routine feature of Indian socialism, in 1956 Lohia formed a new Socialist Party, which lost badly in the second general elections. In order to rejuvenate the party, he put forward a triple programme of caste policy, language policy and price policy (Mehrotra, 1978). Since then he embarked on a tireless mission of exposing the diabolical nature of caste and explored methods of political action to enable the excluded groups to empower themselves. In view of the growing importance of affirmative action and political empowerment of the weak his views on caste, women, Adivasis and minorities need to be revisited and reexamined.

Lohia on Caste

Lohia attributed the decay in the Indian society to the ills of caste system accumulated for thousands of years and dismissed the hoary traditions, gross superstitions, social and religious complexes constituting a bog of history, as 'slime' (Lohia, 1964). He argued that ills like corruption, nepotism and non-adherence to truth sprang from the dysfunctional aspect of caste system and called them the traits of Dvija leadership (ibid.). In an essay titled "Towards the Destruction of Castes and Classes", he remarked that caste is the most overwhelming factor in Indian life and those who deny it in principle also accept it in practice.

He further says, "Life moves within the frontiers of caste and cultured men speak in soft tones against the system of caste, while its rejection in action just does not occur to them. If they are reminded of their acts, which are in such unbelievable conformity with caste, they point out with indignation their thought and speech. ... Who knows if the strange split between thought and action, characteristic of Indian culture more than of any other, is the result predominantly of caste" (ibid., p. 79).

This comment is an indictment on the hypocritical veneer that the elite chose to wear. Caste is the harshest reality of Hindu social life; yet paradoxically people belonging to the upper or privileged castes never acknowledge even its existence though least hesitant to reap the benefits that flow from it. While discussing the preponderance of the Dvijas in all the political parties he found no difference between the Congress, Communist or Socialist that have one big area of national agreement, whether by design or through custom, and that is to keep down and disenfranchise the Shudra and the woman who constitute over three fourths of our entire population (ibid.).

The infamous incident of the then President of India Dr Rajendra Prasad publicly washing the feet of 200 Brahmins at Banaras attracted the wrath of Lohia who was anti-caste and staunch opponent of Dvija dominance. He criticized the President's act as retrogressive, incest of the mind and inbreeding in the realm of ideas and felt that it denigrated the highest office of the land. In the same breath he flayed Nehru for extolling the President's act as Brahmanical spirit of service (ibid.). Lohia saw inter-caste marriages as a tool to break the barriers of caste and wanted Dvija men to marry Shudra women contrary to the practice of Shudra men aspiring to have connections with the twice-born by marrying their women (ibid.). He deplored the attitude of the Socialists who believed that caste fades away once economic inequality is done away with and said that they failed to comprehend economic inequality and caste inequality as twin demons that have to be killed (ibid.). The ties of marriage and friendship are primarily responsible for the unity among the Dvijas (ibid.).

The visionary in him foresaw the dangers of emulation of the Dvijas by the Shudras as he rightly gauged the behavioural change of the Sudra once in office or preeminent position. He lamented that the successful Shudra tries to perpetuate himself by having recourse to dirty methods and in the meantime fail to achieve broadness of outlook (ibid.). This observation has come totally true as his disciples like Mulayam Singh Yadav have thrown their mentor's principles to wind by aligning with controversial businessmen and film personalities and the greatest disgrace is the hobnobbing of the fiery Socialist George Fernandes with the Sangh Parivar – the most obscurantist force which would have been the sole target of Lohia if he were alive.

Lohia's *magnum opus* "Marx, Gandhi and Socialism" gives one a feel of depth of his knowledge of the major doctrines and international affairs. Delineating the interface of class and caste, he pointed out that Marx was not aware of the amazing capacity of class to turn into caste (Lohia, 1964). He wrote, "Caste is immobile *class*. Loosening caste is a class. This slow swing between class and caste has so far been a law of human history. In India alone congealment into caste has taken place, elsewhere it is various degrees of freezing and unfreezing" (Lohia, 1963, xxxiii). In numerous essays and training camps he drove home the point that the *numero uno* position of the advanced among the Shudras in some states was bound to be usurped by the less prosperous but numerically superior Shudras. Thus he made it clear that a cyclical process in caste-based politics is indispensable.

Representations and Reservations

After Ambedkar, Lohia was the greatest votary of representations. Since the forties he contemplated to increase the non-Brahmin representation in all the political platforms. During the Goa liberation struggle, the non-Brahmins complained that the executive committee comprised of Brahmins alone and hence the movement petered out for want of popular participation (Lohia, 1964). Narrating this event he lent his categorical support to the philosophy of positive discrimination. He commented, "As a result of ten thousand year old tradition of cultural supremacy, the twice-born have acquired learning, intelligence, initiative, and it is impossible to bring a new cultural life to the Sudras unless a certain discrimination is allowed in their favour" (ibid., 12).

The fact that the dearth of educated among the Shudras, especially the backward castes and the Scheduled Castes (SCs), stood in their way of empowerment worried Lohia. He lamented that the leaders of all the political parties are university trained and hardly a few were without college education. He, however, never meant that education was a disqualification or illiteracy an asset, but felt that the uneducated too had to be accommodated in politics. What they needed was courage, honesty and a grasp of fundamentals. The suggestion of Lohia in the present context may seem fanciful. But in the fifties when the leadership of all the political parties was in the hands of Dvijas who were fairly educated and had superior airs of learning it was very difficult for someone from a backward caste or even an advanced intermediary caste to become a leader in his or her party. The idea behind his suggestion to make the less educated as leaders was to encourage the backwards and Dalits to take up the leadership.

In the year 1961 at the fifth national conference of the Socialist Party at Hajipur, the party resolved that sixty per cent of its candidates for the coming general elections should be from Shudras, Harijans, Adivasis, women, backward castes and minorities. This resolution based on the philosophy of representations heralded a sea change in the electoral politics of the Gangetic belt as well as other parts of the country. According to Krishna (1968), Lohia visualized a grand coalition of the sections of the disinherited strata of the Indian society. The grand coalition was intended to be a potent force in electoral politics. In the fourth general elections in 1967, the Congress party was defeated in several states and the Samyuktha Socialist Party led by Lohia participated in the non-Congress ministries. Thus the experiment of pitting a combination of intermediary castes against the Congress continued to be replicated throughout the country by many of the non-Congress formations.

Again in 1977, a decade after his death, the backward classes took reins of power in Uttar Pradesh and Bihar, the two largest states. It was because of Lohia's well thought out strategy that the Backward Classes and the Kulak castes were able to halt the victory of the Congress and experience a greater degree of political empowerment. Although this change did not perceptibly benefit the SCs, it nevertheless hastened the process of the empowerment of the weak and paved the way for many political alignments take the centre stage, basing on the principle of 'majority rule'.

Vashishthas and Valmikis

Lohia's exposition of the theory of Vashishthas and Valmikis, in which he described Nehru as the custodian and perpetrator of the Vashishtha tradition, is a scholarly contribution to the discourse on Brahmanism and its ramifications in Indian politics. Vashishtha tradition was Brahmanical, orthodox and reactionary, while Valmiki the indigenous tribesman turned hermit who wrote the Ramayana and founded the heterodox hermitage personified the liberal tradition. During his incarceration in the Lucknow jail in 1957, Lohia was manhandled by some prisoners at the instructions of the administration. After that bad experience he wrote a lengthy letter under the title "Vashishtha and Valmiki" to the Minister of Jails of Uttar Pradesh. The letter qualifies to be described as a treatise on the prevalent social situation and an condemned the practice of considering a woman inferior on the basis of colour (ibid.). In regard to women he held the same views as that of Ambedkar and Peryiar. Linking subjugation of women to the Brahmanical scheme of things he denounced the Shudra who with a little prosperity apes the Dvijas and forces his woman behind the purdah (ibid.).

Lohia (1966) was unduly bitter against English. His anti-colonial stand continued even after independence and in his antipathy towards the Congress and Nehru he brought out a far-fetched proposition that since the Brahmins were well conversant with English they used it as an effective tool to subjugate the rest of Indians. For him those who did not know English were an excluded group and the oppressors were obviously the English-speaking elite. Never content with denouncing racism in any form and on any ground, be it caste or colour, he fought against it tooth and nail. During his visit to the United States of America in 1964, like any other coloured people he was denied entry to a restaurant at Mississippi. He immediately sat in protest and ended it only when the authorities apologized to him.

Lohia: Critical Assessment

Lohia's politics and tireless campaigns against caste and Dvija hegemony had helped the numerically stronger intermediary castes to acquire political power and enhance their negotiating abilities. There are scores of political activists across the country, who proudly proclaim themselves as Lohiates and the tribe is unlikely to dwindle given the ever-increasing assertion of the backwards. His message of equality in spirit and every sphere has developed into an inseparable component of the affirmative action initiatives. Despite his achievements, his politics are found to be heavily loaded in favour of the intermediary castes neglecting the Dalit question. The basic flaw or an unintentional error in his politics was to club the Shudras and untouchable castes together and theorize that all of them were equally oppressed by the Dvijas.

By the early sixties, Shudras or the peasant castes grew so powerful that they could cut the dominance of the Dvijas to size and the fact that their treatment of Dalits was no better than that of the Dvijas, sometimes even worse, was too glaring to ignore. This dimension certainly must not have escaped Lohia's eagle eye and critical assessment. Yet in his mission to overthrow the Congress he sought to unite the intermediary castes who by then were a disgruntled lot and reasonably resourceful and organized. In the process as a tactical ploy he could not have paid attention to the woes of Dalits as they formed a committed vote bank of the Congress along with the Brahmins and Muslims. Notwithstanding such follies, it cannot be denied that Lohia was a relentless champion of social justice and had great concern for the Dalits. There is no gainsaying that he symbolized the just struggle of the people for better life, articulated their aspirations, fought exclusion of every kind, set the tone for sweeping changes in politics and stood as the conscience keeper of the nation for more than two decades.

References

Krishna, Gopal. 1968. 'Rammanohar Lohia: An Appreciation', *Economic and Political Weekly*, Special Number, July.

Limaye, Madhu. 1978. 'Foreword', in N.C. Mehrotra, *Lohia: A Study,* Atma Ram & Sons, Lucknow.

Lohia, Rammanohar. 1963. *Marx, Gandhi and Socialism*, Nava Hind Prakashan, Hyderabad.

——. 1964. *The Caste System*, Nava Hind Prakashan, Hyderabad.

——. 1965. *an Interval during Politics*, Nava Hind Prakashan, Hyderabad.

——. 1966. *Language*, Nava Hind Prakashan, Hyderabad.

Mehrotra, Nanak Chand. 1978. *Lohia: A Study*, Atma Ram & Sons, Lucknow.

various orders of being. We find such barriers erected everywhere in the world" (Gandhi, 1934).

Gandhi tried to fight out social injustice on four fronts: social moral, political, economic and educational. On social plane, Gandhi started a crusade against untouchability and caste system by attacking the very system, much against the will of Hindu orthodoxy and conservatism. He called the religious sanctions as serious stigma on a society that has deep-rooted culture and historical traditions to support its identity (Bakshi, 1987). He assessed the social position of untouchables as follows: "Socially they are lepers. Economically, they are worse than slaves. Religiously, they are denied entrance to places we miscall houses of God. They are denied the use on the same terms as caste Hindus of public roads, public schools, public hospitals, public wells, public taps, public parks and the like The wonder is that they are at all able to eke out an existence or that they still remain within the Hindu fold. They are too down trodden to rise in revolt against their suppressors. It is only ceaseless effort that can raise these down trodden fellow beings from degradation, purify Hinduism and raise the whole Hindu society and with it the whole of India" (*Harijan*, 1933). He tried not to abuse but to invoke the good sense of the people that it is not part and parcel of Hindus, but a plague and it is the bounden duty of every Hindu to combat this (Singh, 1998). Untouchability was essentially perceived by Gandhi as a moral problem, and hence it could be mitigated by changing the hearts and minds of the caste Hindus. Gandhi thought of untouchability as a matter of shame, guilt and sin for the upper castes rather than simply an ordinary evil. Therefore, he sought to change the hearts of the caste Hindus by moral pressure. He strived hard to force on the Indian conscience the problem of untouchability as an issue of national concern. Although the measures of legally abolishing untouchability were adopted in the Constituent Assembly much later he never advocated the same. He did feel that changes must come voluntarily from the heart.

On the political level, Gandhi was the first to grasp the gravity of the problem of untouchability and its significance from the point of view of the national movement (Singh, 1998). Gandhi's desire for removal of untouchability was as strong as his desire for freedom. He has said that freedom would be meaningless if untouchability was not removed. He also said that attainment of Swaraj was a must, but that would not be complete unless a social order based on equality and fraternity was established. In attacking untouchability, Gandhi had gone to the very root of the matter and, therefore, it was an issue of transcendental value, far surpassing of Swaraj in terms of political constitution. He said that such a constitution would be a deadweight if it was not backed by a moral basis in the shape of the present hope engendered in the hearts of the downtrodden millions that the weight is going to be lifted from their shoulders (Yadav, 2006).

Gandhi viewed untouchability as a serious problem for national integration since it was necessary to put up a united front against British imperialism. Removal of untouchability could be an eminently suitable step to defeat the policy of divide and rule employed by the British. Gandhi always held caste Hindus responsible for the plight of the untouchables and he also asserted that the Hindus would have no right to claim Swaraj as long as freedom was not restored to the exploited classes. He believed that the political bondage of Indians was a well-deserved punishment meted out to them for observing untouchability. Therefore, at times it is alleged what Gandhi categorically proclaimed that his Harijan Seva (upliftment) movement was not intended for upliftment of the Harijans but for the salvation of caste Hindus as penance for the crime they perpetrated against the Harijans.

Gandhi stoutly denied that there was any sanction for untouchability in the Hindu scriptures. He said that the *Bhagavad Gita* nowhere shows that a Chandala is in any sense inferior to Brahmin. To him untouchability was a sin. He regarded the practice of untouchability as satanic activity. (Singh and Sundaram, 1996). He reinforced and emphasized, "untouchability is not as action of a religion, it is a device of Satan" (Gandhi, 1921). He often said and wrote, "I regard untouchability as the greatest blot of Hinduism" (Gandhi, 1926). He further emphasized, that untouchability is against the Shastras. He urged Hindus to humanize their interpretations of scriptures used to justify exclusion and servitude and to include Harijans into Hindu Society. He believed in egalitarian form of Varnashrama dharma – the idealized fourfold division of society, a construct grounded in metaphysics and socially impressed in adherence to hereditary occupations, subject to non-competitive mobility over time (Gandhi, 1933). Gandhi was of the firm view that the removal of untouchability is more than building a temple of brick and mortar. Hindus must bleed for it, must pay for it. They must be prepared to forsake wife, children and all for the sake of removing this curse (Gandhi, 1924). Commenting on the movement of anti-untouchability, Mahatma Gandhi says, "If this preference for quality is good, it is specially so, for an essentially religious movement that of anti untouchability. In religion, indifference to quality may even lead a disaster". Mahatma did not believe in external sanctions that enforce obedience to the moral law by external law.

Socialism is embedded in the holistic paradigm. The socialistic ideal of equality is an essential part of Gandhian Sarvodaya. God is the creator of all and, therefore, each human being has an equal status in the holistic plan. The aim of socialism is establishment of a classless, sectionless society in which all the individuals have equal right to welfare and opportunity for self-development. Beteille mentions about three principal rights to equality: "Equality before the law, prohibition of discrimination on ground of religion, race, caste, sex, or place or birth and equality of opportunity in matters of public employment" (Beteille, 1992). Gandhi too laid emphasis upon human equality. In his opinion, there is no such thing as inherited or acquired superiority, and he believed in the rock-bottom doctrine of Advaita and his interpretation of Advaita excludes completely any idea of superiority at any stages whatever (Singh, 1998). "All have the same soul as any other. Hence, he who claims superiority, at once forfeits his claim to be called a man. The terms are many but the informing spirit is one". He, therefore, poses a question: How can there be room for distinction of high and low? For Gandhi, struggle against untouchability was more than securing equal rights and economic betterment; it was a moral and spiritual struggle (Gore, 1993).

The steps for the upliftment of Harijans, taken by Gandhi were unique in our history along with numerous other issues – political, social, economical, cultural and other. He ardently identified himself with numerous causes which had deep connection with the daily life of a downtrodden member of our society (Bakshi, 1986). Gandhi's first interview to the press since entering prison spoke of himself as touchable by birth and untouchable by choice. It was his ambition to represent and identify himself with people of the lowest rung of the society. "What I want, and what I am living for, and what I should delight in dying for, is the eradication of untouchability root and branch. I believe that if untouchability is really rooted out, it will not only purge Hinduism of a terrible blot but its repercussions will be world wide. My fight against the untouchability is fight against the impure in humanity".

He always wished to give Harijans a place of honour and respect in our society, which was denied to them for centuries. In this task what he preached, he professed. He spoke much in their favour by undertaking strenuous tours of all the regions of India. He castigated caste Hindus and criticized their behaviour towards the untouchables. He used to spend some time with the Harijans by living with them. This kind of personal identification of the Mahatma made the Harijans realize their sense of importance in our society. He taught them the sense of cleanliness and advised them to raise their economic and social standards by hard work and honest means. He raised their colonies and advised the workers to devise schemes of their upliftment.

He always preached to the Harijans about cleanliness, abstention from carrion eating and intoxicating drinks and drugs, necessity of educating themselves and their children as well as abstention from eating the leavings from caste Hindu's plates. He stated, on the contrary, "I suggest to caste Hindus that the short comings are not inherent to Harijans but that they are due to our criminal neglect of even deliberate suppression of these brethren of ours ... we must approach Harijans as penitents or debtors, not as their patrons or creditors extending generosity to the undeserving".

Gandhi strongly believed that through education the practice of untouchability can be reformed. He also recommended that common schools and wells should be opened where the existing ones were not available for Harijans either owing to the violent and successful opposition of the neighbours or some other unavoidable cause.

Gandhiji had put this work at the forefront of his constructive programme and Congress was committed to the removal of untouchability. His aim was to regenerate a new spirit, a new thinking and self-reliance among the Harijans. This kind of feeling, he believed, would greatly enhance their prestige and self-respect. They could raise their heads by becoming economically stronger by hard work and incessant labour (Kripalani, 1970).

It can be easily claimed that Gandhi has spoken and written more on untouchability than any other subject. The organizations and newspapers founded by Gandhi are testimony of this effect. At the conclusion of his first fast for the Harijan cause, Gandhiji changed the name of the weekly *Young India*, which he had been editing, to *Harijan*. This was one more effort to boost the work for the eradication of untouchability. Gandhi wrote, in 1931, "Untouchability cannot long endure. Some years ago we obstinately clung to it, to day we are different. It will be a thing of the past only when the indifference is translated into a conscious, deliberate awakening to a sense of the duty of self purification".

Gandhi's contribution to the removal of untouchability was considerable and greater than that of any other Indian leader (Parekh, 1989). No one before him had mounted a formal attack on untouchability and launched a vigorous national campaign. He combined moral, religious and political appeals and his own personal example in creating an anti-untouchability ambience. He cherished an ideal of Swaraj that was attainable through accent on non-political realities – spinning, ruralism, basic education, anti-communalism, etc. (Brown, 1980).

After independence, India enacted laws for the abolition of untouchability. Article 17 of the Constitution of India abolished untouchability and forbade its practice in any form. It was ordained that the enforcement of any disability arising out of untouchability would mean an offence punishable under law. This was followed up by the Untouchability Offences Act of 1955, which prescribes penalties as an aid to the enforcement of constitutional provisions protective of the Scheduled Castes (SCs) and liberal grants have been made for their socio-economic effort (Singh and Sundaram, 1996). Gandhian principle lies in stressing the permanent value of self-abnegation and to enshrine the primacy of goodness and character in the place of the skill of manipulation and self-assertion. Gandhism provides an alternative to solve the problems of unemployment, unequal distribution of wealth, violation of human rights, terrorism and poverty, and he particularly advocated abolishment of untouchability and tried to abolish the social system through non-violent mean. Gandhi gave us a vision of Indian living in largely self-sufficient villages, purges of the scourge of untouchability in which people of all religions did not merely tolerate but respected each other's traditions, customs, thoughts and feelings.

References

Bakshi, S.R. 1986. *Gandhi and Social Thought*, Criterion Publications, New Delhi, p. 165.

——. 1987. *Gandhi and Status of Harijans*, Deep & Deep Publications, New Delhi.

Beteille, Andre. 1992. *Society and Politics in India: Essays in a Comparative Perspective*, Oxford University Press, New Delhi, pp. 198–99.

Brown, Judith M. 1980. 'Mahatma Gandhi', in *History Today*, (30): 18.

Gore, M.S. 1993. *The Social Context of an Ideology: Ambedkar's Political and Social Thought*, Sage Publications, New Delhi.

Gandhi, M.K. 1921. *From Yeravada Mandir*, 6 October, pp. 3, 49.

Gandhi, M.K. 1921. *Young India.* III 19 January, Navajivan Publishing House, Ahmedabad, p. 22.

——. 1921. "From Yeravada Mandir" 6, October, pp.3 and 49, *The Collected Works of Mahatma Gandhi,* 21, Publication Division, Ministry of Information and Broadcasting, Government of India, 1991, New Delhi.

——. 1924. *Young India,* VI, 1 May, Navajivan Publishing House, Ahmedabad, p.16.

——. 1926. *Young India,* VII, 21 January, Navajivan Publishing House, Ahmedabad, p. 30.

——. 1933a. "From Yeravada Mandir", *Harijan*, I, 18, February.

——. 1933b. "From Yeravada Mandir", *Harijan*, I, 11 February.

——. 1937. *Harijan.* V, 6 March.

——. 1954. *The Removal of Untouchability*, Navajeevan Publications, Ahmedabad, p. 25.

Kripalani, J.B. 1970. *Gandhi: His Life and Thought*, Ministry of Broadcasting and Information, Govt. of India, New Delhi, p. 383.

Parekh, Bhikhu. 1989. *Colonialism, Tradition and Reform: An Analysis of Gandhi's Political Discourse*, Sage Publications, New Delhi, p. 241.

Singh, Ramjee. 1998. *The Gandhian Vision*, Manak Publications Private Limited, New Delhi, pp. 51- 52.

Singh, Ramjee and S. Sundaram. 1996. *Gandhi and the World Order*, APH Publishing Company, New Delhi, pp. 37, 43.

Tendulkar, D.G. 1952. *Mahatma*, Vol. III, Ministry of Information and Broadcasting, Govt of India, Bombay, p. 235.

Yadav, Sushma. 2006. 'Gandhi and Untouchability', in S.K. Jolly (ed.), *Reading Gandhi*, Concept Publishing Company, New Delhi, p. 252.

Index